W.E. ADAMS:
CHARTIST, RADICAL AND JOURNALIST (1832-1906)

"An Honour to the Fourth Estate"

Owen R. Ashton

BEWICK PRESS TYNE AND WEAR

First published in Great Britain by
Bewick Press
132 Claremont Road
Whitley Bay
Tyne & Wear
NE26 3TX

ISBN 0-95160-56-1-5

Printed and bound in Great Britain by
Billing and Sons Limited Worcester

CONTENTS

Acknowledgements

My thanks are due in the first place to my institution, Staffordshire Polytechnic, both for funding my sabbatical year (1989/90) and, through their Library and the Department of Humanities, for purchasing on micro-film a complete run of the Newcastle Weekly Chronicle, 1862-1900.

I should also like to record my thanks to the staff of The Bishopsgate Institute, London; The Houghton Library, Harvard, U.S.A.; the Library of the London School of Economics; Manchester Central Library; Newcastle-upon-Tyne Central Library; the Royal Society for the Prevention of Cruelty to Animals at Horsham; and the National Union of Journalists in London.

I am grateful to the following people who helped me either in gathering the research material or by suggesting ideas and lines of argument: P. Adams; J. Airey; J. Ambrose; C. Bassett; S. Blake; B. Bluck; R. Challinor; J. Coutouvidis; S. Dahlin; A. Dalby; D. Dalby; P. Dickinson; M. Fielding; E.& R. Frow; B. Harrison; M. Heaney; A. Jardine; R. Jenkins; C.D. Legge; D. Longhurst; F. Manders; R. Martin; O. Martyn; N. McCord; M. Milne; D. Morrice; A. Munslow; A. Parry; A.W. Purdue; T. & M. Roussos; E. Royle; J. Saville; J.K. Shelton; F.B. Smith; M. Squires; P. Storey; D. Thompson; N. Todd; E.I. Waitt; D.Webb; and D. Vincent. Needless to say, whatever deficiencies remain, they are entirely my own responsibility.

Almost last, but by no means least, I want to thank Maggie Garofall for her skill, precision and speed in typing my manuscript.

Finally, I want to thank my wife, Angela, for her great help and patience during the trying times of attempting to write this biography.

Owen R. Ashton

Stafford, September 1990.

FOR FAYE AND IAN,

AND THE DESCENDANTS OF W.E. ADAMS.

Introduction

In the turbulent and chequered history of nineteenth century working class movements, serious attention has yet to focus on assessing the role and contribution of crucial middle-rank or second-line leaders and activists.[1] A distinct coterie of these "second-lieutenants" emerged following the birth of Chartism in 1838. William Edwin Adams (1832-1906), Chartist, Republican and Radical journalist, by virtue of his vitality and longevity, is broadly representative of a generation of middle-rank luminaries — autodidacts like J.B. Leno, T. Frost, B. Wilson, B. Brierley, B. Lucraft and S. Kydd — who, after 1846 and before the emergence of Socialism, rose above the level of the local grass roots activist to a position of social weight and political influence. Such men often brushed shoulders with the great or revered at the centre of radical movements; but for one reason or another they were largely content to effect change from the fringe rather than thrust themselves, or be thrust, onto the main political stage. Born into humble surroundings, they were not entirely unambitious; nor were they obsequious, self-seeking, vain or opportunist; yet what distinguished them from the ordinary man in the Chartist crowd or even the rank and file membership, and what helped them carve a niche in popular movements of the nineteenth century, was their skill — both artisanal and literary, their intellectual conviction, political acumen and sound judgement. In effect, Adams personified some of the best traditions of the thinking and committed radical artisan.

For a man so frequently self-effacing, W.E. Adams is especially fascinating. His political awareness, organizational flair and administrative efficiency set him apart as that kind of regional Chartist leader who was crucial to the success of the movement as a whole. Rarely the platform orator, his consistency of purpose, combined with an acid pen and trenchant writings for the radical-republican cause, enabled protest movements to flourish, but gave others greater fame or political significance. Attracting international attention in 1858 for his part in provoking Palmerston's ill-fated press prosecutions over the Orsini affair, he went on to play a key role in mobilizing and articulating an incipient urban radicalism on behalf of Joseph Cowen, one of the most advanced Parliamentary Liberals of the day. In turn, Liberal leaders like Gladstone were sensitive to such views when formulating domestic reforms.

Paradoxically, Adams was to achieve material success and political recognition in his own life-time. As the astute editor-in-chief from 1865 until 1898 of the radically-based *Newcastle Weekly Chronicle,* at a time in the history of the "Fourth Estate" widely regarded as the influential heyday of provincial journalism, Adams was able to give full and unadulterated expression to his life-long beliefs and values: that is the weight he attached to such concepts as citizenship, duty, freedom and community. For all his conscious anonymity he was very much his own man; he made important contributions to moulding public opinion in favour of universal suffrage; the struggle for intellectual improvement of his class through propagandism and education; the battle against Negro slavery and the cause of internationalism. It is also testimony to his modernity and breadth of vision that he was passionately concerned about the environment, conservation, folk-lore and legend, special facilities for the young and campaigns against cruelty to animals. At the same time an analysis of such press-based or related activity sheds new light on neglected dimensions to the cultural milieu in certain working class communities in provincial England; it also helps broaden our overall understanding of the forms of control and comparative stability implicit in the relationships which came to exist between those aspects of Working Class Radicalism and Gladstonian Liberalism that derived from patterns of interaction outside the confines of the workplace.

Uniquely, Adams was, in later years, venerated publicly: celebrities and citizens alike joined civic dignitaries, captains of industry and trade-union leaders in Newcastle in June 1898 to recognise and reward his sterling endeavours and intimate association with movements of progress, culture and humanity. Before a large audience in the Central Hall, Nelson Street, the Mayor of Newcastle presented Adams with a cheque for 450 guineas; also a diamond ring for Mrs. Adams, as a mark of regard for her; and an album, bound in red Morocco leather, containing the autographs and addresses, as well as the Mayor's eulogy, on behalf of over 400 subscribers.[2] Indubitably, Novocastrians could feel justly proud of their adopted son, whose work and influence reverberated far beyond the vibrant culture and bustling life of the North East.

Alas, twentieth century observers and historians of popular movements have been less than generous in acknowledging their debt to the remarkable talents and versatility of the unsung middle-rank heroes as an indispensable element of working class movements.[3] It is imperative that they are rescued from obscurity not simply because of what new light they shed on the nature of Victorian social and political protest, its constituent parts and what factors motivated, inspired or repelled the mass following; or for what they themselves did and stood for in different or related causes; they are extremely important because in examining some of the issues which galvanised men like Adams into action — conservation, the environment and cruelty to animals — we are offered a valuable perspective on virtually identical problems that still beset us, albeit in a more acute or urgent form, in the last years of the twentieth century.

My "quest for Adams" grew out of a doctoral study of Chartism in one of the most unlikely of places, the aristocratic, nineteenth century watering resort of Cheltenham Spa.[4] It rapidly became apparent that as Adams rose through the Chartist ranks in the Spa, he gathered around him a group of committed artisan radicals who, much to the delight of national leaders like Feargus O'Connor and Ernest Jones, were vigorously engaged in challenging the establishment values of local representatives of Church and State. In Cheltenham Spa and subsequently at the country house of Brantwood near Coniston — later sold to John Ruskin and now a National Trust property — under the guidance of the owner, W.J. Linton, Chartist leader and famous English wood engraver, he became a Republican soldier in the war to liberate humanity. Yet for Adams it was a cause with a deep respect for the individual and his rights, a refinement of his adherence to Paineite Radicalism. The Republic as they understood it derived from the teachings of Mazzini, who for Adams was "the greatest teacher since Christ": it was not so much a form of government that rejected the monarchy but a system of morals and ethics, a creed, a faith and "a new benign gospel"; it stressed teaching and learning "Duties" as opposed simply to upholding the "Rights of Man". Clearly, it was an educational work to which he felt summoned. Mazzini, Linton and the Brantwood Republican venture left an indelible imprint on Adams's psyche. Henceforth, he was to become a devoted propagandist with an abiding faith in the regeneration of humanity as embodied in Mazzinian ideals.

Unfortunately, one's ignorance of Adams's subsequent career after 1855, in what is clearly a seminal period of the nineteenth century labour movement, was compounded by an absence of private letters, notes and diaries, even though there was some evidence to suggest that Adams had himself at least preserved them for posterity.[5] Nevertheless, through the recovery work of social historians John Saville, David Vincent and Maurice Milne, in weighty biographical reference books, our lost perspective does begin to appear to be a thing of the past.[6] These researches, particularly Saville's, which he extended in his Introduction to Adams's autobiographical work, *Memoirs of a Social Atom*, are suggestive of the many fruitful lives of further and detailed study that this book has undertaken. Hopefully, it has broken new ground, too, by virtue of unearthing and analysing some of the "lost" primary source material. Although the diaries have not been found, a scattering of private letters, pamphlets, press cuttings and, uniquely, ephemera in the possession of identified family descendants has yielded much; indeed, taken together they throw entirely new light on the multi-faceted nature of Adams's interests and involvements.

As we approach the task of assessing the relative merits of the sources, old and new, we appear to be confronted by an inescapable yet enticing truism. On the one hand,

Adams's work is the object of brief mention, passing reference and generous footnoting in countless but diverse material, past and present: witness, for example, the nineteenth century acknowledgments from radical political and trade union leaders like Charles Bradlaugh, Joseph Cowen and Thomas Burt;[7] the leading drama critic, William Archer;[8] the popular novelist, Captain Mayne Reid[9] and the celebrated humanitarian, Florence Nightingale.[10] Among a crop of scholarly writings in the twentieth century, David Jones has acknowledged the role he played both in Chartism and its subsequent historiography;[11] and Alfred Plummer, the biographer of the Chartist Bronterre O'Brien, has paid tribute to the "marked success" he enjoyed as editor of Cowen's *Newcastle Weekly Chronicle* following his graduation from Chartism into the world of radical journalism.[12] On the other hand, a re-assessment of Adams's own works — the political pamphlets, autobiography, American travelogue and a seemingly endless run of newspaper editorials — in conjunction with the fruits of new research, all attest to his considerable talents, wide-ranging public activity and ultimate centrality to radical political issues in Victorian England.

As the author of a series of political pamphlets between 1858 and 1868, Adams has underlined his claim to be considered amongst the radical leaders who were outspoken against the injustices they challenged both at home and abroad. His first pamphlet, "Tyrannicide: Is it Justifiable?" (1858), certainly found its target with a vengeance; it also afforded him widespread notoriety since fundamental questions were raised about what constituted the freedom of the press or rights of the subject in matters of public interest. John Stuart Mill, for example, made the controversy over the reception of this short pamphlet the subject of a note in his second chapter of *On Liberty* in 1859.[13] In language noticeably reminiscent of Cobbettite invective against "Old Corruption", Adams defended Felice Orsini's abortive assassination attempt on Louis Napoleon at the beginning of 1858; he also reflected the bitter indignation felt by ordinary men and women at the conspiratorial activities which underpinned the Caesarist regime of the future French Emperor. The pamphlet provoked a storm of diplomatic protest on both sides of the English Channel because Adams argued stridently and unequivocally that Napoleon's heinous crimes justified his assassination either through guerilla tactics or at the hands of the private avenger. In obedience, it appears, to the dictates of the French Government, an embarrassed Palmerston introduced The Conspiracy Bill and had the pamphlet's publisher, Edward Truelove, a life-long friend of Adams, arrested as part of a concerted campaign against fellow-sympathisers who had also come out in print. Nothing came, however, of the prosecutions. A further ignominy was unexpectedly inflicted on Palmerston's Whig ministry in mid-February 1858: he was defeated during the second reading of the Conspiracy Bill and resigned forthwith.

Adams it must be said could claim only a Pyrrhic victory over Palmerston, for when history repeated itself nearly ten years later the roles were reversed. Just as he prepared to throw down the gauntlet yet again in his pamphlet "Bonaparte's Challenge To Tyrannicides" (the publisher was also Truelove) — the sequel to the first tirade — author and publisher were forced to suppress its publication. The context for the outrage felt on this occasion was supplied by Napoleon's active role in the bloody massacre of Garibaldi's liberation forces at the Battle of Mentana in the first week of November 1867. In Adams's view, Napoleon by such Imperial brigandage in Italy had reopened the question of tyrannicide; and since Italy was powerless and Europe indifferent, the only recourse that remained was the terrorism of the private avenger.

The ultimate significance of this pamphlet war must surely lie in what it tells us about the rights of men such as Adams in relation to the chameleon-like character of the British State at a time when class conflict was visibly in decline and, seemingly, a mid-Victorian consensus was about to, or had, emerged.[14] The cause of suppression is clear: what Palmerston's government had failed to do in 1858, they were to achieve by more subtle and discrete ways in their next in 1861. In July of that year the Conspiracy Bill was cunningly inserted in an Act which merely professed to consolidate the Statute Law of England relating to Offences against the Person (it became law on August 6th 1861). Ostensibly a very harmless Bill, embedded within the act however were a number of provisions over which Palmerston's Ministry had stumbled disastrously in 1858. The legal snare on this occasion — the one which was to trip up Adams in 1867 — hinged on a clause which made it a felony, subject to up to ten years imprisonment, to transmit letters inciting or threatening murder.[15] Adams and Truelove therefore withdrew from the struggle unable to defy the law and unwilling to invite a prosecution, though they were at pains to point out the bitter irony of their situation: that at such a critical moment in liberation movements in Europe the liberty of the subject in England was being circumscribed in order to appease foreign despots.[16] Sections of the Radical press, alert to the implications of the Government's measures, protested but to no avail.[17] In the final analysis, Adams's inter-play with high politics and challenges to bourgeois hegemony in the otherwise more tranquil mid Victorian years are important in a number of inter-connected ways. Firstly, in the 1858 pamphlet and the diplomatic row it provoked we see the principal reasons why, following Palmerston's mishandling of the crisis, the Whigs quickly fell from power; secondly, Adams's uncompromising stand against perceived acts of Anglo-French aristocratic connivance in matters of foreign policy, indicate that the consolidation process by which the ruling class won consent from articulate working men was not easy or straightforward; and lastly by his intemperate pamphlet language Adams drew the kind of coercive ruling class response which was reminiscent of a similar strategy deployed against the Chartists in the confrontations of 1848.[18]

The path to publication which accompanied the remaining three pamphlets was far less problematical. In March 1860 Adams wrote "An Argument for Complete Suffrage" which was simultaneously published in London by Truelove, in Manchester by Abel Heywood and in Newcastle by J. Barlow. Once again his pamphlet was directly concerned with an important national event, the groundswell of working class support for universal suffrage following Whig and Tory hesitancy on the issue of further political reforms. The pamphlet was as Chartist in tone as any radical document of the 1840's: it was extremely critical of Disraeli's (1859) and Russell's (1860) reform proposals, especially with regard to the so-called "fancy franchises" which favoured an element of wealth (for example, holders of £60 savings accounts) and education as criterion for bestowing a limited male franchise in both the boroughs and counties. Adams even went further: by asserting that natural and inalienable suffrage rights recognized no sexual limitations he reminded his working class colleagues, as well as government ministers, that complete suffrage was an arrangement which would brook no compromises.

The pamphlet's immediate importance lay in its educating work for the activities of nation-wide manhood suffrage societies, which sprang up at this time pledged to oppose the 1859 and 1860 Reform Bills. In Manchester, for example, where Adams now briefly lived and worked, Abel Heywood, the pamphlet's publisher, relied heavily on such propagandist activities in his remarkable but unsuccessful attempts to democratize local politics.[19] In the longer term the pamphlet's role served to underline Adams's claim, already well-established in the columns of the *Newcastle Weekly Chronicle*, to have been of considerable help in the successful miners' franchise campaign of 1874 which led directly to the election of Thomas Burt as M.P. for Morpeth.[20]

In 1863 Adams's specialist knowledge of the issues at the heart of the American Civil War was recognised by the Union and Emancipation Society, the object of which was to support the Northern states in maintaining the integrity of the Republic and procuring the liberation of Southern slaves. When the battle-lines in the conflict were finally drawn Adams found himself in a unique position. As "Caractacus" writing in Charles Bradlaugh's *National Reformer*, he was given a free-hand in articulating working class hostility to the slave-owning south and support for the abolitionists in the North;[21] and as a general committee member of the Union of Emancipation Society he became part of a cross class campaign of moral reform embracing radical middle class

Liberals, Nonconformist ministers and ex-Chartists. The high point of this involvement in "moral radicalism" was his third pamphlet entitled "The Slaveholders' War: an Argument for the North and the Negro" (Manchester, 1863). As such it represented a cogent summary of his abolitionist views and arguments: he exposed the shallowness of the claims made on behalf of the so-called Southern way of life based upon codes of chivalry and honour; and then castigated the connivance of the English aristocracy and certain sections of the middle class who, aided by the *Times* at the head of a corrupt and venal establishment press, wished for reasons of self-interest to perpetuate a Southern state system based on the atrocious evils of human slavery. Viewed from these perspectives, Adams's contribution to the Slavery question must be judged as a solid exercise in moral persuasion; it also stands as a testimony to his talents as a promising political propagandist that his pamphlet lay well within the mainstream of the Society's attempts to capture the high ground amongst those sections of the English public opinion entirely uninformed as to the domestic affairs of the U.S.A.[22]

Hitherto it has been widely regarded that Adams's writings included only four pamphlets.[23] However, the present researches have revealed that at least one more, entitled "The Province of Authority in Matters of Opinion", was published by the Secularist, Charles Watts in London, circa 1875.[24] The circumstances surrounding the location of the pamphlet are themselves revealing. Indeed, one might usefully speculate that in its acquisition by the Bishopsgate Institute in London, one can sense the hidden hand of Adams at work helping to build up the Library's reputation. According to Raphael Samuel[25] the Reference Library at Bishopsgate owes its present shape to the man who was librarian there for nearly half a century, Charles William Goss. When he was appointed in 1897, Goss came with solid credentials: he was formerly an assistant Librarian at Newcastle Public Library and a regular contributor to the antiquarian pieces which Adams, as editor, pioneered in the *Newcastle Weekly Chronicle*. It is just possible that Goss's appreciation of radical historical documentation was cultivated in his cultural apprenticeship in Newcastle, where Adams was also a member of the Library Committee; and it is equally feasible that, since no other copy appears to exist, the pamphlet fell into Goss's hands here or followed him for safe-keeping when he arrived in Bishopsgate.

From the preamble of the pamphlet it is clear that it first appeared as a prepared lecture — a rare event for Adams — which he read aloud to large audiences during the course of 1862 before the Secular Societies in its Lancashire strongholds of Manchester, Ashton, Rochdale and Oldham. Reports in the *National Reformer* for that year confirm that this was the case.[26] It is also abundantly clear that whilst Adams was actively involved in the Secularist movement for a brief period between 1860 and 1863, he was not a critic of prevailing religious beliefs and values — that was Bradlaugh's (Iconoclast was his pseudonym) forte. Adams's concerns were with those wider issues which the spectrum of secularism embraced — personal liberty, political reform and liberation movements abroad. The gist of the pamphlet was that in matters of opinion the authority of the State had no province, while the authority of the individual had only such purchase as arguments gave to it. As one whose words had been honoured with a government prosecution in 1858 Adams was well-placed to argue for the rights of free speech, publication and expression. Secularists too continued to face many perils and pitfalls from a coercive state when, as Bradlaugh had done in March 1861 at Plymouth, they disputed the divine origins of the Bible in public places on the Sabbath.[27] On that occasion Bradlaugh fell prey to maltreatment and arrest by the State in the form of the over-zealous Devonport police. The impotent conclusion of his trial in August 1861, for which he received only one farthing in damages, served to reinforce the thrust of Adams's argument through his lectures in 1862, namely how state authority and the persons or institutions attached to it would still menace the rights of those secularists and atheists intent on exercising the utmost liberty of expression.

That a "destiny obscure" was not to be Adams's eventual fate was first ensured when his life and work was subject to a full page pen portraiture and biographical analysis in *Winter's Magazine* on March 25th 1893.[28] At first sight it might appear a little strange that a thinly circulating national magazine, which attempted to reconcile competing ideas about women's occupational and leisure aspirations with a continued emphasis upon appropriate standards of femininity, should be interested in W.E. Adams. The occasion for public acclaim was Adams's unequivocal support for the "No Crinoline League's" campaign by its mildly feminist proprietor, the celebrated Victorian novelist Mrs. Henrietta Stannard (her pseudonym was "John Strange Winter"). No one has accorded Stannard the rightful recognition she deserves as an eminent Victorian woman, although *The Strand Magazine*[29] in February 1895 featured her in one of their long-running series on Victorian celebrities; and the *Dictionary of National Biography for the Twentieth Century*[30] includes an entry for her contributions to public life.

In the second half of the Nineteenth Century Adams and Stannard become close friends because of their mutual interests and shared concerns. These included journalism (Stannard was President of the Society of Women Journalists from 1901-1903[31]), campaigns against cruelty to animals, advocating legal rights for women, and support for the movement known as the Rational Dress Society, in which the "No-Crinoline League" comprised an important element.[32] Doubtless, Adams was kept well-informed on the tyranny of fashion in the form of the crinoline and the wearing of stuffed birds in bonnets by his four teenage daughters who typified in their more practical dress the new woman movement of the 1890s.[33]

Introduced as the shrewd and genial editor of the *Weekly Chronicle*, Stannard made a great play in juxta-opposing Adams's present "days of matured serenity" with the somewhat turbulent character of his Chartist and Radical past, in order to emphasize, Smilesian-like, his remarkable route to upward social mobility and public influence. Next, she paid fulsome tribute to his energetic and able journalism for nearly thirty years on Tyneside. As a ready and effective writer with strong and earnest convictions, she asserted that his advocacy for any genuine cause could be considered valuable and effective; and nowhere more so than in the columns of the *Weekly Chronicle*: a publication of little if any account which he turned after 1864 into one of the most widely circulated and popular newspapers of the time. Pride of place in assessing his journalistic accomplishments however was reserved for two unrelated activities: firstly, the origination and development of the Dicky Bird Society in the Children's Corner in 1876 and which at the time of writing had a world-wide membership of nearly a quarter of a million; and secondly, his trans-Atlantic alignments — a logical extension of his 1860s anti-slavery stand — as evidenced in his first book, *Our American Cousins: personal impressions of the people and institutions of the U.S.A.* (1893), which appeared as a very successful serialised feature in the columns of the *Weekly Chronicle* during 1882.

In doing justice to Adams in Victorian times Mrs. Stannard has unwittingly done an important service to twentieth century historians: she has pointed out the inestimable value of both the *Newcastle Weekly Chronicle* and *Our American Cousins* as substantial sources to quarry in any overall assessment of Adams's life and work; and whilst both these sources have long been neglected, the *Weekly Chronicle* is, for obvious reasons, the most insightful.[34] Assiduous research in the files of the *Newcastle Weekly Chronicle* — partly newspaper, partly a family magazine — reveals a rich vein of source material about Adams's ideas and opinions not found anywhere else. Through his writings as editor-in-chief, but also as "Ironside" (until 1882) and occasionally as a contributor to 'Robin Goodfellow" (a column featuring local and national items of interest), we can attempt three things: firstly, to chart his Radical thought patterns, career and contributions to Tyneside politics; secondly, to appreciate the genesis, form and impact of his homely, domestic reforms; and lastly to assess his skills as a gentleman of the press, the vehicle through which his literary ideas were both the object of innovation and the subject for articulation. Moreover, reading directly or between the lines of the paper Adams offered up in moments of nostalgia, prompted by this Radical's death or that political movement's anniversary, nuggets of biographical information which he judged his discerning readers would find interesting as they shared together their memories of an heroic, radical past. Frequently, too, in the columns of his Children's Corner we can follow a fascinating public dialogue between him, as the amiable Uncle Toby, and his six surviving children over family matters, the care of animals, hobbies for the young and desirable reading material; it was at once an association with which yet again many of his readers, young and old alike, could empathise.[35]

To date, the content and significance of his travelogue, *Our American Cousins* (published in London and Newcastle, 1883) has received scarcely the briefest attention, even in the twentieth century texts cited above. This is a great pity because the book represents an important milestone in his journalistic work for which he won warm praise from newspaper critics on both sides of the Atlantic.[36] The book is of value in a number of ways: it records Adams's successful and triumphant tour through the U.S.A. and Canada, where he was fêted as a distinguished Englishman with an Abolitionist pedigree; secondly, it shows him again to be the indefatigable campaigner for Negro Civil Rights, including by now in his arguments an advocacy of the still frowned upon concept of miscegenation; thirdly, it offered important insights into the American way of life for the would-be working class emigrant; and lastly it reveals a man with a trans-Atlantic frame of mind whose admiration for the progress of the American Republic — "that greater Britain beyond the Atlantic"[37] — had in no way been stunted by his first hand knowledge of its political scandals, corruption and misgovernment. Adams had commented favourably on the wonderful courtesy of the people, the utter absence of restraint or formality in connection with all the institutions, and, above all, on the amazing energy and enterprise which Americans imported into all aspects of life; but he did not hesitate to criticize such odious features as the Tammany Ring, lynch-law and the partiality of the courts. The book's endearing quality as a piece of investigative journalism rests upon its balanced appraisal of the United States at a time when in England the stock image of its people and institutions still drew on either Charles Dickens's caricatures in *American Notes* (1842) or George Augustus Sala's racist and pro-South observations in *America Revisited* (1881).[38] The influential *New York Herald* certainly felt that in using his eyes, ears and pen purposively, Adams had provided a much needed corrective on English perceptions of America. Commenting on the book's attributes in 1883, the *Herald's* literary editor also offers this verdict on what is in effect Adams's endearing professional qualities:

> "The author brings to his work acute penetration, a keen observation, a graphic, picturesque style of presenting his impressions, and a quiet humour that finds expression in quoting amusing scraps from

> newspaper stories and sayings that aptly illustrate the case in point."[39]

The precise motives that prompted Adams to write his *Memoirs* at the beginning of the twentieth century remain tantalizingly veiled in both family and work-related circumstances. When he effectively retired in 1898 — he had been wintering in Madeira for up to three months at a time for some years before this date — his eldest son, Ernest Welles Adams, succeeded him as editor in chief. There is no doubt that Adams always loved to be at his desk in the *Chronicle's* office; but since the onset of bronchitis, a health problem compounded by advancing years, he reconciled medical advice with a little writing carried on in semi-retirement from the warmer climes of Funchal, the capital of Madeira. Invariably on these civilised sojourns he was accompanied by his eldest daughter, Mrs. Gertrude Amy Smith, a very energetic, capable and outgoing woman.[40] Circumstantial evidence suggests that having exhausted local material for a weekly column devoted to the island's charms — a pleasant diversion for the paper's readers during the dreary English winters — Adams cast around for something to do to fill his leisure time. A number of factors appear to have converged to produce a situation propitious to the *Memoirs'* appearance during the winter months of 1900-1 in serialised form for his beloved *Weekly Chronicle*. Firstly, with the unexpected death in February 1900 at Stella Hall, Blaydon, of his long-standing friend and employer, Joseph Cowen, was lost the unique device by which Adams had been able to flourish in print virtually free from proprietorial interference for over thirty years; and not surprisingly when the *Memoirs* were published by Hutchinson in 1903,[41] the book was respectfully dedicated to Joseph Cowen. Secondly, Adams himself was an enabler: he had consistently encouraged former radicals, especially Chartists (for example, James Burns, R. Gammage, G.J. Harney and G.J. Holyoake), to contribute their recollections in the form of letters or weekly reminiscences to the magazine features of the *Chronicle*; and now having outlined most of these friends he must surely have been conscious that as one of the last of a band of activists capable of effective writing about Chartism, he too should do his duty. Thirdly, whatever reservations he may have had about publication were seemingly removed by his balmy surroundings, daughter's persuasive company and loyalty to his son, who, anxious to sustain the paper's long-standing circulation success, wished to include what remained of such delightful nuggets of Radical nostalgia. Naturally, Adams did not disappoint. His presentation of the self was precisely the kind of thing which made good copy in the *Weekly Chronicle*. In self-contained weekly episodes, mediated via his son's editorial care, Adams offered a highly-constructed but extremely selective life-history: it was at once a wide ranging survey of social and political events as he had known or participated in, but it kept up his readers interests because there was always on offer something of interest for everybody to enjoy.

Adams's *Memoirs*, of course, fall squarely into the distinctive genre of working class autobiography, the nature, quality and content of which has been extensively researched by J. Burnett and D. Vincent.[42] Any consideration therefore of the *Memoirs* as source material for a full-blown biographical study must proceed by reference to their findings. For all the opening protestations of ordinariness,[43] Adams's *Memoirs* were essentially a celebration of success on behalf of the radical artisan's persevering and self-help mentality. As such the core of his self-image is one with which many of his readers, particularly the skilled engineers or "advanced" sections of the working classes, could meaningfully identify or aspire: a humble but happy childhood; a printer's apprenticeship; an appetite for books and rational culture; the struggles of a journeyman or tramp; bouts of unemployment and in a penniless condition; and then a more regular cycle of work leading, like a fairy story, to the rare path of geographic and upward social mobility; finally public recognition and financial security. Such a pinnacle of achievement uniquely serves to underline Adams's degree of differentiation from the undifferentiated mass of the working class; it is a process which he reinforces by consciously employing his remarkable literary skills and reliable memory to document both important and trivial aspects of socio-political and cultural life in which he, the self, actively or passively interacted. Among the many topics that enrich the personal narrative are nostalgic recollections of the demise of popular pastimes, customs and rituals on the eve of the railway age; delightful anecdotes or snippets about travelling theatre, circus, crime and trials, the changing character of cheap literature and of fashions and dress; fascinating snapshots of a number of political movements and their personalities, particularly valuable being those recalling Chartism and European liberation movements; and interesting but all too brief insights into the joys, as well as the responsibilities, that befell the compositor turned provincial editor in chief in the mainstream of North East journalism. Occasionally, too, it is important to recognize that he moves outside the narrative form to interpret current events or trends. Witness, for example, the way in which the tension between his Radical-Liberal values and an abhorrence of the centralising tendencies of the State are deliberately foregrounded in the chapter entitled, "Coddling and Culture."[44] Perhaps this was a deliberate attempt to enter the contemporary debate — articulated amongst others by both the *Daily* and *Weekly Chronicle* — about challenges the Liberal hegemony faced from an incipient Labour movement. The North East had long been a bastion of Liberalism and the *Weekly Chronicle* one of its most important acolytes; but the last twenty years of the Nineteenth Century witnessed the beginning here of a slow but steady erosion of Liberal conceptions of reality. Adams's timely intervention can therefore be seen as an attempt to re-affirm the efficacy of practical political ideas within the Liberal creed: a faith in human progress through the virtues of self-reliance and freedom of action, vindicated by the serialised life-history, is paraded in the arena of public space as infinitely preferable to new-fangled Socialist values which, given their reliance on state agencies, were purported to stifle human initiative, sap individual energy and circumscribe personal liberty.

The *Memoirs* weaknesses however stem from their journalistic character, as A.L. Morton has indicated: "sometimes the material is stretched out, sometimes truncated."[45] Consequently, whilst Adams writes expansively and sometimes vividly on important events or people he has met — presumably because he felt them intuitively to be of more interest to his readers — he holds to the literary conventions of the genre of working class autobiographical silence governing the treatment of personal and private life.[46] This is all the more surprising in Adams's case, given his journalistic skills, command of language and public persona on Tyneside. In essence, what Adams yields up is his public not private memories. For example, he is extremely reticent about the circumstances surrounding his courtship; his feelings towards or wife's role in their marriage; the nature and quality of shared familty life in and around Holly Avenue, their home in the leafy suburb of Jesmond; the traumatic emotional experiences which confronted them on the untimely death of their teenage daughter, Florence Annie, and the indifferent health in childhood of their youngest, Hilda Kate; nor do we know anything about his relationship with the *Weekly Chronicle* staff (was he a good employer?), or for that matter how he filled his leisure time and who were his social friends and acquaintances. Equally disappointing are Adams's attempts at self-analysis. Apart from the opening game of pretence discounting any uniqueness and a few perceptions about the qualities of the discerning artisan, we learn very little about how he perceived himself in relation to other professionals in public life on Tyneside. For example, his nostalgic evocations of the idyll of rural childhood are intended more for the delectation of readers living in the anonymous smoky city or coal-mining communities than a return to the past in search of a greater understanding of his present self. Still more problematic is our ability to find clues from a textual analysis in order to tease out of an oblique reference the experiences of the unconscious, its conflicts and unresolved tensions which perhaps might manifest themselves in the form of some kind of internalised identity crisis. In this respect an obvious and interesting line of speculation might be Adams's dependency on Joseph Cowen; that he only existed as a subject in and through the actions of his wealthy and powerful patron. We know, for example, from surviving private papers[47] that their relationship was characterised on more than one occasion by severe strain and tension, but there is very little, if anything in the *Memoirs* — quite the reverse in fact — to suggest that Adams felt in any sense circumscribed, as other employees did, by Cowen's actions as the interfering press baron.[48] It is of course still possible that, apart from judging the needs of the market, Adams, the autodidact, felt ill-equipped to talk about the innermost self because he simply did not possess the necessary linguistic skill to articulate his ideals and prejudices. In the final analysis, however, given the context in which he worked, lived and had his being, and for which he had earned a reputation as a "clever, able journalist",[49] one senses that the *Memoirs* are the product of an adroit and considered process of selection, one in which family advice, both personal and professional, played a modest part.

All the source materials reviewed so far suffer from one obvious defect: they were printed public documents dovetailed to a particular purpose — be it a pamphlet or book by Adams himself or press recognition by his own admirers; and, as such, they throw little light on the private nature of the man, behind the scenes activities or important moments of tension in radical battles and journalistic activity. Fortunately, additional information and valuable correctives can be glimpsed from an assortment of private papers in which his name or correspondence, or both, appeared. The *Cowen* and *Holyoake Papers,*[50] for example, if taken together, tell us a little more about the fact that Adams's talents were increasingly recognized and favoured over those of G.J. Holyoake by Joseph Cowen, for whom they both worked, in the contest to fill the vacant editorship of the *Newcastle Weekly Chronicle* in 1864. Subsequently, judging by the tone and content of their association in the *Cowen* papers, it was a position that Adams was to make virtually his own precisely because Cowen trusted to his integrity, deftness, sense of fair play and, when necessary, a firm hand — attributes also underlined sharply by the exchanges in the *Howell Collection*[51] between Adams in his professional position and George Howell, the aspiring Radical columnist, who was prone to slips of the pen, solecisms and a discursive style.

By far the most helpful is the little used but extensive collection of letters (119) from W.J. Linton to Adams, a remarkable testimony to their life-long friendship following the disbanding of the Brantwood Republic venture in 1855.[52] This correspondence between 1855 and 1897 reveals much about a whole range of subjects and issues surrounding Adams's personal life and subsequent public career. For example, in the sphere of politics we begin to appreciate the stamina required to sustain a mid-Victorian Radical movement in which Adams acted as Linton's peripatetic Republican envoy; their debate about effective strategies for promoting propaganda via the printed word; their disappointments and flagging morale in the face of public apathy; the responses of the authorities to their presence and organisation, including a classic piece by Linton advising Adams on how best to proceed following Truelove's arrest during the Orsini crisis. We also learn something about Adams's personality, his enthusiasm for work, ability to reconcile a hectic editorial schedule with a love of travel (he visited, for example, France, Norway and Ireland) and a thirst for knowledge. Above all, we begin to penetrate the completely private spheres of the man himself: thus revealed are references to his health problems even before the onset of bronchitis; a warm sense of humour amongst friends and work colleagues, and a close bond with Linton's son, Willie, a man as anxious to learn the skills of the compositor as Adams was eager to teach him. There are useful insights, too, into family matters including the closeness of the relationship with his wife, Elizabeth Jane Owen (amongst Radical friends like Linton and James Glover she is affectionately referred to as "Lizzie"), the welfare of the family and, as evidenced also in the few personal family ephemera, a great interest in his children's reading materials, their upbringing and a reflective pride in old age at their's and their children's success, particularly with regard to the latters' academic achievement in school during the time of the Boer War.[53]

Inevitably, at the end of the day the historian is confronted by the fact that some aspects of and periods in Adams's life remain either impenetrable or shrouded in mystery. Yet the detective work implicit in this Introduction suggests that sufficient source material both in quality and range now exists to form the basis of an introductory study to, rather than a conjectual history about, Adams's life and work. The aims therefore of this book are twofold: firstly, to fill many of the gaps in our existing knowledge in order to provide a more rounded overview of the man and the multifaceted nature of his interests and involvements; and secondly, to try to assess critically his contribution, as a middle-ranking radical leader, to a number of nineteenth century working class struggles and related humanitarian concerns, starting with Chartism. In addressing these aims the study also hopes to throw more light on a number of important historical and cultural debates in which Adams consciously or otherwise played a part. These include: the regionalism of English culture and how it developed in relation to the Nation; the growing interest in late nineteenth century conservation and a deep love of the countryside; the existence of a broad Liberal-Radical political culture, whose relationship was not directly determined by conflict in the workplace, and which connected Chartism to Gladstone; the role of the press in local as well as national politics; and the construction of the self both through writing and through the conscious making of a career.

To suggest the relative autonomy of culture in social and political relations as this work does, necessitates a methodological framework which draws heavily on the concept of hegemony (leadership) articulated by the twentieth century Italian Marxist, Antonio Gramsci.[54] In essence, Gramsci utilizes this concept to explore political, ideological and cultural forms through which a dominant class in society is able to win consent to its leadership or its "conceptions of reality" from a subordinate class in ways other than simply by means of coercion or main force. The core feature in this activity for Gramsci is a perception of culture as a space or arena that is always contested and yet never won; it is a space for complex negotiation, though mechanisms of transformation, inclusion and exclusion, between dominant culture and the oppositional or resistance elements within popular culture (for example, an area of negotiation over such sites as popular rituals, customs and pastimes; shared beliefs and values). Thus, in assessing W.E. Adams as the Chartist and Radical in conflict with an Anglican dominated Cheltenham Spa and a coercive British state; as the participator in or recorder of forms of popular plebeian culture susceptible to "modernization" at the hands of middle class rational recreationists; and as an outspoken radical journalist in the vanguard of North East Liberalism — in all of these activities, themselves specific sites for the production of hegemony, it is important we do not conclude that Adams was easily or automatically incorporated by the cloying embrace of Gladstonian Liberalism.

W.E. Adams was a life-long Radical, the product of a particular political culture. It is axiomatic therefore that we cannot understand such a figure without examining first the formative influences of life in Cheltenham Spa where he spent the first twenty three years. Hence the structure that follows is broadly chronological. Chapter 1 attempts to explore the early influences on Adams, the child of a poor but politically active family; his rudimentary education and a thirst for political knowledge which did not prevent him — even in his apprenticeship years — from enjoying those aspects of a balanced, happy youth, which derived from a time for play, for pranks and a deep attachment to the countryside and all living things. Chapter 2 explores early manhood in the context of Adams's role as an active local Chartist. Along with fellow artisans he shared a common hostility, inspired by the writings of Tom Paine and ideals of Mazzini, towards the Spa's traditional rulers as personified by Craven F. Berkeley, M.P., the local Whig representative of "Old Corruption", and the Rev. Francis Close, the energetic and zealous evangelical "Pope of Cheltenham". The Cheltenham years are important not only for moulding his political views, but also for underlining his artisanal virtues of self-reliance and self-improvement through education and sobriety — all aspects of a cultural broadening which Adams led his colleagues into establishing in opposition to the dominant values of the clerical supporters of F. Close. Chapter 3 charts his Radical endeavours both at Brantwood and in that club life in London which eventually led to his involvement in the Orsini affair. His literary and political talents clearly recognised and notwithstanding precarious employment prospects as a printer, Adams wrote for Charles Bradlaugh's *National Reformer* as well as for a number of

Radical Societies composed of ex Chartists and advanced middle class radicals, who saw eye to eye on such issues as freedom of speech, extension of the vote and support of the oppressed people abroad. Invited by Joseph Cowen, the advanced radical tribune on Tyneside, Adams went North in 1864 to the thriving and bustling centre of Britain's capital goods industries. Here he found a situation highly conducive to his missionary work. Chapter 4 examines the ways in which, until the feature closed in 1882 on the eve of his visit to America, Adams was able to give full expression in his "Ironside" leader column to advocating political democracy, the abolition of primogeniture, freedom of expression and human rights in countries on both sides of the Atlantic. It was these beliefs and values, entirely alien and abhorrent when articulated in stuffy Cheltenham Spa, to which Joseph Cowen, captain of industry and M.P. had, at the head of a remarkable group of advanced Liberals, moved steadily leftwards to embrace. Moreover, in as far as the *Weekly Chronicle's* readership was synonymous with the Newcastle electorate, it may be safely assumed that, in conjunction with its stable-mate, the *Newcastle Daily Chronicle*, Adams's propagandist work helped provide a basis for that kind of political loyalty which saw Cowen returned to Parliament on four successive occasions between 1874 and 1886; it also played a part in politicizing the miners' cause in the North East which resulted in the election of Lib-Lab M.P.'s Thomas Burt, Charles Fenwick and William Crawford.

Chapter 5 recognises the unique journalistic skills and devices by which Adams, independently of Cowen, built up the *Newcastle Weekly Chronicle* into one of the most successful and respected quality newspapers of its time. In utilizing, too, the *Chronicle's* columns as a vehicle for publicizing a number of homely reforms — kindness to animals, libraries and parks for the people, tree-planting and smoke abatement — the paper came to play an important role in shaping and reflecting North East public opinion, a focus for family life and community consciousness. The wider, political importance of Adams's *Weekly Chronicle* is also recognised in that it represented a site for the intersection of oppositional and hegemonic values: it upheld the old voice of Chartism, the traditions of working class independence and cultural autonomy; but it also seemed to be furthering the development of better class relationships within the orbit of the dominant culture by articulating the language of community politics of an advanced Liberal type. Thus Newcastle and much of the North East became areas whose Liberal political "commonsense" embraced, on the one hand, attacks on the unrepresentative State, the iniquities of the House of Lords and European despotism; and, on the other, an uncritical acceptance of bourgeois hegemony, whereby freedom of the indiviudal was dovetailed to the workings of a laissez-faire, competitive capitalist system.

The penultimate Chapter argues for the centrality of Adams's family life in order to better understand or suggest the personality of the subject. Evidence gleaned from the various primary sources strongly suggests that the companionship, love, interests and tranquillity of home life provided important emotional props with which to sustain his busy and demanding position in bourgeois waged labour. The Chapter also attempts a short genealogical history in order to reveal the enduring nature of his remarkable talents and range of interests as bequeathed to successive generations, some of whom are still actively involved in public life in the 1990s.

The last Chapter reveals how in the period after the American visit Adams, having gradually retreated from politics into local good works, became increasingly old-fashioned and out of touch politically. There is an essential continuity of thought and action in Adams's life. Consequently, his artisanate view of the world with its stress on individual freedom of action, dislike of bureaucracy, state aid and interference when confronted by the emergence of New Unionism and Socialism, both of which addressed what he failed to do namely the position of the unskilled, evoked a predictable outburst of hostility. There followed a brief flurry of anti Socialist commentary from which attention was shifted to his final crusade: a growing dislike for the Boers and their maltreatment of Black Africans in South Africa. To the last, Adams was a sincere, courageous and genuine Radical; in private life a caring and decent man; he was also honest and straightforward in public service to the people of Tyneside; and in his own editorial work and writings ranks amongst the best of press men: indeed, he was "an honour to the Fourth Estate".[55]

Notes

1. A start has been made on an analysis of the "second lieutenants" of Chartism. See C. Godfrey, Chartist Lives — The Anatomy of a Working Class Movement, New York, 1987 (originally presented as a Ph.D thesis, Harvard University, 1978). He offers a thumbnail sketch of W.E. Adams's career up to the 1860s; see pp.457-458.

2. Report of proceedings and copy of presentation address to William Edwin Adams (after thirty-five years' editorial work), Newcastle Upon Tyne. The original is in the possession of his great grand-daughter, Miss Margaret (Peg) Adams of Newcastle-Upon-Tyne. I am grateful to Mr. Frank Manders, Local Studies Librarian at Newcastle Central Reference Library, for his help in cross-referencing old and new source material.

3. Two obvious exceptions are: D. Thompson, The Chartists, London, 1984 and J. Saville, 1848: the British State and the Chartist Movement, Cambridge, 1987. See generally.

4. See my unpublished doctoral thesis 'Radicalism and Chartism in Gloucestershire, 1832-1847', University of Birmingham, 1980.

5. See W.E. Adams, Memoirs of a Social Atom, London, 1903, two volumes; Reptd. in one volume, New York, 1968, with an Introduction by J. Saville. p.112, p.117, p.268, p.291. Hereinafter, references to this book appear as Memoirs. According to Peg Adams her great-grandfather's library was donated to Newcastle Central and Gosforth Public Libraries at various stages between 1902 and the 1950s. Apart from a small number of extremely useful personal family papers, the bulk of his private correspondence may well have been lost from sight following the death in the mid 1950s of her grandmother, Kate, W.E. Adams's daughter-in-law by his eldest son, Ernest Welles Adams.

6. J. Saville and J. Bellamy (eds.), Dictionary of Labour Biography, Vol.VII, London, 1984, pp.1-4; J. Burnett, D. Vincent, D. Mayall (eds.), The Autobiography of the Working Class, an Annotated, Critical Bibliography, Vol.I 1790-1900, Brighton, 1984, pp.2-3; and J.O. Baylen and N.J. Gossman (eds.), Biographical Dictionary of Modern British Radicals, Vol.III, 1870-1914, Brighton, 1988, contribution by Maurice Milne on W.E. Adams, pp.14-18. See also a very good review article of Memoirs by A.L. Morton, Bulletin of Society for Study of Labour History, No.17, 1970, pp.32-35.

7. See Hypatia Bradlaugh Bonner, Charles Bradlaugh, A Record of his Life and Work, London, 1908, p.123; Thomas Burt, Pitman and Privy Councillor, An Autobiography, London, 1924, pp.185-186. These pages also report a glowing tribute by J. Cowen on Adams (the former did not write an autobiography).

8. W. Archer, William Charles Macready, London, 1890, Preface. Archer was indebted to Adams for his knowledge of the Northern theatre and the fact that he was a friend of the Macready's. (One of Macready's descendants, Louisa Mary Macready, was a subscriber to the 450 guinea fund for Adams in 1898).

9. G. Pollard, "Novels in newspapers: some unpublished letters of Captain Mayne Reid", Review of English Studies, Vol. XVI, Part II, 1942, pp.72-85. These letters from Mayne Reid to Adams indicate his respect for both the quality of the Newcastle Weekly Chronicle and Adams's business acumen as its editor.

10. B.M. Nightingale Papers, Vol. LXXIV, Add. Ms 45,812. Letter No.203, Oct. 13 1894. Florence Nightingale was accepting the honour of becoming a patron of Adams's Dicky Bird Society. Through the columns of the Children's Corner in the Newcastle Weekly Chronicle, the Society tried to instill in the minds of children and young people humane ideas, particularly about the duty of kindness to all living things.

11. D. Jones, Chartism and The Chartists, London, 1975. He lists nine references to Adams in the Index.

12. A. Plummer, Bronterre: A Political Biography of Bronterre O'Brien, 1804-1864, London, 1971, p.242.

13. John Stuart Mill, On Liberty (1859), Reptd. Middlesex, 1974, Introduction by G. Himmelfarb, pp.75-76.

14. For a critical scrutiny of this concept see D.G. Wright, Popular Radicalism: The Working-Class Experience, 1780-1880. London, 1988, pp.150-182.

15. National Reformer, July 27 1861. "An Old Foe With a New Face".

16. Ibid., Nov. 24 1867.

17. Idem.,

18. J. Saville, 1848: the British State and the Chartist Movement, op.cit., see generally.

19. F.E. Gillespie, Labor and Politics in England, 1850-1867, Durham, North Carolina, 1927, pp.164-165.

20. Newcastle Weekly Chronicle, Feb. 7 and March 7 1874.

21. National Reformer, Aug. 23 1862.

22. Beehive, Sept. 5 and Dec. 12 1863.

23. J. Saville, Introduction, Memoirs, op.cit., pp.25-26.

24. I am particularly grateful for the help of Mr. D.R. Webb, the Bishopsgate Librarian, and for his efforts in unearthing this pamphlet. Adams's name has been hand-written in parenthesis beneath the pseudonym, Caractacus.

25. R. Samuel, 'The Bishopsgate Institute', History Workshop Journal No.5. Spring 1978, pp.163-171, particularly pp.165-166.

26. See National Reformer, March 22; August 16; Oct. 11; Nov. 1 1862.

27. Ibid., April 6 1861, Article by Caractacus on "Dangers to the Right of Free Speech" with regard to the arrest of Bradlaugh at Plymouth. For reports of the trial see National Reformer, Aug. 10 1861; and Hypatia Bradlaugh Bonner, Charles Bradlaugh, A Record of his Life and Work, op.cit., Chapter XVII, "The Devonport Case, 1861", pp.175-188.

28. Winter's Magazine started as Golden Gates in 1891; became Winter's Weekly in 1892 and then in the same year Winter's Magazine, still a weekly. In 1895 it was absorbed into Mrs. Stannard's long established Wit and Wisdom. I am indebted to Peg Adams for loaning me the family's copy.

29. The Strand Magazine, No.187, Feb. 9 1895. Mrs. Stannard's inclusion in this magazine was kindly drawn to my attention by my English colleague, Mrs. Ann Parry.

30. D.N.B. 1901-1911, Vol.I 1920, pp.394-395. Her novels, some of which sold in excess of two million copies, were essentially simple, sentimental tales of military life which appealed irresistably to the Victorian public. A noted admirer of her work was John Ruskin. See also H.C. Black, Notable Women Authors of the Day, Glasgow, 1893. Mrs. Stannard, pp.45-57.

31. The Times. Dec. 15 1911, Obituary of Mrs. Stannard.

32. See, for example, Newcastle Weekly Chronicle, Aug. 21 1869 in support of the campaign for the Married Women's Property Bill by E.C. Wolsenholme and L. Becker. For the Rational Dress Society see D. Rubinstein, Before the Suffragettes, Women's Emancipation in the 1890s, Brighton, 1986 pp.214-220. An estimation of the size of the "No-Crinoline League" is given by the Newcastle Weekly Chronicle, March 25th 1893 when a figure of 16,000 members is quoted in the weekly Ladies Column.

33. Newcastle Weekly Chronicle, Jan. 28 1893. Ladies Column: "Geraldine's Letter". Geraldine was the pseudonym for Adams's daughter Ada Eveline

Adams who later married the Rev. Leonard B. Dalby, a Methodist Minister, of Whitley near Newcastle. I am particularly grateful to Mr. David Dalby of Whitstable, Kent, a great-grandson of W.E. Adams, for this lead in my explorations of the Newcastle Weekly Chronicle.

34. Some of its potential has in fact been utilized by W.H. Maehl (ed.) in his Introduction to R. Gammage: Reminiscences of a Chartist, Society for the Study of Labour History, Aids to Research, No.4, Manchester, 1983. pp.7-19.

35. A summary of Adams's work as Uncle Toby appeared in his commemorative History of the Dicky Bird Society, Newcastle, 1887.

36. The book was reprinted in a cheap second edition in 1887 by Walter Scott. On this occasion the publisher's preface, VII-VIII, lists a number of periodicals which had commented favourably on the original. These include: New York Herald, Washington Republic, Manchester Guardian, Spectator, Morning Post and The Sheffield Daily Telegraph. Its place in Chartist and Radical reaction to post-Civil War America has been recognized by A.R. Schoyen, The Chartist Challenge. A Portrait of George Julian Harney, London, 1958, pp.264-265.

37. Newcastle Weekly Chronicle, March 31 1883. Impressions of America, Conclusion by Viator (the pseudonym Adams adopted for the tour). See also Our American Cousins, op.cit., p.357.

38. G.A. Sala, America Revisited, London, 1885 (VIth edition). Sala had toured America in 1879 and 1880 and America Revisited first appeared in serial form in the Daily Telegraph in the early 1880s. See, for example, p.201, for his prejudices: "The Negro is, from many different aspects, a bad job; but the Southerners are trying hard to make the best of him."

39. New York Herald, Oct. 1 1883. I am grateful to my Americanist colleague, Dr. Alun Munslow, for supplying me with this information.

40. I am grateful to Mrs. Sheila Dahlin of Galashiels for information concerning her grandmother, Mrs. Gertrude Smith, and also for material relating to Adams's descendants through his eldest daughter's issue.

41. Bradlaugh Papers (National Secular Society Collection, Bishopsgate) Letter 2692 from Adams to Hypatia Bradlaugh Bonner, May 8 1902 indicates that with regard to the Memoirs he was looking for "somebody to publish them or the reminiscent portion of them". In reply, letter 2693 May 12, Adams thanks Mrs. Bonner for her suggestion of Fisher Unwin with whom he intended "to communicate in a day or two". Within a year however they were published by Hutchinson. According to the latter, records of this period were destroyed by aerial bombing during World War II.

42. J. Burnett, (ed.) Destiny Obscure: autobiographies of childhood, education and family from the 1820s to the 1920's, London, 1982 and D. Vincent, Bread, Knowledge and Freedom: A Study of Nineteenth-Century Working Class Autobiography, London, 1981.

43. According to R. Gagnier, "Social Atoms: Working Class Autobiography, Subjectivity and Gender", Victorian Studies, Spring, 1987, Vol. 30, No.3 pp.335-363, in particular p.338: "most working class autobiographies begin not with a family lineage or birthdate but rather with an apology for their author's ordinariness" encoded in title's like that of Adams's Memoirs.

44. W.E. Adams, Memoirs, op.cit., Chapter XII, pp.109-119.

45. A.L. Morton, Bulletin of Society for the Study of Labour History, Review Article, op.cit., p.33.

46. For a general consideration of the emotional experiences in working class autobiography, see also D. Vincent, "Love and death and the nineteenth century working class", Social History, Vol.5. No.2, May 1980, pp.223-247.

47. Cowen Collection (Newcastle Central Reference Library). See, for example, B415.27,1881, Letter from J. Cowen to W.E. Adams disapproving "of the general tone, and a good deal of what has been written in the Weekly for some time".

48. E.I. Waitt, "John Morley, Joseph Cowen and Robert Spence Watson: Liberal Divisions in Newcastle Politics, 1873-95", Unpublished Ph.D thesis, Manchester, 1972, see pp.86-89, for Cowen's dramatic clash with James Annand, his editor of the Newcastle Daily Chronicle, over their differences concerning the Eastern Question in 1877. Annand felt obliged to resign.

49. T. Burt, Pitman and Privy Councillor, An Autobiography, op.cit., p.185.

50. The Holyoake Papers from the Bishopsgate Institute, London and the Co-operative Library, Manchester, Microfilm Copy with Introduction by E. Royle, Cambridge, 1969. There are eight letters directly by W.E. Adams to G.J. Holyoake, but a further six make reference to him.

51. The George Howell Collection at the Bishopsgate Institute contains seventeen letters from Adams to Howell.

52. At the Houghton Library, Harvard University, U.S.A. MS, Eng 180, Letters to W.E. Adams from W.J. Linton, 1855-1897. Although this collection is listed in J.F.C. Harrison and D. Thompson, Bibliography of the Chartist Movement, 1837-1976, Brighton, 1978, p.24, as far as I am aware only Prof. F.B. Smith has utilized them briefly in Radical Artisan, W.J. Linton, 1812-97, Manchester, 1973.

53. Ephemera in the possession of Peg Adams, Newcastle Upon Tyne.

54. For Gramsci's influence on Nineteenth Century British Social History, see, for example, T. Bennett, G. Martin, C. Mercer, J. Woollacott (eds.), Culture, Ideology and Social Process, Milton Keynes, 1981; see particularly Section 4, Class, Culture and Hegemony, pp.185-260.

55. Memorial to W.E. Adams, Newspaper cuttings (Newcastle Central Reference Library), L920A219, 1907, 113pp. See in particular p.107, Letter 15 from Wigham Richardson, local industrialist, to Basil Anderton B.A., Librarian at Newcastle, May 8th 1907.

1 A Radical Upbringing

For an early political baptism, W.E. Adams could almost claim a head's start. He was born in Cheltenham Spa on February 11 1832 in humble circumstances to a radical family, amid the resounding and unsuccessful struggle by fellow members of the British working class for a programme of advanced political reform. Adams was one of four children belonging to John and Sarah Adams (née Wells) who, because of the relative poverty of their circumstances and the perennial disruption consequent on the father's tramp for work as a plasterer, was brought up within the kinship structure of his maternal grandmother's home in the Spa. It was here under the protective eye of the Wells' three unmarried daughters — described by Adams proudly as his "upright, honourable, considerate, thoughtful, industrious" aunts[1] — that he enjoyed a settled, stable and happy childhood. It should not be inferred of course from this situation that Adams was spoiled or in any way the subject of his family's undivided attention — far from it. In this poor family the values which Adams inherited viewed time as precious, rationalised all labour as honourable and worthwhile, and attacked the idleness of the feckless and unrespectable poor. Superimposed were his own artisanal values of the virtues of self-help, self-reliance and independence. Both his elderly grandmother and her daughters were hardworking washerwomen enslaved to the drudgery of the wash tub; they were part of that politically invisible yet vitally necessary economic order — the other face of Cheltenham — which was needed to maintain their wealthy residents' mantle of finery and fashion. Indeed, as Adams well-remembered, it was the unsightly hands of these family heroines, disfigured by large calluses and corns,[2] the result of years of hard scrubbing for little financial return, who provided the very basis for the Spa's outward show as a genteel, fashion conscious tourist centre, the "Queen of Watering Places".[3]

The thriving and bustling Spa town in which Adams's family found a role derived its vitality from the unique intersection of two ways of life: the traditional, self-contained rural world of a country market town on which was then superimposed the sophisticated, urbane and polished world associated with seasonal visitors and a residential professional élite, retired Anglo-Indian military personnel and, as Adams observes, "lords and ladies of high degree".[4] Until the rise of the mineral springs in the mid-eighteenth century, Cheltenham was a small market town straddling a two-mile-long thoroughfare which was known as the High Street, and interrupted only by the Parish Church of St. Mary's in the centre. The visit of George III in 1788 however confirmed its role as a rapidly rising and fashionable Spa resort which, with its supply of health-giving waters at the Sherborne and Montpellier wells, could rival the pump rooms at Bath. Social brilliance and a programme of building expansion then followed hand in hand. Visitors, including the Duke of Wellington and the poet Tennyson, as well as country gentry, retired colonels and metropolitan aristocrats, flocked to take the waters. By 1820 Cheltenham was almost overflowing: balls and concerts were crowded; seven hundred lodging houses full; and walks, wells and streets aglow with fashion. Country land speculators as well as architects and solicitors cashed in on the boom. New estates, stately mansions, grass verges and tree-lined crescents were developed at Pittville, Lansdown, Montpellier and off the Promenade. In addition, in the fashionable upper High Street, new developments in the form of exclusive villas or terraced town-houses were built in Berkeley Place, Oxford Parade and Portland Street. To many of the visitors, the whiteness of the buildings presented a magnificent aura; and their impressive balconies, fantastic domes and ornamental ironwork added that touch of grandeur which helped distinguish resorts like Cheltenham as a haven of the wealthy.[5] Given its charms, a large number of visitors understandably stayed on and the recorded population statistics underline the mushrooming development. In 1801 the population was 3,076; in 1821, 13,396; but by 1831 on the eve of Parliamentary reform, Cheltenham became eligible for an M.P. with over 24,000 inhabitants.[6] A year later, as if to confirm its social exclusiveness, Craven F. Berkeley, a powerful patron of, and focal point for, the gay, idle and pleasurable life, was returned by its wealthy and unrepresentative electors. For the next fifteen years and then from 1852 until his death in 1855, this scion of the leading Gloucestershire gentry made Cheltenham Spa a virtually unassailable Whig proprietary borough, notwithstanding the separate attempts by the Rev. Francis Close, the Spa's leading Tory evangelical, and the Radical-Chartist alliance to diminish his influence.[7]

Amidst the airs and graces of the Spa's social scene, the old character of the town as a market centre contrived to stay, even though the handicraft trades that were to be found amongst the labouring population after 1830 were geared increasingly to serve the diverse needs of the genteel residents, and the demands of new and flourishing public schools. The survival of both the old horse and cattle markets, as well as a flourishing centre for the sale of locally produced agricultural products, meant that the town did not become detached inAdams's time from a region it still served: the surrounding catchment area of rich Gloucestershire farmland. The old market town ethos also ensured that for its labouring population their loss of an overall sense of community, as mushrooming Cheltenham polarised socially and geographically, was offset by the ability to relate within the working class locality to an almost organic rural world with such familiar features as the attendant fairs, seasonal mops, strolling ballad-singers and plebeian customs and pastimes.

Adams was certainly conscious of these changes from an early age: "Our street was in Lower Dockum — a locality that is unknown even by name to the genteel residents in the parades and squares and crescents of Lansdown and Pittville."[8] Geographically, the select areas of 'young' Cheltenham were to be found in the Eastern, Southern and South Western parts of the Spa. They stood in sharp contrast to the poorer quarter, or lower part of the town, that had long existed and to which Adams referred on the North, North East side of the Spa. By 1840 one can recognise a fairly well-defined area of working class housing in the vicinity of the coal wharfs on the Gloucester Road, and along the cluster of little streets that connected the Swindon Road to the trading area at the lower end of the High Street. It was here amongst a thriving community of politically conscious shoemakers, carpenters, tailors, small shop-keepers, gardeners, domestic servants and general labourers — at once the expected support force of the genteel residents and the seed-bed for Chartism — that Adams learnt the laws of the Street, received a radical schooling and was immersed in those communal customs long embedded in the culture of the Spa's incipient working class.

From the mid 1830s, the vogue for taking 'the Cheltenham Waters' went into decline and, as the number of visitors fell, the wells gradually closed. At the same time the force of the evangelical movement began to make strong headway and transform the social scene in Cheltenham: no longer by 1845 could it be described as the "merriest, sick resort on earth";[9] rather, it had become as the poet Tennyson, now a local resident, described: "a polka, parson-worshipping place of which Francis Close is Pope."[10]

Close had been the minister of Holy Trinity Church (1824-6), and was then appointed by Reverend Charles Simeon to Cheltenham parish church. Throughout his long career, like Simeon his mentor, Close fearlessly extolled a deep attachment to the Liturgy, the Book of Common Prayer and biblical study, as part of an unswerving loyalty and obedience to the Church of England. Like Simeon, too,Close's chief objection to Dissenters was not on theological grounds but from fear that they were in no way tied to the status quo and wanted fairly sweeping reforms. For Close, good government meant a Conservative government and the preservation of the Protestant ascendancy. Not surprisingly, he was strongly anti-Roman and thundered forth against the teachings of Newman and the "Tract for the Times". He was, therefore, both the product and powerful exponent of an evangelicalism that came to establish over home and will in Cheltenham so supreme and inquisitional an empire that his opponents nicknamed the Spa 'the Close Borough', and his thirty-year clerical dynasty the 'Close Season'. Indeed, 'the authorities of the town sank into insignificance when their influence was placed besides that of the potent Vicar'.[11]

The range of Close's activities as the Spa's spiritual autocrat was impressive.[12] Only a year after his appointment the thirty-year-old minister began to mount a formidable attack on both aristocratic decadence and popular leisure pursuits. Much to the dismay of the racing fraternity he called in his sermons for the ending of the three-day Cheltenham races, a major attraction for all social groups in the Spa, and remained undaunted by attempts on the part of the Berkeley household to thwart plans for eliminating 'the turf'. Backed by the *Cheltenham Chronicle* (founded 1809) and the *Cheltenham Journal* (founded 1834), to the proprietor of which Adams was apprenticed, Close also waged a ceaseless campaign against excessive drinking, gambling, card-parties and the theatre. In Adams's opinion "the most remarkable example of his authority in secular affairs was the power he exercised in preventing the reconstruction of the Theatre Royal", which had been destroyed by fire in 1830.[13] No doubt he achieved much in reassuring the minds of staid, orthodox and respectable people whose numbers, particularly among the ladies of the town, began to grow more influential in the wake of his repeated exhortations.

It was in his earnest desire to spread the gospel through church building, to found schools and charities, to extol sobriety and to uphold strict sabbatarian observance that Close, the defender of an existing social order, rudely encroached on the life of the Spa's working class enclave. To this end he persuaded many of the wealthy residents to subscribe and the government to grant £3,000 for the building of a new and more 'popular' church. Thus was conceived a symbol of society as settled and god-ordained, each class content to do its duty in that sphere of life in which providence had placed it. Accordingly, in 1831 the 'Free Church' of St. Paul's, with accommodation for 1,600, was erected north east of the High Street expressly to serve the needs of the poor in that area, who could not otherwise afford either those pew rents or payments at the door required of wealthy worshippers in the Spa's more fashionable churches.[14] Within a few years, as the evangelical crusade against organised working class political behaviour gathered momentum, Close found himself engaged in two spectacular confrontations. The first of these occurred in August 1839 when in response to his pulpit attacks on Chartist aims and objectives, the Chartists ruffled the placid surface of Cheltenham society by defiantly "invading" the parish Church of St. Mary's; it was a peaceful protest to register both their dissatisfaction with the hypocrisy of professing Christians and disgust for the Anglican Church's connections — reaffirmed regularly by Close himself — with an aristocratic state, which denied the artisan his right to political liberty. Secondly, following the celebrated incident in May 1842 when the Owenite Socialist, G.J. Holyoake, publicly exercised his right to free speech in an open lecture, a more wily Close on this occasion had him successfully convicted and imprisoned for blasphemy. Thus encouraged, men like Adams fared little better from the fruits of Close's more intrusive sabbatarian advances. At the beginning of his apprenticeship, for example, Adams had promised that he would not "haunt taverns or playhouses";[15] but while he was able to find a way around Close's theatrical boycott he could do nothing to obviate the unsocial hours for printing copy: the *Journal* was always published on Monday mornings. It was an arrangement which would have ordinarily necessitated normal Sunday labour, and Adams recalled with great displeasure how, at his expense, their employer deferred to Close's wishes:

> "Mr. Hadley avoided desecration of the Sabbath by obliging us to work till twelve o'clock on Saturday night and resume operations at twelve o'clock on Sunday night. This preposterous regulation almost completely destroyed three days of the week so far as any enjoyment or sensible pursuit was concerned."[16]

The extended family unit within which Adams grew up remained remarkably unconditioned by the respectable straight-jacket of Close's evangelicalism. His family were not anti-religious: he had been baptised into the Christian faith[17] and sporadically attended morning service and Sunday School at a local Wesleyan chapel;[18] but they were anti-clerical and viewed Close as a symbol of an establishment Church which functioned as an ideological prop for the corrupt political system so starkly reproduced on their doorstep. Excepting the few visible signs of a dissenting religious affinity and mindful of the writer's tendency to idealize retrospectively, Adams nevertheless enjoyed what can only be described as a progressive childhood and home life — the antithesis of a strict puritanical regime endured by some other middle-rank radicals.[19]

As a child he showed a great love of animals, a joyful impulse that was not repressed even though the close-knit family home was small and already full to capacity. His aunts patiently watched on as, like Topsy, Adams's aptly named pet-dog, the menagerie steadily grew in number to include fantail pigeons, rabbits and a canary![20] An appreciation of the surrounding countryside was also allowed to thrive when he was free from domestic chores. Robust in health,[21] he enjoyed the liberty to play either on his own or with his street mates on the open spaces and wonder in the fields and woodlands that existed just beyond his backyard. It was here, of course, that he first began to appreciate the wonders of nature, show a love for all living things and enthuse the sheer beauty of the rolling Gloucestershire landscape. Such influences as he derived from the idyllic rural life were not always progressive. Adams painfully recalled his sense of shame not for any religious transgression, but at being an accomplice, albeit protestingly, to his chums' cruelty on their regular Sunday afternoon ramble: they had deliberately taken a bird's nest and sadistically tore the little fledglings to pieces.[22] To Adams looking back this was an important moment in his boyhood; and as he became more conscious of what was right and wrong he resolved to sever the connection with some of his more unsavoury friends; no longer was he content simply to "follow the crowd".

Adams's formal schooling was brief and intermittent. The family's meagre resources saw him denied access to the National and British schools. Instead, he went first to an inefficient dame's school, a lowly institution recalled only for the way in which "the old lady shook and touzled me";[23] and then to a private seminary in the town called Gardner's Academy, the proprietor being Joseph Aldan Gardner — a fiddler, dancing master, pen-man as well as a teacher of youth. However, because of the family's impecunious state his grandmother, unable to pay the small fee, agreed to an equivalent amount of laundry work. This arrangement proved unsatisfactory; but from an indifferent Gardner Adams at least learnt both how to write and appreciate his own talent for calligraphy. Acute financial circumstances in 1844 finally interrupted Adams's schooling. He was obliged to leave and took service as an errand boy with a book-seller. Amongst the less onerous of his duties was the job of carrying books and magazines from his employer's circulating library to the homes of gentry subscribers. Thus was opened to him the joys of English literature, for he had opportunities of learning about, for example, the inside pages of those novels by Dickens and plays by Shakespeare with which he had to deal. But the work at the library became too heavy for the twelve year old and he was sent to a Wesleyan day school for a brief season. There were in fact two day schools run by the Wesleyans in the Spa at the time and Adams attended the one housed under the new Chapel, which was built in 1839 in St. George's Street. For all its religious mould it was here that young Adams, judging by his comments, first felt a thirst for knowledge and found the basic means of self-education. "The Schoolmaster knew his business" he declared, and "the lessons were made intelligible; the classes were made interesting; ... There was no more mooching ... It was a delightful time",[24] A heavy burden at this time was also thrown on the free Sunday Schools, but as to the role the Wesleyan one played in Adams's life he had no doubts: "the vague remembrances I retain of it are not pleasant ... the small tradesman who conducted it was severe in his dealings with the children ... I had a dreary time there."[25]

A dislike of school and fear of teachers were feelings frequently expressed by nineteenth century working class autobiographers. This is understandable given the fact that while some of the educational institutions which Adams attended overtly aimed at inculcating discipline, order and obedience both in and outside the class room, others — the Sunday School for instance — operated more subtle but equally effective methods of accommodation to middle class priorities about respectable behaviour.[26] Adams's boyhood recollections suggest that, however protean in form, the forces of the evangelical movement were as yet singularly unsuccessful in their work as "social policemen". For one thing there was the individual resourcefulness of lads like Adams to contend with. On absenting himself from school he recalled that he went to great lengths to reach one of his favourite hiding places.

> "I got on to a plank bridge over a stream in Jessop's Garden, now the site of the Great Western terminus; the swirl of the running water turned me giddy; I jumped right into the middle of the stream; and dried my clothes, running about naked the while under one of the arches of the new railway bridge."[27]

A more formidable problem for clerics like Close was the fact that Adams's family were part of a wider, working class community in which were embedded what Close perceived to be those disreputable rites and rituals derived from an eighteenth century plebeian, rough culture. Adams certainly confirms the fact that, notwithstanding the stamp of rudimentary schooling, there was a range of such "pleasures" of an extremely colourful kind in which he showed little personal restraint. For example, the boisterous street life[28] with its emphasis on fighting amongst peer groups within and between localities, the running into shops, knocking doors of unpopular elderly people or knocking down tradesmen's goods, as well as the half-tolerated anarchy when "beating the bounds"[29] — all this involved Adams in prankish behaviour which was, as he himself admitted, "often reprehensible, sometimes dangerous, nearly always annoying".[30]

The stability of this street culture was also underpinned by a seasonal interest in such every day frivolous pursuits as marbles, peg-tops, leap-frog, rounders and running games; and at Christmas time by the singing of un-liturgical carols. Two lines of one popular carol he recalled ran thus:

> "It was the joy of Mary, it was the joy of one
> To see her infant Jesus sucking at her breast bone."[31]

As a rule the carol-singers closed their serenades with an appeal for money.

Much of the adult example set to Adams and his boyhood friends stubbornly upheld the practices of an older, traditional rural culture. He recalled some of their ceremonies:

> "May Day used to be recognized by the sweeps of the town, who exercised a sort of prescriptive right to dress up a Jack-in-the-Green (a wickerwork cage covered with ivy leaves, with a man inside to carry it), dancing round the figure in grotesque fashion,

> and collecting pence from the small crowds which witnessed the performance ... later in the month (May 29th) came Royal Oak Day, when the innkeepers decorated their premises with oak boughs, and the inhabitants, especially the lads, carried oak apples or oak leaves in their button holes. The lad who failed to adorn himself in this manner was an object of derision to the rest who saluted him with cries of "Shick Shack". (Adams never knew the meaning).[32]

Custom it should be remembered operated not simply as a bastion against clerical control; it was also advanced "to defend and promote the rights of the labouring poor at a time when new ideologies of private property and capitalist enterprises threatened to extinguish those rights".[33] In this respect Adams could certainly claim to have personally played a minor historical role in perpetuating a popular Spa ceremonial activity. At Whitsuntide in 1841, at a time when the conflict between Close's evangelical zeal and popular-based calendar customs was particularly noticeable, Adams defiantly established an entirely new company of Morrismen. Later in life he claimed that:

> "The dancers appeared at that time, and for many years afterwards, appearing as regularly in the streets at Whitsuntide as Jack-in-the-Green on May-Day."[34]

Clearly, in the 1830s and 40s there was little that Close could do by way of preventing either the public gaiety associated with popular beliefs, customs and ceremonies, or the more private habits of dear old dames like Adams's grandmother who, in a practice more reminiscent of Hogarth's day, took a pinch of snuff and half a glass of gin before bedtime.[35]

Adams's intermittent schooling had provided him with an elementary grasp of reading, writing and a passion for books; it also ensured that he was able to appreciate at an early age the single most important activity in the family's life: a deep commitment to radical politics. Both his grandmother and aunts were politically aware: they read such radical newspapers in the 1830s as the *Weekly Dispatch* and *Political Register*; they warmed to the writings of Tom Paine because the poverty and decadence of Cheltenham itself fitted closely his critique of government through "Old Corruption"; and they became staunch Chartists attending meetings and abstaining from all excisable articles during the sacred month of August 1839.[36] Not surprisingly, the young Adams imbibed the household's radicalism. His whole interest in books first came via a political medium as he listened to his grandmother reading aloud from Cobbett, and when able to read himself recalled how "I revelled as a boy in the politics of the

Dispatch".[37] Political knowledge grew; and the family offered their humble kitchen as the venue for Sunday morning Chartist gatherings:

> "The most constant of our visitors was a crippled shoemaker ... we called him Larry ... [who] made his appearance every Sunday morning as regular as clockwork, with a copy of the *Northern Star*, damp from the press, for the purpose of hearing some member of our household read out to him and others "Feargus's letter". The paper had first to be dried before the fire, and then carefully and evenly cut, so as not to damage a single line of the almost sacred production."[38]

Hand in hand with this kind of political education came an early exposure to the activities of the local Chartist movement of which Cheltenham itself was the epi-centre in Gloucestershire. When only a boy of nine he recalled being taken to his first political meetings, a spate of which took place in the early months of 1841. In early April that year, for example, he went with his aunts to hear a reformed Henry Vincent extolling the virtues of temperance to a receptive audience;[39] and in late April 1842, when the weather was unusually hot, to hear the great Chartist leader, Feargus O'Connor, holding forth on Chartist principles in his shirt sleeves to large crowds in the markets.[40] But perhaps the most revealing example of the impact of this "radical schooling" was the occasion of G.J. Holyoake's first visit in January 1841 when he came to lecture on "the freedom of the press".[41] Reminiscing over fifty years later in *The Newcastle Weekly Chronicle* Adams vividly recalled how, amidst mounting speculation amongst fellow townspeople about what to expect from the tongue of an Owenite infidel, his eager curiosity was satisfied and imagination freed from the shackles of small-town popular superstitions about Holyoake's visage:

> "Well, I, as a boy, had heard the elders talk about the stranger and the fearful things he was saying: so I peeped into the room in which he was lecturing, not without fear and trembling, for I expected to see a monster with cloven hoofs and forked tail. What I saw and heard was a tall, thin young man, with a still thinner voice."[42]

Just as Adams was beginning to appreciate the solid advantages of school, he had to leave and choose a trade. This was certainly an important stage in his life, a point when he became conscious of his identity:

> "I was a boy still, but I thought myself a man. No other boy was half my importance; no man, even, strutted the streets with anything like the dignity I

> assumed during the first few week of my apprentice days.[43]

The family's sacrifices in order to place their grandson in what was undoubtedly one of the most "aristocratic" of skilled trades — one incidentally which was not strongly represented in Chartism[44] — were enormous. He was apprenticed as a printer to the proprietor of the *Cheltenham Journal*, John Joseph Hadley, on June 6 1846, the indenture arrangements costing his grandmother the princely sum of £15.[45] The work for Hadley — Close's eyes and ears — sharpened his awareness both of social snobberies and the power of the Anglican Church in the Spa. The nature of his trade was not particularly arduous or dangerous, although, as we've noted, the hours were long and anti-social. This did not blunt his enthusiasm for self-improvement as he embarked upon a remarkable career of self-education. Distancing himself from those street companions with bad habits, he gradually became the autodidact in his private hours at home or in the few slack moments between the plebeian demands of the weekly press work. His new companions in this cultural interplay of knowledge with experience were, as he recalled, John Cassell's *Popular Educator*, his inspirational *Family Friend* and William Cobbett's *Grammar*;[46] and with their aid he studied French, Latin, English grammar and stenography, assiduously. Such self-directed intellectual activity not only thrived in a home conducive to study, but was also extended as Adams was attracted to the stimulating company of fellow tradesmen like-mindedly intent upon the pursuit of knowledge.

The range of mutual improvement societies in which Adams now became immersed was impressive. Perhaps the best known and enduring was the Working Men's Club movement associated with the rational recreation work of the Rev. Henry Solly.[47] In 1847 Solly was the Unitarian minister in Cheltenham; he was also mildly involved with Chartist activities;[48] but he was also experimenting with self-improving artisans like Adams in creating a drink-free, educational and social programme that caught on nationwide. Adams was fortunate, too, on occasions to procure tickets to attend lectures at the fairly exclusive Philosophical Institution, situated in a handsome Grecian-style building on the prestigous Promenade. Here, he heard "people of some importance in their day", including the spell-binding George Dawson elucidate on various topics. These ranged from geology and astronomy to poetry and travel guide books, and, in Dawson's case, to an exposé of "the weaknesses and foibles of mankind".[49] Usually, however, Adams was involved in institutions more suited to their humble means and needs. At least three can be identified. The first was the local Mechanics' Institute, already under Chartist control by the time Adams joined.[50] Its well-stocked library and spacious rooms in Albion Street offered a means of preserving a completely independent tradition of adult education for the politically conscious Spa artisans. Adams had access to books on a wide range of subjects, including the natural sciences, history, geography and European languages. The second grew out of the embryonic Working Men's Club, for when Solly left the Club folded; but his successor, the Rev. John Dandy, allowed them to use the vestry rooms for meetings of the Cheltenham General Literary Union.[51] That Adams's talents were above average from an early age is borne out by the fact that he founded the third: the People's Institute in Regent Street,[52] it became extremely popular in his time. This is understandable given the fact that it developed, often under his presidency, into a working class literary and debating society, as well as a Chartist stronghold after 1847. Adams recalled proudly the fruits of his adolescent labours at the Institute:

> "Books and newspapers could be read in one of the rooms; classes for the study of various subjects were held in other rooms; debates on topics of current interest or speculative value took place once a week; and occasionally essays that had been awarded prizes in competition were read by ingenious writers. We were fond of controversy in those days..."[53]

Such powerful educational experiences as were gained by young Adams within the Spa's radical political culture, had a profound impact upon his perceptions of, and purposes behind, the content of public reading material being consumed across the terrain of mid-Nineteenth century popular literature. If we view popular literature as "one of the sites where a struggle for and against a culture of the powerful is engaged"[54] — "a divided territory"[55] of domination, negotiation and exchange between dominant and subordinate classes — then we may begin to appreciate how, on the one hand, the cultural practices of politically discriminate and temperance orientated Chartists like Adams and, on the other, the orientation by middle class individuals at proselytization through moral reading works and "useful" knowledge, or more unwittingly through commercially produced forms, were transacted or negotiated.

It was in streets inhabited by poor families like Adams's that a distinctive form of popular literature, the broadside ballad, was hawked, sold and read. The broadside ballad or tale was a sheet of verses printed on one side of a piece of thin paper, usually decorated with a crude woodcut, and sold for 1d. or $\frac{1}{2}$d. Sung or read aloud the broadside gave, according to Martha Vicinus, "a very large number of people access to current events, trade customs, local legends and the cultural life around them".[56]

Much to Close's annoyance, at his printing office in Oxford Passage, High Street, Thomas Willey, an active Chartist and colleague of Adams, earned both a livelihood and an unrivalled reputation in the Cheltenham community as the vendor of broadsides, the contents of which were dovetailed to suit almost every whim, fancy and occasion.[51] Many related to the bawdy rural world, to fairs, festivities, crime and the gallows; but some were new, reflecting the developing political consciousness of the working class and the problems of urban and social life. Such literature, with a meaning and appeal that reached to the roots of the harsh realities of earning a living in the Spa community, was, until "the penny papers and recognised reporters drove the flying stationers (the ballad hawkers) from the streets",[58] the popular literature par excellence of working people.

Such everyday literature co-existed uncomfortably alongside solid literary works of a more substantial nature, but access to them was often difficult for poor families. In Adams's situation, work as an errand boy gave him a brief but unique opportunity to appreciate solid reading material. He missed entirely however the religious meanings of Bunyan's *Pilgrim's Progress*, the staple literary diet of a God-fearing home;[59] nor did he take to the literature churned out by the Society for the Diffusion of Useful Knowledge. Its *Penny Magazine*, propagator of the "steam intellect", was "full of facts, often very dry facts — interesting, but not enlivening";[60] but he did enjoy the penny editions of Shakespeare's plays, *Gulliver's Travels*, *Arabian Nights* and, most of all, the adventure stories of Fenimore Cooper.[61]

A significant new dimension to the popular reading literature in Adams's day — one which he looked back on as degenerative — was that of the cheap, commercially produced forms for the mass market; it was just beginning to find favour in larger centres of population like Cheltenham. For example, "I remember best", recalled Adams, "the *Family Herald*, *Reynolds's Miscellany*, and Lloyd's "penny dreadfuls".[62] Within the pages of these low brow weeklies[63] were to be found serialized articles dealing with crime, romance, cruelty and adventure, as well as more innocent material on gardening, biography, topical events and odd bits of information that were likely to provide harmless stimulation. In the case of *Reynolds's Miscellany*, sensationalism existed side by side with a more overt radical political content as Reynolds, an active Chartist himself in 1848, went through the motions of attacking, for example, the aristocracy and clergy over inadequate public health provision and inefficient local government in the mushrooming cities.[64] Yet pride of place in the cheap weeklies, so it appears from Adams's recollections, was reserved for Edward Lloyd's penny fiction (e.g. "The Horrors of Zindorf Castle"), which would "make the blood curdle and the flesh creep".[65] Such titillation as Adams gained from these sensational chap-books was augmented by an important literary adjunct: the travelling booth or theatre. Francis Close had successfully prevented regular drama in the town by 1839, but as

23.12.10 Todmorden, West Yorks

In January 1845, the Chartist newspaper the *Northern Star* requested that readers send in ideas for a hymn book, which was duly printed later that year. The only surviving copy has now been discovered by Mike Sanders of Manchester University, in Todmorden Public Library. The tiny pamphlet, containing sixteen hymns, had the boards of a cigar box glued to its covers. Dr Sanders argues that this "amazing find . . . opens up a whole new understanding of Chartism – which as a movement in many ways shaped the Britain we know today". Couplets such as "Men of England, ye are slaves; / Beaten by policemen's staves" did not find house room in that quintessential product of Victorian endeavour, *Hymns Ancient and Modern*, first published in 1861.

and political controls exerted from the mother country on which their ascendancy depended. For Swift's subtlest critics, such as Claude Rawson, the anti-colonial dimension of his satire is disrupted by startling gestures of self-implication, and by elements of aggression and disgust against the colonized too fierce and compelling to be sanitized by the ironies around them.

The problem here is that the "soft" interpretation of Swift, in which his work is wishfully retrofitted as a monument of liberal humanitarianism or postcolonial analysis, keeps popping back up. Though acknowledging that Swift never objected to the penal laws enacted by the Dublin Parliament (some of which were rejected in Westminster as too draconian), Fabricant and Mahony remain wedded to a view of him as a strenuous activist and sympathetic advocate for the indigenous poor. In Dublin, "he daily wandered through the streets . . . getting to know the weavers of the nearby Coombes (whose interests he espoused in several prose tracts and poems) and the beggars entreating passersby in the vicinity of the cathedral".

Swift did indeed espouse the interests of the Dublin weavers in several tracts, and it was with reference to this group, and especially to his courageous campaign in the *Drapier's Letters* against currency warfare from the Whig ministry in London, that he rested his claims to popularity with the Irish "mob". The weavers were mostly Dissenters, but he would have been on safe ground with them so long as he avoided his favourite topic of the Test Act, which he most memorably upheld against the threat of repeal in his poem "On the Words Brother Protestants and

ship with them? Perhaps he wanted to anti-colonialism or proto-nationalism – Swift's mind was nothing if not versatile, a multiple in its impulses and commitme and other possibilities are worth keeping mind. Since many of these beggars w refugees from the impoverished hinterla he would probably have kept clear of "Legion Club" theme, the maintenance of tithing system that supported the Anglic clergy in Ireland (though not of course th Presbyterian and Catholic counterparts) fr the fruits, if fruits is the word, of agricultu labour. But he also had bracing opinions share about their present occupation. In sermon on the "Causes of the Wretch Condition of Ireland", he insists that begg owed their poverty and disease "to their o Faults; to their present Sloth and Negliger . . . to their foolish Expensiveness, to th Drunkenness, and other Vices". And if t was too commonplace and predictable, also had views on begging that were all own. In recent scholarship as well as otl textbook selections from Swift, simplis understandings of his irony as merely means to humanitarian ends have been uns tled by startling similarities between the rh oric of disgust he exaggerates in *A Mod Proposal* (1729) and the dour vituperatio of his lesser-known *Proposal for Givi Badges to the Beggars of Dublin* (173 Again, Fabricant and Mahony exclude th awkward work, which Swift published und his own name to advance another pet proje that Dublin beggars should be forced to we badges on pain of whipping, and that the "fo eign" beggars now infesting the city shou be whipped out of town. This rebarbati booths were not mentioned in Adams's indentures he assumed that he was quite at liberty to haunt this relatively recent form of popular urban-based culture.[66] The greatest drawing force of the many evenings of entertainment he recalled were those colourful comedians, conjurors and actors who performed farce, tragedy and stock pieces of the "blood-and-thunder sort" in Tommy Hurd's travelling theatre.[67]

Notwithstanding the continuing attractiveness in the 1830s and 1840s of the Spa's traditional plebeian culture and its noted embryonic commercial penetration, for Adams, in the "divided territory" of popular literature, "the taste of reading, once acquired, came in due course to need higher pabulum to satisfy it."[68] His conscious choice was to reject demeaning pulp literature in favour of acquiring that political reading material which questioned every aspect of the established order.[69] Not surprisingly, in the various mutual improvement societies the works of leading radicals were in demand in the reading rooms. Undoubtedly the most important ideologue in Adams's initial intellectual and political development was Tom Paine. Writing at the time of the stirring events of the French Revolution of 1848 Adams recalled vividly how:

> I had previously read the "Rights of Man" and other political works of Thomas Paine, which had seduced me from bed at five o'clock for many mornings in succession. And now I was fairly in the maelstrom.[70]

Another firm favourite with Adams was Reynolds's *Political Instructor*, which echoed the familiar anti-aristocratic critiques of William Cobbett's *Political Register* — one of his grandmother's radical heroes. Pride of place amongst his radical newspaper reading was, of course, reserved for the *Northern Star*. A common sequel to those Sunday morning gatherings at his home, held primarily for their friend Larry's benefit, was the mid-week political discussion classes centred around the contents of the *Star*, and at which they reaffirmed their faith in the justice of the Chartist demands.[71]

Adams's radical schooling in the 1830s and 40s suggests that amongst Spa Chartists like himself, there was a real conflict of values within the surviving plebeian culture. On the one hand, we have noted his boyhood identification with the culture of communal custom, the street-life and the broadside ballad, much of which was riotous, semi-pagan and pub-centred; on the other, his attachment in adolescence to the improving political culture of the sober, self-educated and radically conscious workman. In Cheltenham it is clearer than in most places that this radical culture was not that of an upper stratum of workmen with pretensions to a middle class way of life, but it nevertheless did define itself against aspects of traditional popular culture as well as against Francis Close and Evangelical control.[72]

For Adams, the desire for culture and a passion for politics were mutually reinforcing. He came into a local Chartist movement as a precocious young man firmly imbued with radical ideas and artisan values, which were both resistant to clerical controls and appalled by aristocratic corruption and incompetence. Moreover, as his remarkable talents were realised, so he began to make the running in that movement culture which characterized much of Chartism in the Spa before 1848. By the time he joined the Cheltenham branch of the National Chartist Association at fifteen — a "very youthful atom indeed" —[73] in 1847, he was well into an apprenticeship in which trade consciousness and political awareness enhanced his separate working class identity. Already, his record of achievement was impressive: founder and president elect of the People's Institute; co-auditor of the Cheltenham branch's Land Plan accounts;[74] and earmarked for the chairmanship of the local N.C.A. branch activities. Within a year the French Revolution of 1848 took place: the stirring events in Paris and the newer literature that began to be issued sent the young men of Adams's age in Cheltenham "wild with excitement and enthusiasm".[75] Typical of many areas, the local Chartist activity was not in any sense damaged by confrontations with the bourgeois state; but after the dust had settled on the momentous events in France and London in 1848, Adams became, as we shall see, "a Chartist and something more".[76]

Notes

1. W.E. Adams, Memoirs, op.cit., p.40.

2. Ibid., p.33.

3. Ibid., p.2.

4. Ibid., p.3.

5. For Cheltenham see G. Hart, A History of Cheltenham, Leicester, 1965 and George Rowe, Illustrated Cheltenham Guide, 1845, Reptd. Gloucester, 1981, with Introduction by Dr. Steven Blake.

6. Victoria County History of Gloucestershire, London, 1907, Vol.II, p.177.

7. A. Courtenay, "Parliamentary Representation and General Elections in Cheltenham Spa, 1832-1848: A Study of a Pocket Borough", Unpub. M.Phil, Open University, 1991. See generally.

8. W.E. Adams, Memoirs, op.cit., pp.61-62.

9. G. Hart, A History of Cheltenham, op.cit., pp.186-210, the title of Chapter XV.

10. Ibid., p.211.

11. Ibid., p.200.

12. For a more detailed analysis of Close's attempts to control Chartists, Owenites and Dissenters before Adams was active in radicalism, see my "Clerical Control and Radical Responses in Cheltenham Spa, 1838-1848", Midland History, Vol.VIII, 1983, pp.121-147.

13. W.E. Adams, Memoirs, op.cit., pp.11-15. "The Close Season", particularly p.12.

14. G. Hart, A History of Cheltenham, op.cit., p.224.

15. W.E. Adams, Memoirs, op.cit., p.92.

16. Ibid., p.86.

17. There is some disputing the actual date of his baptism. According to the Memoirs, p.1, it was in the old Parish Church on Feb. 11th 1832, but in the Bishops' Transcripts of the St. Mary's Parish Registers in Gloucester Record Office his baptism is recorded as having taken place on 18th March 1832 at the hands of C. Winstanley. I am grateful to Dr. S. Blake for supplying me with this information.

18. W.E. Adams, Memoirs, op.cit., p.72.

19. D. Vincent (ed.), Testaments of Radicalism: Memoirs of Working Class Politicians, 1790-1885, London, 1977, Introduction pp.1-25, see also, for example, the solemnity of the home for Adams's friend and future Lib-Lab, George Howell, in F.M. Leventhal, Respectable Radical, George Howell and Victorian Working Class Politics, London, 1971, pp.5-16.

20. Newcastle Weekly Chronicle, The Children's Corner, Feb. 23, 1878 and March 2 1878.

21. Apart from an attack of small-pox, all the evidence in the reminiscences in the Newcastle Weekly Chronicle during the early and mid 1890s points to a healthy childhood.

22. W.E. Adams, Memoirs, op.cit., p.107.

23. Ibid., p.72.

24. Ibid., p.79.

25. Ibid., p.72.

26. The process by which the Sunday Schools played into the hands of the middle class is developed by C. Reid in "Essays in Review: Class and Culture", Bulletin of the Society for the Study of Labour History, No.34, Spring, 1977, pp.56-61. Reid reviews T.W. Laqueur's Religion and Respectability, Sunday Schools and Working Class Culture, London, 1976. Laqueur argues for the increasing integration of the Sunday Schools into working class life, rather than simply existing as overt agencies of social control under middle class manipulation.

27. Newcastle Weekly Chronicle, Jan. 21 1893, The Gossip's Bowl, Reminiscences of "An Old Cheltenham Boy".

28. See W.E. Adams, Memoirs, op.cit., pp.61-70, part of Chapter VII, "The Laws of the Street". See also my article "Chartism and Popular Culture: an Introduction to the Radical Culture in Cheltenham Spa, 1830-1847", Journal of Popular Culture, Vol.20, No.4, 1987, pp.61-81.

29. Ibid., p.53. This was the old custom of defining the parish boundaries.

30. Ibid., p.68.

31. Ibid., p.53.

32. Ibid., pp.51-61, Chapter VI, "Yielding Place to the New".

33. See Conference Reports: "Custom, Crime and Prerequisites, "Bulletin of the Society for Study of Labour History, Vol.52, No.1 1987 pp.33-45, in particular, R.B. Bushaway, "The Ideology of Custom in Eighteenth-Century England". pp.37-38.

34. M. Heaney, "Morris Dancers at Cheltenham "The Morris Dancer, No. 17, Nov. 1983, pp.18-20. I am grateful to Mike Heaney for drawing my attention to Adams's contribution on Morris Dancing in Notes And Queries, London, 6th Series, July-December, 1881, Vol.IV. p.524.

35. W.E. Adams, Memoirs, op.cit., p.32. But see Cheltenham Journal, May 29th 1858: "Whitsuntide has passed by in Cheltenham without any public festivity." (and quoted in Heaney's "Morris Dancers at Cheltenham" op.cit., p.19). For the wider significance of popular custom and the successful suppression by a process of selection, rejection, approbation and disapprobation of many customary activities by the middle classes, see R.B. Bushaway, By Rite: Custom, Ceremony and Community in England 1700-1880, London, 1982, particularly Chapter 7, The Control of Custom pp.238-279.

36. W.E. Adams, Memoirs, op.cit., p.158.

37. Ibid., p.39.

38. Ibid., p.166.

39. Cheltenham Free Press, April 24 1841. Henry Vincent gave several meetings in Cheltenham on behalf of the initiative known as "teetotal Chartism". It was a very different Vincent in tone and temper to the one his aunts had listened to March 1839. At that stage he was a fiery and reckless orator; by 1841 he had become sober and restrained; and Adams's aunts had a strong suspicion that the government had somehow found means to influence or corrupt him whilst imprisoned in 1840.

40. W.E. Adams, Memoirs, op.cit., p.167.

41. Cheltenham Free Press, Jan.23 1841.

42. Newcastle Weekly Chronicle, July 1 1893; The Gossip's Bowl. An abbreviated version also appeared in the Memoirs, op.cit., p.15.

43. W.E. Adams, Memoirs, op.cit., p.80.

44. For an analysis of the artisan component in Chartism see I. Prothero, "Chartism in London", Past and Present, Vol.44, 1969 pp.76-105; and also "London Chartism and the Trades", Economic History Review, 2nd series, XXIV, May

1971, pp.202-219. The situation in Cheltenham was similar to that in London. Compositors or printers were the most upper of skilled trades; along with coach-makers, watch-makers and jewellers, they constituted virtually a labour aristocracy. For the most part the strength of Cheltenham Chartism (as in London) was drawn from what Dr. Prothero calls the "lower" or humbler skilled trades: shoemakers, tailors, book-makers, plasterers, carpenters, cabinet-makers and printers.

45. W.E. Adams, Memoirs, op.cit., p.82. Adams proudly recalled "Fancy £15 for a poor old washerwoman! It had to be paid in instalments, of course; but the obligation was discharged to the last penny".

46. Ibid., p.112.

47. For an assessment of Solly's work see P. Bailey, Leisure and Class in Victorian England, London, 1978, pp.106-118.

48. H.A. Solly, These Eighty Years, London, 1893, pp.40-41.

49. W.E. Adams, Memoirs, op.cit., p.114. The Rev. George Dawson was a leading Birmingham Unitarian, editor of the Birmingham Journal and in the 1850s a friend of W.J. Linton. The latter described him as "the popular lecturer and preacher ... A fluent and good orator ... He was not an original thinker, but did very good work in popularising Carlyle, and in general politics", See W.J. Linton, Memories, 1894, Reptd. New York, 1970, p.159.

50. For the radicalization of the Cheltenham Mechanics' Institute see my article "The Mechanics' Institute and Radical Politics in Cheltenham Spa, 1834-1840", Cheltenham Local History Society Journal, No.2. 1984, pp.25-30.

51. W.E. Adams, Memoirs, op.cit., p.116.

52. Idem.,

53. Idem.,

54. S. Hall, "Notes on Deconstructing 'The Popular'" in R. Samuel (ed.), People's History and Socialist Theory, London, 1981, pp.227-239, in particular p.239.

55. T. Bennett, "Popular Culture: Divided Territory", Social History Society Newsletter, Autumn, 1981, p.5.

56. M. Vicinus, The Industrial Muse, London, 1974, p.9. See also pp.10-46 for the importance of the broadside ballad in nineteenth century popular literature.

57. W.E. Adams, Memoirs, op.cit, pp.141-3.

58. Ibid., p.141.

59. Apart from Pilgrim's Progress, Adams makes no reference whatsoever in his career to any religious work (e.g. bible) that he might have read or owned.

60. W.E. Adams, Memoirs, op.cit., p.100.

61. Newcastle Weekly Chronicle, June 4 1898, The Gossip's Bowl.

62. W.E. Adams, Memoirs, op.cit., p.101.

63. See A. Humphreys, "G.W.M. Reynolds: Popular Literature and Popular Politics", Victorian Periodicals Review, Vol.16, Part 3/4, Fall 1983 pp.79-89.

64. Ibid., pp.82-83. Humphreys argues that Reynolds' work articulated a fine point in the popular mind where "escapism and activism touch". It was his ability "not to try to blend the various elements of the popular mind into a unified position" that made his work successful both as a fiction writer and editor. Humphreys employs the concept of "negative capability" to assess Reynolds as editor. Thus defined it is "an ability to absorb the contradictory impulses and desires of the populace without any 'irritable' effort at resolution. His instinct for doing so may have been at bottom commercial — one group of his critics certainly thinks so — but the result was the creation of a form that was popular in the best sense of the word because it was inclusive".

65. W.E. Adams, Memoirs, op.cit., p.103. For the "penny dreadfuls" see L. James, Fiction for the Working Man, London, 1973, pp.28-30.

66. For such new forms see S. Easton (ed.) Disorder and Discipline: Popular Culture from 1550 to the present, London, 1988. See her chapter, "A Much Improved World", Popular Culture and Society 1700-1914", pp.52-79.

67. W.E. Adams, Memoirs, op.cit., pp.92-97.

68. Ibid., p.107.

69. For an analysis of the quality of domestic working class reading material and what the middle class thought they should be reading see D. Vincent "Reading in the Working Class Home" pp.207-226 in particular pp.221-222, in J.K. Walton and J. Walvin (eds.), Leisure in Britain 1780-1939, Manchester, 1983.

70. W.E. Adams, Memoirs, op.cit., p.119.

71. Ibid., p.116 and p.119.

72. See also my "Chartism and Popular Culture: An Introduction to the Radical Culture in Cheltenham Spa, 1830-1847", Journal of Popular Culture, op.cit., pp.69-71.

73. W.E. Adams, Memoirs, op.cit., p.151.

74. Northern Star, Jan. 9 1847.

75. W.E. Adams, Memoirs, op.cit., p.119.

76. Ibid., p.151.

2 The Cheltenham Chartist

The Spa Chartists' counter-culture within which the young Adams was reared, represented, of course, an important complement to their central objective: a radical political campaign to secure the six points of the People's Charter. As he grew older, so in the work-place, amongst other Chartist families and in the sizeable Cheltenham branch of the N.C.A.,[1] Adams came into close contact with seasoned activists — shoemakers, bricklayers, plasterers, coach-makers and even small shop-keepers — who were resentful of their exclusion from full social and political rights. Most were craftsmen in middle-age — some could even date their political involvement back to the ferment of the Spa Fields Riots of 1817 — who had turned to Chartism as the only effective political vehicle for the removal of a parasitic ruling class of aristocrats, clergymen and pensioners. And like them, Adams's thinking was the product of a distinctive artisanal culture: it stressed the virtues of personal independence, self-reliance and respectability through intellectual improvement and temperance; and in political ideals, a strong individualist component firmly rooted in Paineite democratic beliefs. Indeed, such values and what they stood for, formulated in the experiences of simultaneously having to earn a living from yet resenting the very nature of the representatives of "Old Corruption" in Cheltenham Spa, were to frame most of Adams's subsequent ideals and prejudices.

Cheltenham had been by-passed by the classic saga of the industrial revolution; it was rather a thriving tourist centre; and economic factors as such cannot account for the intensely political character of Chartism amongst its artisan community. For example, a couple of fellow Chartist leaders Adams mentioned by name — J.P. Glenister and T.J. Hemmin — were actually in possession of the franchise by 1852;[2] but for the rest of the leadership, including Adams himself, they, as tradesmen, were sufficiently and consistently impecunious so as to be excluded from the stringent property clauses conceded by the Whigs in 1832.[3] However, they viewed their individual hardship not so much in economic but in larger and more political terms: they saw themselves as "producers" self-consciously fighting what Stedman Jones has argued was the political oppression of a tyrannical state;[4] and the limited scope for change in 1832 had simply served to deepen their sense of political outrage. Cheltenham had become a pocket Whig borough in 1832 which was practically owned by the Berkeleys, Gloucestershire aristocrats and implacable opponents of universal suffrage. Craven F. Berkeley was the political representative of those parasitic residents that William Cobbett had contemptuously described in 1826 as: "East India plunderers, West India floggers, English tax-gorgers, together with gluttons, drunkards, and debauchees of all descriptions."[5] There was also hostility from another direction: the overburdening evangelical influences of Francis Close, the Tory cleric, who encroached on their freedom of action and sense of self-determination both at work and play, particularly in the latter arena by curtailing customs and popular pastimes. In essence, therefore, Chartism for Adams, the journeyman printer, was classically a political movement directed against both the local aristocratic representative of an oppressive State and the symbol of a hypocritical, reactionary Church. The passage of time, too, served only to reinforce the centrality for Adams of this political reaction to explain the rise and, in the wake of a more liberal State, the demise of Chartism:

> "People who have not shared in the hopes of the Chartists, who have no personal knowledge of the deep and intense feelings which animated them, can have little conception of the difference between our own times and those of fifty or sixty years ago. The whole governing classes — Whigs even more than Tories — were not only disliked, they were positively hated by the working population ... Then a transformation was marked in the sentiments of the great body of the people. Thanks to the political earnestness but still more to the political intrepidity, of later statesmen, working men, enfranchised by household suffrage, commenced for the first time to associate themselves closely and actively with the orthodox parties in the State."[6]

Given the fact that Cheltenham Spa represented in microcosm some of the most glaring political inequalities which fuelled the Chartist movement as a whole, it is perhaps understandable that Tom Paine's works, which attributed popular distress to aristocratic power and its corruptions, provided the greatest inspiration for change. Indeed, just the mention of his name evoked great reverence and affection, as Adams vividly recalled:

> "One night, while he (referring to J.P. Glenister) was so presiding, somebody spoke of Tom Paine. Up jumped the chairman. 'I will not sit in the chair', he cried in great wrath, 'and hear that great man reviled. Bear in mind he was not a prize-fighter. There is no such person as Tom Paine. Mister Thomas Paine, if you please."[7]

What Paine's works, particularly the *Rights of Man* (1791&2), offered Adams and his colleagues was a clear critique of "Old Corruption": it argued that popular misery derived from the class legislation of unrepresentative governments that were monopolised by an inept landed aristocracy and buttressed by a parasitic and equally unproductive Church. Together, they acted to ensure a self-perpetuating system of material inequality through heavy and mass taxation, by lavish spending on wars and pleasurable pursuits, and by granting pensions and sinecures to those favourably connected — "the hangers-on" — within a vast undergrowth of patronage and preferment.

For Paine, all men were created equal and with natural rights, and on which were founded civil rights. Governments should not be based upon those holding hereditary titles, honours and privileges, but subject to the sovereign will of the people through universal suffrage and a written constitution. Paine's radicalism centred on the achievement of political freedoms and not social equality, for he stressed that all property acquired by honest endeavour would not be taxed. The artisan was therefore left clear to improve his individual economic position since Paine believed that "social and economic inequalities were the result of an unjust political system, rather than of the maldistribution of wealth".[8] Indeed, as another historian of Paine's works has commented in respect of the marked absence of social levelling: "his proposals on wealth re-distribution would hardly have destroyed the existing property system".[9] Little attention was given thus to industrial wealth and middle class political economy, because the problem as early Radicals saw it was not that of the poor against the rich, or employers against employees, but of producers — artisans, shopkeepers, professional men, but not the very poor — versus the non-producers or parasitic lords and priesthood.

Paineite radical ideology was absolutely crucial then both to Adams and to his colleagues' thinking. It affirmed their belief in popular sovereignty, the importance of individual freedom and the tyranny of centralised State authority; it also upheld their sense of the value of personal independence, self-reliance and self-improvement, which was characteristic of contemporary English artisan attitudes.[10] In two further, yet still vital, respects Paineite radicalism was a fundamental and life-long inspiration to Adams. Firstly, he assimilated through Paine's works some of the ideas of the Enlightenment — a faith in reason, belief in progress and confidence in the capacity for society to change when "Old Corruption" had been swept away. A corollary to this, of course, was the great importance attached to political education to remove the impediments to progress. Secondly, the class hostility that characterised Cheltenham was not that between employer and employee; rather it was between, on the one hand, "producers", — the artisans and small shop-keepers — and, on the other, parasites — the landlords, retired genteel residents, "tax-gorgers" and staid followers of Francis Close. Such a perspective could and did allow co-operation to exist on occasions, as in mid 1840s, between Chartists and radical middle class nonconformists, small businessmen and liberal professionals over non-payment of Church rates, vote by secret ballot and the release of Chartist prisoners.[11] History was to repeat itself shortly: Adams found common ground with a small group of Spa middle class liberals over the issue of, and movements for, freedom amongst oppressed nationalities in Europe, following the failures of the 1848 revolutions.

By December 1847 Adams, "having all the effrontery of youth"[12] was "whirling and swirling round the political maelstrom".[13] His fellow leaders in the Spa branch of the N.C.A. were "earnest and reputable men — much above the average in intelligence".[14] Together, they were intimately involved in a whole constellation of socio-political activities, which were so closely interwoven that they are difficult to disentangle without losing sight of their overall significance in relation to Chartist objectives nationally. One important theme, separable for analysis, running though the late 1840s was Adams's concern with, and support for, Feargus O'Connor — "the idol of the day"[15] — and his Chartist Land Plan. This was an attempt to give Chartism new life through a practical scheme of self-supporting agricultural communities of independent small-holders, and with it freedom and enfranchisement. Undoubtedly, the scheme captured an artisan consciousness concerned with self-reliance and individuality.[16] Additional stimulus was provided for the Cheltenham enthusiasts when two of the land colonies were actually purchased on estates only seven miles away at Lowbands and Snig's End.[17] The scheme depended on the purchase of land with money subscribed by the people at large; and the Cheltenham Chartists, for whom Adams acted as financial scrutineer, made generous contributions. For example, between the beginning of December 1847 and the middle of January 1848, a period when Adams was actuarialy involved, the local branch contributed just over £32 in shares to the National Land Company;[18] and for many months thereafter it systematically levied members over and above their regular subscriptions.[19] By April 1850, however, O'Connor had financially and administratively overeached himself and the viability of the Chartist Land Society was called in to question. As a government enquiry was mounted into its affairs, amidst mounting disquiet both in and outside the Chartist ranks, those at Cheltenham publicly stated their loyalty by petitioning Parliament. In it they reaffirmed their confidence in both the National Land Company and O'Connor's honesty and integrity; they also expressed the hope that Parliament would "grant him a short Act to render the Society legal".[20] Alas, this was not to be and the land ventures were soon wound up.

Such enthusiasm for the Land Plan is all the more remarkable since it does not square with the hostile verdict ostensibly offered by Adams in the *Memoirs* in 1903:

> "The Land Scheme which he (O'Connor) grafted onto the demand for political reform was one of the wildest and maddest schemes that ever entered into the mind of a rational being. It was doomed to disaster from the very beginning."[21]

The explanation is quite simple. Adams was an unqualified supporter of the principle of peasant proprietorship, but felt that O'Connor had picked the wrong personnel. Writing on subjects of radical nostalgia in his "Notes and Queries" column in the *Weekly Chronicle* in March 1882, Adams clarified his own position in response to a correspondent's request for information on the "Land Plan":

> "There is an all but universal impression that the scheme was a great failure, and that serious loss was entailed upon the unfortunate shareholders. In a sense this is correct. The men who got the allotments under the scheme, in the first instance, were unfitted for making them. When tailors and shoemakers with little capital, and less knowledge, got planted down on a couple of acres of land they made a bad fist at cultivating it, and of course they did not succeed.[22]

In the thirty years that had elapsed since the Chartists' failure, Adams, it is clear from this and earlier reports,[23] had noted how new and more appropriate occupiers had turned the estates into a highly prosperous condition. As a result, he was better-placed by this time to declare with some confidence that:

> "To describe the scheme as a failure is not in any sense correct. I know, for example, that last summer a holder of one of the allotments made as much profit on the stawberries he sent to London markets as nearly kept his wife and himself for one year. If I were called upon to adduce evidence as to the practicality of a project of peasant proprietory, I should certainly cite O'Connor's oft denounced scheme as the best illustration of it."[24]

It is a great pity that Adams, the possessor of a remarkable memory for facts, forgot or ignored this in 1903; in so doing he perpetuated wholesale the unfortunate myth that the Land Plan speculation was a dead failure.[25]

The second important business in which Adams was concerned in the early months of 1848, was the public collection of signatures for the third National Petition requesting the House of Commons to enact the Charter.[26] Animated scenes accompanied this and the overlapping exercise amongst branch members for the election of another convention delegate — J.P. Glenister — to represent them and Gloucestershire at the National Chartist Convention, summoned in London for April 1848. Even greater excitement followed: aware that momentous political events in France had begun to trigger off a series of nationalist and liberal revolts across Europe, a monster Chartist demonstration was planned for April 10 at Kennington Common to give the Petition an appropriate send-off on its way to Parliament. Tension mounted in the capital as the authorities feared that, given the popular revolution in France and the forced abdication of Louis Philippe, threats of physical force might be translated into open violence by Chartists on the London streets.

For his part, Adams invariably eschewed violence in England, except in situations requiring self-defence; but he justified its offensive use in Europe as necessary for the overthrow of brutal and despotic regimes. Inevitably, debates about the employment of physical force, if the Chartist demands were not conceded, surfaced at the National Convention in April when delegates reported on the preparedness of their regions. The assessment amongst Cheltenham Chartists was very much in line with Adams's own thinking, as Glenister duly reported:

> "He could not say as others had done, that his constituents were prepared for such things (physical force), but they desired agitation, and a long pull and a strong pull for the obtainment of their rights."[27]

Such a commitment to moderation, of course, did not prevent Francis Close simultaneously denouncing them and the new provisional French government as "bloodhounds" from the pulpit of St. Mary's.[28] In fact, Close was to mount a barrage of criticism against Adams and his colleagues as events unfolded in the turbulent months of 1848. He even interspersed his annual November 5th anti-Catholic sermon with anti-Chartist references, calling them "an ignorant, violent body unacquainted with history and not knowing the different between the British Government and the Government of the Grand Turk".[29] Such tirades were part of the scorn and ridicule which the authorities initiated in order to traduce the Chartist movement over the coming months and years.[30] But in Cheltenham, as elsewhere, the Chartists remained undeterred and undaunted; as far as they were concerned the events of April 10th and the performance of O'Connor was no mere fiasco. A groundswell of activity, which had begun in March with Spa Chartists, their wives and even children signing first the National Petition and then an address to congratulate the French people on their success, was mobilized behind the policies of the Chartist leaders in London during the difficult months of April and May 1848. Thus at Spa meetings there followed resolutions demanding the people's right "to have the Constitution of England fairly carried out";[31] a strategy to rebutt the lawyers' charges that the Petition was falsified by fake signatures; and support for the authority and influence of O'Connor, the Convention and the proposal for a National Assembly.[32] Not to be outdone, Adams and his fellow leaders also delivered Close a smack in the eye. Following his vituperations delivered on November 5th, they quickly retorted with counter-arguments about the hypocrisy of the Anglican Church; and in a specific charge levelled at Close, personally, suggested that in sending his son to the Army, there was no greater example of a physical force man than he![33]

The National Assembly met in May in order to frame an appropriate set of ulterior measures. Before it could deliberate at length the government acted: it assumed a more coercive stance on the basis of spy reports of likely insurrectionary plots and risings; and as a result by early June a large number of arrests were made including that of Ernest Jones, Peter McDouall and Joseph Williams. Once again the Cheltenham Chartists redoubled their efforts in order to try and help those who were put on trial and subsequently placed in prison. Adams's administrative skills were now recognised as he personally chaired meetings and corresponded with Grantley Berkeley over the treatment of Chartist prisoners.[34] Although courteous in his replies, little joy could be expected from Cheltenham's Whig representative and opponent of Chartism. Financial success, however, was more forthcoming within the Chartist ranks as money was collected for a number of specific funds. These included the Liberty Fund established by O'Connor; the respective Defense funds for Ernest Jones and P. McDouall; and indicative of their wider concern, the Fund for the families of Chartist victims.[35] Given that weekly subscriptions were still being made to the Land Company, the collection of just over £5[36] in funds for these additional and unforeseen demands was impressive; it also reflected well on the remarkable talents of the young Adams — not yet seventeen — who was intimately associated with their procurement.

Inevitably, in the wake of the July trials and the severe sentences inflicted upon leaders like Ernest Jones, the knock-on effects of confrontations with the State began to be felt at branch level. Although the Cheltenham Chartists were called upon "to do their duty and rally round the banner of Chartism",[37] there is ample evidence in the second half of 1848 and for some time to come that the branch had lost its way. On the one hand, financial and moral support for the Land Plan activities continued steadily;[38] but, on the other, Joseph Hume's more limited "Little Charter" for household suffrage, which Feargus himself gradually came round to support via the platform of the radical middle class dominated Parliamentary and Financial Reform Association, received a very mixed reception.[39]

Already for Adams, with a passionate aspiration for a better world, the new political initiative by Hume was not good enough. He recalled that:

> "even at that time I was 'a Chartist and something more', for it appeared to me that the Charter fell far short of the ideal that ought to be sought and must be

> attained before society could be constituted on a proper basis."[40]

Increasingly, Adams, followed by a few associates, looked to the leadership of George Julian Harney, attracted as they all were by his editorial style and choice of material in the *Northern Star;* he also voted for Harney as a member of the N.C.A. executive in 1850 and joined his Fraternal Democrats Society (fd. 1845) to satisfy a growing interest in and support for those principles of self-government and nationality set in motion by the struggling and oppressed peoples of Europe in 1848.[41] In the short term at least Adams was not to be disappointed. After Harney joined O'Connor's opponents early in 1850 in defeating the old leader on the Chartist executive, he started to carry the principles of the Fraternal Democrats into the country. To further this end he had begun to satisfy Adams's "higher aspirations and ideals".[42] Adams also subscribed to Harney's subsequent literary ventures: *The Red Republican* (1850) and *Friend of the People* (1850-1).[43] Both these publications reflected not only propaganda for openly socialist objectives, but also a growing and profound sense of Chartist internationalism; both reveal, too, Adams and such old colleagues as Sharland, Glenister, Hemmin and Glover, making generous financial sacrifice to alleviate the plight of Polish and Hungarian refugees, and defending publicly the Democrats' line, against attack from O'Connor now, of progress towards "the fraternity of nations".[44]

On the face of things support for Harney, who was joined by Ernest Jones after his release from prison in July 1850, and to whom an open invitation was extended to visit Cheltenham,[45] continued up until the London Chartist conference in March 1851, which adopted the social programme behind the ringing slogan, "the Charter and something more". For Adams, however, all was not well. What Harney had offered was "better. But we longed for something better still".[46] In his *Memoirs* Adams was, as John Saville points out, "at pains to dissociate himself from the implications of the *Red Republican* title":[47]

> "We did not like the title. It savoured of blood. Also it seemed to suggest a return to the Reign of Terror, with new Marats and Couthons to horrify the world. We were Republicans, but not Red Republicans. The title was altered to the *Friend of the People*. The paper was the same though the name was changed."[48]

Such emphatic language may have been intended to reassure predominantly Lib-Lab *Chronicle* readers of his own anti-socialist pedigree. However, the fact remains that until the summer of 1850 Adams was aligned very much with the Harney-Jones Socialist grouping; it was a stance, too, that represented a retreat, consciously or otherwise, from supporting the mainstream radical ideas of their old hero, Feargus O'Connor.

The great sea-change in Adams's thinking about what constituted the "something more" was supplied by W.J. Linton, a member of the Chartist executive; and it was through the columns of the *Red Republican*[49] in the first instance — a touch ironic perhaps in view of Adams's underlying feelings against the title — that his future friend and lifetime associate wrote "a series of articles in exposition of the principles of Republicanism".[50] Linton was a very talented radical, poet, propagandist and wood-engraver.[51] By 1850, he wanted to adapt Chartism to the new conditions consequent on the "failure" of popular uprisings against tyrannical regimes in Russia and Austria; and regarded the Republican movement as "a development forward from Chartism and superior to it".[52] The stimulus and inspiration behind Linton's articles was a "Proclamation to the People" in July 1850, the work of the great Italian patriot, Guiseppe Mazzini; it was written by the latter on behalf of the Central European Democratic Committee in order to advance "Humanity" for the international democratic and republican cause.[53] For Adams therefore, the concept of "something more" meant "republicanism of the Mazzinian variety as interpreted by W.J. Linton".[54]

The central idea of Mazzini's republican teaching — the one that Adams found most compelling — stressed duty to be the basis of human action; not the thought of self-interest, but sacrifice and endeavour the beginning of all real progress. Hitherto, men had talked and political movements been inspired by their ideas about rights; but Mazzini contended that while the individual had rights to maintain, they were only valuable as the means of discharging duties — to the family, to the country and to promoting the progress of humanity at large. In the universality of duty Mazzini found the need for freedom for every people, towards growth into nationhood: that nationhood no longer mapped out, as in 1848, to suit the convenience of a few royal families, but constituted according to natural fitness and attraction, for the sake of closer fellowship and greater power in the world's work. For Mazzini, the individual right was to be free and fitted for public duty; governments fully representative and democratic; and nations, constituted on the principles of nationality, interacting within a wider fraternity committed to the progress of humanity.[55] Embedded, too, in these lofty ideals were, as Linton himself was to stress in his *English Republic* (1851-55), a deep respect for the individual, the inviolability of personal property, the holiness of work, the sacredness of the family and a commitment to the value and role of national education "for the common amelioration".[56]

There is no doubt that in the evolution of Adams's radical political thought if Tom Paine's works had acted as a first stimulus, then Mazzini's doctrines represented a vitally important water-shed. For the rest of his life, as Adams recalled shortly after Linton's death in 1898, he remained steadfast in his adherence to Linton and Mazzinian republicanism:

> "Something higher than material welfare entered the ideas and aims of us young Chartists then. There was nothing selfish or sordid in their methods or objects. It was not to benefit themselves, to increase their own leisure, advance their own interests or promote their own enjoyments, that they combined. Rather did they find satisfaction in sacrifice — the sacrifice of time, energy and such poor resources as they possessed ... They set before themselves a noble ideal — nobler than ever the demand of the present day for more wages and more football."[57]

According to Adams Mazzini's teachings supplied a religion, a system of morals, a creed and a faith.[58] And so these ardent young men in Cheltenham responded to Linton's appeal to create a new world: they formed societies, not for forcing republican institutions upon a people unprepared for them, but for teaching republican principles — the principles of "a newer and diviner political faith than either radicals or Chartists had yet preached".[59]

In this educational, not revolutionary, work to which they felt summoned, Adams led propagandist activity by forming a Cheltenham Republican Association; he was only eighteen, but colleagues saw fit to elect him as their branch president.[60] Part of their method of procedure, in keeping with Linton's views on how best to propagate the republican faith, was to hold family meetings for instruction at each other's houses "after the manner of the old Methodists".[61] Here, the works of revolutionary leaders for the regeneration of mankind were discussed, Linton's *English Republic* — a blueprint for the new society — closely followed, the prospects of the cause abroad and at home pondered, tracts circulated and candidates credentials for membership closely scrutinised. There was almost an inverted Corinthian feel about the activities of the small band as "old Chartists looked askance at our proceedings, called us foolish striplings, and would have nothing to do with us".[62] Ultimately, of course, as Adams himself admitted, with under a score of members "we were never strong enough to impede anything".[63] Such statements should not detract from the remarkable and wholly non-sectarian nature of Chartist activity from this time and until the formal abandonment of the movement in 1858. Adams, for once, exaggerates when he states that they were ostracized, for the evidence tells a different story: Republican and social-democratic Chartists worked together successfully over a range of concerns of both local and national importance.

Common cause was made first over a successful campaign to save a number of public footpaths in the vicinity of Cheltenham and Prestbury from further enchroachment by residential development.[64] Adams, we have already noted, had a deep love of the countryside; and by exercising, in the company of colleagues, the right to "rural rambles" and drawing attention to the baleful effects consequent on the loss of open spaces in the town, was already showing himself to be something of a proto-conservationist.

Undoubtedly, the most important aspect in the radical political culture after 1850 was the ongoing interest in foreign affairs and the receptiveness of men like Adams to the plight of European political refugees, who were fleeing the hoof of a restored continental despotism after the failure of the 1848 revolutions. As Adams recalled:

> "The idea of Fraternity was as sacred to us as any of the ideas expressed in our republican formula. And Fraternity if it meant anything, meant the offer of such help as we could give to the struggling peoples of the Continent."[65]

Spa Chartists responded energetically: they issued resolutions and addresses of moral support for the republican causes in newspapers and at protest meetings; they printed tracts and leaflets reminding the British people to be on their guard lest their government caved in to demands of European reactionaries not to provide political asylum for refugees; they also made generous financial contributions to Mazzini's Shilling fund for European Freedom, and, on their own initiative, channelled specific aid in the direction of Poles and Hungarians, who were escaping to Britain. Adams was in the thick of all such consciousness raising activities. Unfortunately, no trace has been found of the tract "Right of Refuge" which he wrote in defence of the refugee's traditional right to political asylum in Britain,[66] but his first contribution to the press, an emotional appeal on behalf of the 250 strong Polish-Hungarian Legion who had landed at Liverpool, has been preserved. The context for Adams's open letter published in the radical-Liberal *Cheltenham Free Press* on May 17th 1851 was the consternation felt amongst fellow republicans over the hostile reception afforded to the refugees by the British government. According to Peter Brock,[67] an authority on Anglo-Polish relations, the aristocratic based Society of Friends of Poland, alarmed by the potential accession to the numerical strength of their opponents that the Legion's arrival posed, had succeeded in persuading the government to refuse them all support unless they agreed, which they would not, to continue their journey to the United

States. In stirring language Adams reminded readers that the "fair lands of the Pole and Magyar" were decimated by "the rope and the bullet" of the uncivilized Cossacks and the brutal Austrian soldiers; he then argued that by their heroic struggle for liberty under the banner of Kossuth, the Legion had strong claims on the help and support of English liberal sympathy. Public opinion was to be mobilized, therefore, according to the inspiring Mazzinian doctrines:

> "the holy dogma of Fraternity ... implies both a right and a duty — the right of the Refugees to expect from us assistance; our duty, as far as in us lies, to afford it them."[68] [Adams's underlining]

The appeal stimulated further letters by fellow republicans[69] and a fund for the refugees which was sent to James Spurr, the secretary of the republican operatives committee in Liverpool.[70] For Adams, this was also an intensely private moment. The feelings of personal satisfaction at experiencing his first printed public article was to be something he always treasured: "The printing of that letter produced an exaltation that no similar honour has ever produced since".[71]

Adams was also heavily involved in getting Chartist leaders to the town in order to lecture, whenever possible, on foreign affairs. During the course of his second visit to the Spa for two nights in October 1850, Thomas Cooper gave a splendid lecture on:

> "The European Revolutions of 1848, the Present State of the Continent, and the Prospects of Coming Changes at Home and Abroad."

Cooper offered "cheering prospects of the future" and urged the branch to be prepared for the "inevitable uprising of their glorious principles". At the the close, following a collection of 7/3 for the Polish and Hungarian brethren, they passed a resolution in support of an incident which was having national and international ramifications:

> "Thanks are due to Barclay and Perkins' men for thrashing the Austrian hyena, Haynau, and sparing the life of a fellow who never spared the lives of his fellow-men, when in his power, nor the feelings of honourable and virtuous women."[72]

Equally memorable for Adams, but for entirely different reasons, was the second night's lecture at the Montpellier Rotunda. As branch secretary, Adams had been responsible for all the arrangements — the hiring of the room and the placing of the chairs — but when Cooper was deep into his oration he remembered an important matter of business in connection with the proceedings. In his youthful eagerness,

Adams leaned across to a colleague and whispered what he had got to say. Alas, the mercurial Thomas Cooper caught-sight, stopped, and

> "then covered us with confusion as he solemnly assured the company that he would only resume his discourse when these two young men have finished their conversation."[73]

Embarrassment apart, Adams always found him an admirable lecturer and subscribed to his *Journal*.[74]

Nine months later when Ernest Jones came the group was treated, much to Close's annoyance, to some stirring Sunday lectures; but this time they were given on the subject of social-democratic issues in the Chartist cause. It is quite likely that during informal discussions between the afternoon and evening lectures, Jones admonished Adams's moral republicanism: that "it was just another division in the ranks, and as such calculated to impede the general advance of the popular cause."[75] Differences, however, appear to have been minimised: Jones affirmed at the close of his lectures that "he had come out of prison a republican, to work with renewed vigour in the people's cause"; and it was young Adams himself who finally terminated the proceedings with a warm note of thanks.[76] In 1855, after his return from Brantwood, Adams was to vote for Jones as a member of the National Chartist Executive.[77]

James Finlen of the Executive followed Jones to Cheltenham with lectures on more familiar ground — "Mazzini and Kossuth, the Heroes of Hungary and Italy."[78] However, the peak of this intense working class interest in foreign affairs was reached during the British military catastrophes associated with involvement in the Crimean War. The Spa Chartists did not subscribe "to the hysterically anti-Russian views of David Urquhart";[79] but, like Linton, they favoured a strong war effort to defeat Russia in order to usher in a new era of European freedom.[80] Accordingly, they linked the long-standing campaign for "the freedom of Poland" from Russian interference with a specific domestic issue thrown up by press reports over aristocratic military incompetence in the Crimea: the need for a Soldier's Charter to guarantee the rights of and justice towards the ordinary and gallant British soldier. At a large and widely supported meeting in Cheltenham Town Hall in mid-February 1855 to organize petitions on these two issues, Ernest Jones spoke for nearly two hours: he called for the creation of a free and strong Poland "as an effectual barrier against the encroachment of Russia"; and for sweeping reforms in the British army as embodied in the "Soldier's Charter". Adams was not at this meeting — he, James Glover and Thomas Hailing had already left home and kin (mid 1854) to assist Linton at

Brantwood in the promising work of producing a new republican educational literature;[81] but they had all been instrumental in helping to arrange what was, in effect, a familiar Paineite-inspired attack by Jones on aristocratic treachery in general and the political guilt in particular of Lord Palmerston, who was shown to be "the most active cause of Russian aggression and the bitter enemy of liberty at home".[82]

The post-1848 social structure in Cheltenham was also conducive to a growing sense of internationalism . Amongst a more radical section of its literati were to be found those who took strong exception to the brutal repression inflicted upon the men who had organized the 1848 revolutions. Their main hope for change rested on the romantically inspired freedom campaigns of Garibaldi and his Red Shirts in Southern Italy. Their organization was the influentially composed and widely supported, Society of the Friends of Italy, which also had strong Cheltenham connections. Two individuals, Henry Solly, the Unitarian Minister, and Sydney Dobell, a lesser known English poet, literary critic and friend of Tennyson, were the unofficial leaders in the Spa of a radical middle-class groundswell in favour of the cause of persecuted nationalities. It was Solly who had first welcomed the great upheaval in France in February 1848 at a political meeting in his Chapel on the first Sunday after the Revolution.[83] Thereafter, Sydney Dobell[84] made most of the running. Late in 1848, for example, he helped found, in conjunction with such eminent literary figures as Douglas Jerrold and George Dawson, and the radical reformer, James Stansfeld, the Society of the Friends of Italy — some of whose meetings were held at the Dobell's family home in the Spa.

It is clear from Adams's writings that whilst he felt his "friends of freedom" campaigns to be part of a wider, working class struggle to awaken and aid the emancipation of suppressed peoples, on occasions sufficient common ground existed to suggest inter-class co-operation in foreign affairs with radical liberals. This is precisely what happened over the issue of Italian freedom in 1850. In Adams's view the Dobells were beyond reproach: they stood aloof from the balls and parties; they rejected the patronage of both the Berkeleys (Whig) and the Agg-Gardners (Tories); and "they shared the Chartists' enthusiasm for the struggling peoples of Italy and Hungary".[85] There was also the knowledge that Linton, their mentor, increasingly favoured a bourgeois alliance.[86] Consequently, as Adams pointed out, "we in Cheltenham were members of the Society also".[87] The wisdom of such pragmatism was repaid by Sydney Dobell's subsequent literary activity on behalf of the "Friends". In 1850, for example, he published the famous poem entitled "The Roman" first over the signature of Sydney Yendys (Yendys being Sydney transposed), and afterwards by the appearance of a series of patriotic songs in conjunction with another young poet of the time, Alexander Smith.[88] The object of this material, particularly "The Roman", which was praised by the critics, was to awaken still further the interest in Italy and aid her patriots (Mazzini was a friend of Dobell's) in their endeavours to achieve Italian liberty from the Habsburgs.

Loyalty to the political framework offered by the Six Points as a declaration of rights[89] — a prerequisite to the republic — was the other great issue which gave Chartists of different perspectives in the Spa a sense of unity; it was a consciousness brought sharply into focus during political election times when unrepresentative working class influence was concertedly mobilized on the hustings against aristocratic Whigs, Tories and their propertied supporters alike. As in 1841 and 1847, so once more in the elections of 1848 and 1852 their influential voice was heard on the hustings, advocating the rights of the working class to political representation. Adams distinctly remembered the excitement generated in 1847 when the unexpected happened: Sir Willoughby Jones, the Conservative candidate, succeeded in defeating the sitting Whig member, Craven F. Berkeley. The victory, however, was shortlived: Berkeley petitioned successfully and Jones was unseated. Ironically, in the new election of July 1848 C.F. Berkeley, who defeated James Agg Gardner, a former candidate, was himself unseated after the Conservatives presented a similar petition complaining that the Whigs had only won by bribery and treating.[90] Yet another election was necessary. C.F. Berkeley decided to stand down in favour of his cousin, Grenville Berkeley, when the election was fixed for September of that year. Given the new political instability and the inexperience of both candidates (Bickham Escott was the Conservative), the Chartists went on the offensive at the hustings. Adams, once again, was in the midst of all Chartists attempts at radically-inspired electioneering. Close interrogation by Chartist members revealed that Escott's was a stand-still policy and Grenville Berkeley's support only for the secret ballot from the radicals' programme. At the poll itself, of course, the Chartists had little or no influence. Grenville Berkeley was returned and the Berkeley hold remained intact; but at least the admission by the successful candidate of his conversion to the efficacy of the secret ballot principle offered the Chartists some encouragement.

In July 1852 the Spa Chartists turned their attention to what was, in effect, their last great electoral challenge to the two party domination in Cheltenham politics. In this election two former candidates, Sir Willoughby Jones and Craven F. Berkeley, were opposed, unexpectedly, by a Chartist nominee, the well-known Robert Gammage of the National Chartist Executive. According to W.E. Adams:

> "Chartist candidates were often nominated, not with the idea of going to the poll, which would have been useless in the then state of the franchise, but for the

> purpose of making a speech, which pleased the populace at all times."[91]

Until Gammage's arrival two days before the election,[92] Adams and his colleagues had more or less resigned themselves to a perfunctory campaign against the two candidates since no Chartist candidate was forthcoming. Whig confidence was high. They had organzied an open air meeting of the working classes (2,000) in the Montpellier Gardens in the preliminary stages of the contest.[93] According to Adams the resolutions for the meeting were "ingeniously framed to propitiate the Chartists and at the same time assist the candidature of the Whig nominee".[94] Adams and Glenister were on the platform addressing the crowd, but aware of Whig machinations. One of Adams's aunts then observed "her precocious nephew ... proclaiming at the top of his voice the inalienable right of every man to the suffrage!"[95] As the Chartists expected, the Whigs' purse exploited the power of the printed word by having distorted reports of the meeting advertised in all the local papers so as to indicate mass support for them.[96]

Used or not, however, a few weeks later, Adams and his colleagues had the real satisfaction of hearing their own candidate "propound the true doctrine from the hustings".[97] Before an assembled crowd of over 10,000 people at the hustings in Sandford Mead on July 8th 1852, Gammage was nominated, much to the Whigs' surprise and anger.[98] Already, he had addressed one public meeting since his arrival, but the Whigs, sensing problems, had made every effort to obstruct him by tearing down the bills advertising the meeting and threatening him with hustings expenses if he persisted. Undeterred, Gammage went forward into the contest, having been proposed by two of Adams's colleagues, Charles Hiscox and James Gardner. To the delight of the crowd Gammage lost no time in attacking Whig and Tory candidates alike with what were, in effect, standard radical arguments of the day.[99] Both Berkeley and Willoughby Jones had been proposed as "free-traders" and "advocates of progressive reform" but as Gammage pointed out:

> "neither were prepared to acknowledge the rights and interests of the working classes by adopting universal suffrage."

Identifying with the lot of many in the crowd, Gammage emphasized his humble background and cherished loyalties. "He stood before them" he declared:

> "as a working man: he was not ashamed of his class. He could not boast of broad acres or of millions in the fund. It was his lot to earn his bread by the sweat of his brow."

He dwelt then on the importance of universal suffrage since it was

> "from the ranks of the people that the greatest characters that ever saw the light had risen to adorn the political, scientific and literary world."

For his part he was confident that:

> "as there was no aristocracy in point of talent, so neither ought there to be in politics."

To immense cheering he concluded his speech by emphasising that:

> "we want not to rob the rich men of political power; we only want that the rich men shall no longer rob us."

Speeches completed, the show of hands was taken. There was an immense show of hands for Berkeley and Gammage, somewhat less so for Jones. The moment or two which followed was quite exciting for the Chartists since the Returning Officer was puzzled over which way to decide between Gammage and Berkeley. At last, the crowd was asked to go through the ceremony again, but with orders to exclude Gammage! The second show, surprisingly, revealed a majority for Jones![100] A ruffled Berkeley then demanded a poll which he went on to win.[101] Although Gammage did not stand at the poll, the Chartists were extremely pleased with his performance. Adams was one of a deputation who subsequently expressed their thanks in person for the fine speech he had made at the hustings.[102]

Although reports in the *People's Paper* suggest that Chartist activity in Cheltenham continued in a desultory fashion until the formal end of the movement in 1858, one senses that around 1855-56, at a time when the old enemy Francis Close was preparing to leave for his new post as Dean of Carlisle, much of the richness and vitality of earlier years was beginning to disappear. The reasons are quite obvious. The departure of J.P. Glenister for Australia in 1853 and of Adams, Glover and Hailing for Brantwood in 1854, robbed the movement of important and talented leaders. It is also evident that local Chartists became sadly disillusioned by the squabbles amongst the Chartist executive. In effect, the politics of exhaustion were gaining the upper hand amongst the depleted ranks.

Amidst the gloom there was one bright spot. In August 1856 the last great Cheltenham Chartist gathering took place to organise celebrations marking the return of the Welsh martyr, John Frost, from penal servitude in Tasmania. Many of the old leadership, including Adams, who had returned from Brantwood in the Spring of 1855 following an eventful period on tramp "amongst the freemasonry of the road",[103] gathered at a large meeting in the Carpenters' Arms in Henrietta Street.[104]

They were also joined by some of the veteran Spa Owenites — now secularists in G.J. Holyoake's new movement — who wanted to show their respect, too, for Frost's services in the cause of oppressed people.[105] Adams was one of a small committee duly elected onto a Frost Reception Committee to prepare a demonstration to honour his imminent visit. As they set about preparing a grand public reception, it must surely have crossed their minds that they were also celebrating the triumph of a well-tried form of Chartist political agitation: the granting of free pardons to the "Welsh Martyrs" (Frost, Williams and Jones) had vindicated yet again the efficacy of the petition as a prized public weapon with which to pressurise unrepresentative governments into respecting popular opinion.[106] Equally important for the sense of occasion was the element of working class consciousness and perspective. According to the report in the *People's Paper*:[107]

> "a large double banner made of red, white and green colours (was prepared), bearing the following motto, Welcome John Frost, the martyr for liberty and victim of class Government."

The Chartist years in Cheltenham illustrate important characteristics in the life of W.E. Adams. He rapidly gained a reputation as a tenacious, enthusiastic and hard-working local leader: a man who worked well with rather than dominated his Chartist colleagues. At a time, too, when the value of the printed word was widely appreciated, we also catch a first glimpse of what was undoubtedly to become Adams's first love: an ability to write lively and vigorous political prose that was at once comprehendable and persuasive.

In relation to the wider significance of the Chartism, Adams's activities are also important. T.R. Tholfsen and J. Saville, for example, have tended to see in Adams's commitment to moral-force republicanism traces of a new phase of more cautious, constitutional activity by a working class which was rapidly coming to share "a romantic-progressive sensibility" with elements of the hegemonic middle class.[108] This is a rather unfortunate and narrow conclusion: it ignores the politically combative strategy that Adams adopted, for example, in the 1850s and over the Orsini affair; it also neglects his fervent support for Bradlaugh's freedom campaigns and the uncompromising class conscious tone of the "Ironside" column of the *Newcastle Weekly Chronicle*. We should not accept at face value therefore Adams's hindsight comments printed in the highly constructed *Memoirs* as principle evidence linking his Chartism unproblematically to later reformist political activity. Secondly, alongside the long campaign for political freedom at home, Adams's involvement suggests a heightened sense of internationalism amongst Cheltenham radicals. It is surely time then that Henry Weisser's sweeping generalisation, proclaiming how

> "outside London internationalism was not an important element in the Chartist movement, and no number of quotations from G.J. Harney or from the addresses of the Fraternal Democrats can ever make it so."[109]

is largely discarded.

Notes

1. The size of the Cheltenham branch of the N.C. A. varied between approximately 90 and 120 rank and file members; the leadership which Adams identified was, including himself, about ten in number.

2. On the eve of the Cheltenham election in July 1852, the Cheltenham Examiner, July 7, 1852, printed a list of persons entitled to vote. John Putman Glenister and Thomas John Hemmin are the only identifiable Chartists in the list.

3. W.E. Adams, Memoirs, op.cit., p.169. Apart from Hemmin (occupation unknown) and Glenister (coach-axletree maker), James Glover was a gardener; Charles Hiscox, a tailor; William Knight and William Ryder, shoemakers; Charles Winters, a stonemason; and Edward Sharland, a newsagent (formerly a shoe-maker). Apart from Glenister, only Adams and Thomas Hailing, both compositors, were members of the "upper" skilled trades; but at this time they were still journeymen and unlikely to be in possession of the vote.

4. See G. Stedman Jones, Languages of Class: Studies in English Working Class History, 1832-1982, Cambridge, 1983, pp.90-178, "Rethinking Chartism", particularly pp.161-163. See also Northern Star, Aug. 31 1839, Cheltenham: "Progress of Chartism Amongst a People Comparatively not Distressed". A correspondent from Cheltenham had sent the editor "a few facts which ought to convince our rulers that Chartism, the principle of political equality, is a thing deep down in the heart of man".

5. W. Cobbett, Rural Rides, London, 1830, Reptd. Middlesex, 1967, with Introduction by George Woodcock, p.401.

6. W.E. Adams, Memoirs, op.cit., pp. 237-238.

7. Ibid., p.169.

8. D. Wright, Popular Radicalism, The Working Class Experience, 1780-1880, op.cit., p.43.

9. G. Claeys, "Republicanism versus commercial society: Paine, Burke and the French Revolution debate". Conference Report, B.S.S.L.H. Vol.54, No.3, Winter 1989, pp.4-14, particularly p.6.

10. There are remarkable similarities between the political thinking of Cheltenham radicals and artisan radicals in London. Compare I. Prothero, Artisans and Politics in Early Nineteenth-Century London: John Gast and his Times, London, 1981, pp.328-337; and G. Crossick, An Artisan Elite in Victorian Society, London, 1978, pp.200-220.

11. See my "Clerical Control and Radical Responses in Cheltenham Spa, 1838-1848" Midland History, 1983, op.cit., pp.137-139.

12. W.E. Adams, Memoirs, op.cit., p.170.

13. Ibid., p.151.

14. Ibid., p.169.

15. Ibid., p.157.

16. J. Epstein, The Lion of Freedom: Feargus O'Connor and the Chartist Movement, 1832-1842, London, 1982. pp.312-313.

17. For the evolution of these two estates see my "Chartism in Gloucestershire: the contribution of the Chartist Land Plan 1843-1850", Transactions of the Bristol and Gloucestershire Archaeological Society", Vol.104, 1986, pp.201-209.

18. Northern Star, Jan.1; Jan.8; Jan.15, 1848.

19. Ibid., April 29, 1848.

20. Cheltenham Free Press April 20, 1850, The National Land Company. The petition was presented by Granville Berkeley, the cousin of C.F. Berkeley, who was elected in September 1848 after C.F. Berkeley had been unseated.

21. W.E. Adams, Memoirs, op.cit., p.209.

22. Newcastle Weekly Chronicle, March 18, 1882, Feargus O'Connor's Land Scheme.

23. See, for example, Newcastle Daily Chronicle, Feb.10, 1875, and quoted by J. Saville in Introduction to R.G. Gammage, The History of the Chartist Movement, 1894, second edition, Reptd. London 1969, p.60, in support of the viability of the Land Plan.

24. Ibid., March 18, 1882.

25. W.E. Adams, Memoirs, op.cit., p.160 and p.209. For a major revision of the traditional picture of failure associated with Feargus O'Connor's Land Plan, see J. Saville's Introduction to R.G. Gammage, The History of the Chartist Movement, 1894, op.cit., pp.48-62; D. Hardy, Alternative Communities in Nineteenth Century England, London, 1979, pp.65-105; and K. Tiller, "Charterville and the Chartist Land Company", Oxoniensia, Vol. L, 1985, pp.251-266.

26. W.E. Adams, Memoirs, op.cit., p.170.

27. Northern Star, April 8, 1848; See Also R.G. Gammage, History of the Chartist Movement, Merlin Press facsimile of the 1894, second edition, London, 1969, speech by J.P. Glenister pp.306-307. It is just possible the young Adams believed that to threaten violence was a strategy which would wring changes from the Government. See Memoirs, op.cit. p.183: "The fear was general that the great gathering (at Kennington Common) would end in a deluge of blood. I remember reading in the newspapers of the time (and not without a glow of satisfaction on my own part) how an Irish orator had

exclaimed that London would be in the hands of Chartists on April 10th, and that that would be the signal for insurrection in all parts of the kingdom."

28. Northern Star, April 8, 1848.

29. Cheltenham Free Press, Dec. 2, 1848.

30. See J. Saville, 1848:the British State and the Chartist Movement, op.cit., pp. 200-229, for the manner in which Chartism after 1848 was misrepresented by contemporaries in the press, parliament and from the pulpit.

31. Cheltenham Free Press, March, 25; April 22, 1848; see also Cheltenham Examiner, March 29; April 12, 1848.

32. Cheltenham Free Press, April 22, 1848.

33. Ibid., Dec. 2, 1848.

34. W.E. Adams, Memoirs, op.cit., p.151 and p.171.

35. See Northern Star, July 15; July 22; Aug. 5; Aug.19; Aug. 26, 1848.

36. Idem.,

37. Ibid., Aug. 26, 1848.

38. Ibid., Oct. 21, 1848.

39. See Cheltenham Free Press, June 16, 1849. The Chartists were conspicuous by their absence from a meeting of the Parliamentary and Financial Reform Association. See also Cheltenham Free Press, March 2, 1850, great meeting at Cheltenham of the Parliamentary and Financial Reform Association at which Glenister made a policy statement declaring that "what they really wanted was the Charter, but they were prepared to join".

40. W.E. Adams, Memoirs, op.cit., pp.151-2.

41. Ibid., p.223.

42. Newcastle Daily Chronicle, May 15, 1906, Obituary on W.E. Adams.

43. W.E. Adams, Memoirs, op.cit., p.223.

44. Red Republican and Friend of the People, 1850-1851, Reptd., London, 1966 with Introduction by J. Saville Vol.I & II. See, for example, Red Republican Vol.I p.100, Saturday, Sept. 14 1850 Subscriptions (8) from Cheltenham; see also Friend of the People, Vol,II, p.200 resolution repudiating "with extreme disgust the anti-democratic sentiments contained in Mr. Feargus O'Connor's letters published in the Northern Star of 29th March and 5th April, reiterating the foul and caluminous statements of the enemies to democracy against our foreign brethren".

45. Friend of the People p.264, July 12, 1851. E. Jones first came in June 1851, then again in August 1853.

46. W.E. Adams, Memoirs, op.cit., p.262.

47. J. Saville, Introduction, Memoirs, op.cit., p.10.

48. W.E. Adams, Memoirs, op.cit., p.262.

49. See F.B. Smith, Radical Artisan, W.J. Linton, 1812-97, op.cit., pp.99-100.

50. W.E. Adams, Memoirs, op.cit. p.262.

51. F.B. Smith, Radical Artisan, W.J. Linton 1812-97, op.cit., see generally.

52. J.F.C. Harrison, "Chartism in Leeds" pp.65-98; in particular pp.96-97 for Linton, in A. Briggs (ed.) Chartist Studies, London, 1959.

53. W.E. Adams, Memoirs, op.cit., pp.262-264.

54. J. Saville, Introduction, Memoirs, op.cit., p.11. For the reformulation of British Republicanism, see also G. Claeys, "Mazzini, Kossuth, and British Radicalism, 1848-1854", Journal of British Studies, Vol. 28(3), July, 1989, pp.225-261.

55. For Adams's admiration of Mazzini, his teachings and work, see Newcastle Weekly Chronicle, March 16, 1872, Political Letters by Ironside; Newcastle Weekly Chronicle (supplement), Jan.23, 1886; and Jan.8, 1898, in connection with the death of W.J. Linton.

56. W.E. Adams, Memoirs, op.cit., pp.263-264 sets out a few inspiring passages from Mazzini.

57. Newcastle Weekly Chronicle, June 25, 1898.

58. W.E. Adams, Memoirs, op.cit., p.266.

59. Newcastle Weekly Chronicle, Jan. 8, 1898, The Gossip's Bowl. New Chartist republican societies were found in many parts of the country, including Newcastle-upon-Tyne. Here, Joseph Cowen was already active in the mid 1850s with his National Republican Brotherhood.

60. W.E. Adams, Memoirs, op.cit., p.152.

61. Ibid., p.267; see also F.B. Smith, Radical Artisan, W.J. Linton, 1812-97, op.cit., pp.101-102.

62. Ibid., pp.267-268,

63. Ibid., p.268.

64. Cheltenham Free Press, June 8, 1850.

65. W.E. Adams, Memoirs, op.cit., p.270.

66. Ibid., p.275.

67. P. Brock, "Polish Democrats and English Radicals 1832-1862: A Chapter in the History of Anglo-Polish Relations", Journal of Modern History, Vol.25, Part 2, 1953 pp.139-156, particularly p.152.

68. Cheltenham Free Press, May 17, 1851, Letter to the Editor by W.E. Adams.

69. Ibid., May 24th, Letter by James Glover on the Hungarian Refugees; May 31st, Letter by Edward Sharland on the Polish and Hungarian Refugees.

70. Ibid., May 24th, 1851.

71. W.E. Adams, Memoirs, op.cit., pp.271-272.

72. Northern Star, Oct.5, 1850, Thomas Cooper's Lecture at the Cheltenham Town Hall.

73. W.E. Adams, Memoirs, op.cit., pp.170-171. See also Newcastle Weekly Chronicle, July 23 1892, The Gossip's Bowl. Here Adams dates the lecture to 1850, as reported in the Northern Star above. It was not in March 1851 as suggested by him in the Memoirs, p.171.

74. Newcastle Weekly Chronicle, July 23, 1892, The Gossip's Bowl. See also Cooper's Journal, London, 1850, Vol.1., Reptd. New York, 1970, No.18, May 4, 1850, p.280.

75. W.E. Adams, Memoirs, op.cit., p.268.

76. Northern Star, June 28, 1851. E. Jones at Cheltenham.

77. Newcastle Weekly Chronicle, Sept. 22, 1900, The Gossip's Bowl; People's Paper, Sept.1, 1855.

78. People's Paper, May 28, 1853.

79. See C. Godfrey, Chartist Lives — The Anatomy of a Working Class Movement, op.cit., pp.405-421 on the influence of David Urquhart (1805-1877), Britain's leading Russophobe.

80. Ibid., pp.422-423.

81. Newcastle Weekly Chronicle, Jan. 8, 1898, The Gossip's Bowl.

82. People's Paper, Feb. 17, 1855. According to Adams in the Newcastle Weekly Chronicle Feb.6 1897, Edward Sharland headed the Cheltenham republicans after he left for Brantwood.

83. H. Solly, These Eighty Years, op.cit., Vol.II, pp.40-41. He left Cheltenham in the latter part of 1851 to work at Carter Lane, London.

84. For Sydney Dobell (1824-1874) see D.N.B. Vol.V.pp.1,038-1,039. The entry states: "A radical reformer in some directions, he held the tyranny of mobs and autocrats in equal aversion". See also Contem Ignotus, The Golden Decade of a Favoured Town, London, 1884, pp.154-193, for Sydney Dobell and his poetry.

85. Newcastle Weekly Chronicle, Jan. 21, 1893, The Gossip's Bowl.

86. F.B. Smith, Radical Artisan, W.J. Linton, 1812-97, op.cit., p.98.

87. W.E. Adams, Memoirs, op.cit., p.274.

88. Newcastle Weekly Chronicle, Jan. 21, 1893, The Gossip's Bowl. The Roman was a monk preaching the regeneration of Italy by covert and indirect methods.

89. W.E. Adams, Memoirs, op.cit, p.261. Adams wrote that "The Charter, as a declaration of rights, was excellent".

90. G. Hart, A History of Cheltenham, op.cit., p.250.

91. W.E. Adams, Memoirs, op.cit., p.254.

92. W.H. Maehl (ed.), R. Gammage: Reminiscences of a Chartist, op.cit., pp.31-33.

93. W.E. Adams, Memoirs., op.cit., p.172.

94. Idem.,

95. Ibid., p.173.

96. Idem.,

97. Idem.,

98. R.G. Gammage, The History of the Chartist Movement, London, 1854, p.416. I am grateful to Mrs. Dorothy Thompson for the loan of this rare copy.

99. Gammage's speech was fully reported in the Cheltenham Free Press, July 10, 1852. See also Cheltenham Examiner, July 14, 1852 and People's Paper, July 17, 1852.

100. Cheltenham Examiner, July 14, 1852.

101. W.R. Williams, The Parliamentary History of the County of Gloucester, 1213-1898, Hereford, 1898, p.147. C.F. Berkeley 999; W. Jones 869.

102. W.H. Maehl (ed.), R. Gammage: Reminiscences of a Chartist, op.cit., p.32 Gammage, accompanied by Ernest Jones, paid another visit to the Chartist group in August 1853.

103. W.E. Adams, Memoirs, op.cit., p.301.

104. People's Paper, Aug. 2, 1856 and People's Paper, Aug. 9, 1856.

105. Reasoner, Aug. 10, 1856, p.49. Gazette of Secularist Societies.

106. D. Thompson, "Chartism, Success or Failure?" in D. Rubinstein (ed.), People For the People, London, 1973, pp.90-97, particularly p.95.

107. People's Paper, Aug. 2, 1856.

108. T.R. Tholfsen, Working Class Radicalism in Mid-Victorian England, London, 1976, pp.153-154 for his arguments about Adams's political behaviour in the 1850s. J. Saville, Introduction, Memoirs, op.cit., p.12.

109. H. Weisser, "Chartist Internationalism, 1845-1848", The Historical Journal, XLV, No.1, 1971, pp.49-66, in particular p.64. There is no mention either of Adams or of Spa Chartist involvement in foreign affairs in Weisser's British Working Class Movements and Europe, 1815-1848, Manchester, 1975.

3 A Peripatetic Radical

In the spring of 1854, on completion of his apprenticeship as a hand compositor, Adams tramped to W.J. Linton's home at Brantwood, a small mansion estate on the eastern side of Lake Coniston in the beautiful but rugged terrain of the Lake district. In the company of fellow Spa republicans, Thomas Hailing, a printer, James Glover, a gardener-handyman and another bachelor volunteer, George Vine, a staymaker from the north of England, Adams worked unstintingly and earnestly in the labour of love: to produce their mentor's monthly, the *English Republic* and Joseph Cowen's Newcastle based radical-republican magazine, the *Northern Tribune*.[1]

The vision which had dominated Linton's retreat to Brantwood in 1852 was said to be "the awkward figure of Louis Napoleon, looming large and threatening through mountain visits".[2] Both Linton and Cowen were equally convinced that because of their outspoken anti-Napoleonic invective they were objects of dread to the man "who had just strangled the French Republic",[3] and that, as he could not reach them by any legal process, he would try to have them kidnapped. Professor F.B. Smith has graphically detailed the realities of life in the Brantwood venture: the unworldliness of Linton himself; the unconventional "free growth" his seven children enjoyed; the more familiar domestic tensions with their servant, Agnes, the wife of Karl Stolzman, a Polish refugee to whom Linton had generously provided a home; the considerable suspicion shown to the household by wary neighbours and surly shopkeepers; the primitiveness of everything, the privations the majority happily endured; and, above all, the impracticality of the scheme which in such isolated and forbidding countryside, led to its untimely demise in the spring of 1855.[4] Adams's own account, too, in the *Memoirs* was no mere "playing to the gallery" attempt to stimulate *Chronicle* readers eager to absorb snippets of radical nostalgia. In that spartan regime and seclusion of Brantwood which he readily enjoyed as a youthful and unpaid republican idealist, we are offered a snapshot on an experience that left an abiding impression: the production of new radical literature was part of the duty of sacrifice; it was an essential endeavour in life's mission — "nothing less than the conversion of England to Republican ideas".[5] Later in life Adams, it is clear, made more than one pilgrimage to this old and inspiring haunt.

In the Brantwood Printing House Adams was Linton's indispensable printing assistant. He was not, however, simply a back-room boy walking to and from the unfurnished cottage he shared with Hailing at Yewdale Bridge, some three miles away. The camaraderie of the experiment threw up moments for reading, discussion and "dreaming together the establishment of an English Republic".[6] In Linton's company

Adams became intimately associated with his master's ideas, projects, and "exalted faith in the regeneration of humanity".[7] Here they imbued at first hand a Mazzinian inspired mystical republicanism based on the fullest possible sovereignty and an equal participation in society through universal suffrage; it all led to a belief:

> "in a social state having God and His law at the summit — the People, the universality of the citizens, free and equal, at its base — progress for rule, association as means, devotion for baptism, genius and virtue for lights upon the way."[8]

Karl Stolzman's presence also helped: the Polish refugee's insights into his own country's terrible plight at the hands of Russian expansionism served simply to reinforce everyone's personal attachment to the lofty ideals and eloquence of Mazzini; and it was a chance to speculate on the enormous possibilities within a free, united and republican Poland where, as in the English republic, the people could realise for the first time their own potential for duty and altruism in an ameliorative and cumulative manner.

In a little more than a year, however, the short-lived Brantwood venture came to an end. Adams was the first to leave by the spring of 1855. Glover and Hailing stayed on for a time "to sweep up"; the former then left to engage in gardening work in London, the latter to resume his printing trade in Cheltenham.[9] Not surprisingly, all three retained their faith in republican principles and for proselytizing the cause; and the network of republican associations, never large by radical standards, was at least strengthened for some time in both London and Cheltenham with the arrival or return of these activists. Between the trio, too, there seems to have been forged a personal bond and friendship which Adams certainly valued highly. Glover, for example, became for a time Adams's gardening correspondent in the *Newcastle Weekly Chronicle*.[10]

Adams prepared to set off on tramp with only 17/- in his pocket and a distance of 274 miles separating him from the familiar surroundings of home and friends in Cheltenham Spa. Admittedly, he travelled light: a few personal belongings accompanied a bundle of tracts to be distributed on route; a handful of letters of introduction from Linton to be given to fellow republicans or printing houses where he might apply for work; and, in confident anticipation that he would be selling his skills, a composing stick and an apron, the printer's basic tools.[11] Yet life on tramp was far from easy; but it certainly widened Adams's experiences in ways profoundly different from those he had imagined, even romanticised, when in his apprenticeship days. For one thing, as Adams recalled:

> "The times were out of joint. It was the winter of the Crimean War — the severest as regards weather, the dreariest as regards depression, the direst as regards distress, that we had had for years."[12]

Fascination for the itinerant's life had been naively identified in young Adams's mind as a summertime experience: a chance to enjoy and enthuse the natural beauty and restless activity of the countryside. The stark reality, however, for our intrepid artisan on his departure south from Coniston was a landscape universally numbed: the severe and lingering effects of the winter cold left him no chance "of communing with Nature"[13] as he had dreamed tramp life would embrace. The effects of the trade depression also ensured a rude shock to his youthful optimism. Work was extremely scarce, the printing trade over-stocked and Adams was both alarmed and dispirited by the number of men he met on tramp vainly in search of employment.[14] His own particular difficulties were compounded at this time by the fact that he was not a member of the Typographical Association or Union. This was not through choice, for no branch existed either at Coniston or Cheltenham. Unlike Association members he could not therefore take advantage of their well-established tramping systems or arrangements, which had houses of call and paid relief to skilled but out of work migrant members.[15] The reason he was able to gain 1/- relief but no work in Birmingham by showing his indentures, was probably due to the influence of one of Linton's letters, which had directed him to George Dawson, a friend already well disposed to Mazzinian ideals and a possible source of printing employment on his paper, the *Birmingham Daily Post.*[16] Elsewhere, not even the letters of introduction to republican brethren in a string of towns between Manchester and Birmingham brought the remotest employment success. Indeed, the situation was so desperate that the plan, whereby Adams should retain some of the proceeds of the sale of *English Republic* tracts in order to subsist and forward the rest to Linton, was abandoned.[17] Instead, he forlornly distributed some of them amongst school children, some to the equally unreceptive inmates of the common lodging-houses he frequented, and the remainder was simply hung on bare bushes and trees for the benefit of passing itinerants.[18]

For another thing, Adams's industrious up-bringing, his political maturity and the social habits of independence and temperance which he shared with fellow artisans in Cheltenham were completely ill-suited to the cultural practices of life he discovered on tramp. He had always eschewed tap-rooms and looked down on the shiftless poor for the coarseness of their language and the improvidence of their life-style. Tramping brought such prejudices sharply into focus. Although often footsore, weary and at times depressed he soon learned how to avoid the more sordid taverns and lodging-houses, and to cope with the nocturnal excesses of ignorant room or bed-mates in that "vagabond class" prone to drunken and disorderly behaviour.[19]

The difficulties of travel were at times mitigated by the freemasonry of the road. "Every tramp", recalled Adams, "chums with every other tramp, just as if he had known him from boyhood".[20] He was particularly fortunate to be befriended by an ex-sailor and fiddler who insisted on paying his accommodation at a Preston tavern. Typical of Adams, he never forgot a good turn. For the tramping hospitality shown to him by one knight of the road, John Connolly, he retained cherished memories, which he clearly felt duty-bound to share with readers in the *Memoirs*.[21]

Gregariousness notwithstanding, his determination, resourcefulness and tramp's fitness — he walked thirty-two miles on one day — brought him home to Cheltenham, albeit penniless, in a little over a week.[22] Unfortunately, the prospects of work in 1855 in the Spa were even gloomier. At a time when many skilled workers or labour aristocrats were considered to be making steady material advances,[23] Adams came home to penury. Undeterred, he resolved to leave his native town almost immediately in order to tramp again in search of work. On this occasion his departure was virtually for good, because the wider world was to offer new involvements and interests which prevented all but the briefest of visits to ageing relatives and friends.

In this next peripatetic phase Adams fared better: he found his first regular employment since his apprenticeship days at a printing establishment in Hereford, to where he had initially tramped. By early June he had moved on again. This time he went directly to London, but not before trying in vain, at Linton's request,[24] to place Anton Zabicki, another Polish refugee and mutual friend,[25] in the printing work he had vacated in Hereford.

Life in London was to prove more stimulating and certainly more exciting than anything he had ever known at either Cheltenham or Brantwood. Adams certainly went prepared: "There I had friends, introductions and the promise of work."[26] Republican agitation rather than work appears to have come top of Adams's priorities as he was attracted straightaway to the radical tradition and intellectual life on which the capital thrived. He re-joined James Glover and Agnes Stolzman in a small republican club which included Edward Truelove, the radical bookseller, made contact with a now frail Stanislaus Worcell, the veteran leader of the Polish refugees, and introduced himself into the first of a network of popular political discussion halls, the John Street Institution, "a well-known rendevouz for Reformers in the middle years of the century".[27] It was in connection with republican proselytization that Adams also found himself caught up in support of the so-called "Free Sunday Movement": the protest campaign in 1855 and 1856 against all sabbatarian restrictions on popular Sunday recreations.[28] Linton had always stressed to Adams that in their propaganda work the most effective strategy for individual conversion lay with the role of the printed word:

> "I feel certain that tracts to awaken thought and personal conversation are the two best means. Preaching doubtless may be good sometimes — but words so uttered do not, I think, have the weight of well-digested tracts."[29]

Accordingly, their plans envisaged that a maximum impact would be achieved amongst those large often fashionable and wealthy crowds which gathered on Sundays for recreation or celebration in the venue provided by Hyde Park. All went well, for example, when Adams and his fellow band of dedicated republicans distributed republican tracts on the family, property and religion amongst the well-ordered assembly celebrating the conclusion in 1856 of peace after the Crimean War.[30] However, the scene in Hyde Park a year earlier was far from peaceful. The discontent which spilled over into riots and clashes with the police in June and July 1855 could not be attributed to public sensibilities outraged by the content of Adams's republican fly-sheets, even though the focus of agitation — the free Sunday movement — had attracted a whole spectrum of radical sympathies.[31]

Opposition to the Christian sabbath was a fundamental part of the Paineite tradition shared by radicals such as W.E. Adams.[32] They felt that Sunday recreations need not interfere with Sunday worship any more than Sunday worship interfered with wholesome and rational Sunday recreations. The long running battle between Radicals and Sabbatarians was given a new twist in the summer of 1855 when Sir Robert Grosvenor's Sunday Trading Bill attempted to regulate in some manner the sale of alcohol in the metropolis on Sundays. According to E. Royle "Sunday trading had long troubled Christian consciences and the police".[33] Employers paid wages at public houses on Saturday nights where working men were induced to remain, often in a drunken state, until Sunday mornings at which point they confronted outraged worshippers on their way to church. On the face of it respectable artisans like Adams might be expected to welcome such a move, but not so. The Bill was regarded not as a temperance, but as a Sabbatarian measure:

> " — as a measure, too, for circumscribing the rights and enjoyments of the poor, while leaving untouched the customs and recreation of the rich. It was felt, indeed, by the people whom it concerned, to be in every sense a class measure."[34]

The cry went up in London for working people to go "to Hyde Park and see how the aristocracy keep the Sabbath".[35] The conduct of the first Sunday gathering on June 24th was notable for its lively hooting, jeering and hissing at wealthy Londoners; but the second Sunday — July 1st — saw comparative self-restraint completely break down into mass disorder. The mobbing of fashionable people in their luxurious coaches escalated into missile throwing and the destruction of property in some of the palatial Mayfair residences nearby. Orders were then given by the police to clear the Park. Adams was a first hand witness to the indiscriminate brutality of the bâton charges which characterised the speedy execution by the police of the authorities orders. After some weeks of protest and an inquiry into the heavy-handed conduct of the police, which vindicated the public outcry, the obnoxious Bill was withdrawn.

The riots had a profound impact on the young Adams, new to the rigours of London life. After all, such boisterous and violent behaviour was light years away from the ways in which public affairs had been conducted in the comparatively calm backwaters of his native Cheltenham. The issues nevertheless remained clear. The whole episode indicated the insidious manner in which freedom of expression and civil rights could be eroded by a coercive state; it also revealed an over-zealous law enforcement agency that only paid lip-service to upholding the rights of the individual. His anti-Close prejudices thus rekindled, Adams became a fervent supporter against any move to control the individual's freedom simply for religious purposes. As part of a broad campaign to educate people into drink-free recreations on their rest days, Adams was to be found in the next thirty years actively subscribing to the aims of the National Sunday League, namely the Sunday opening of galleries, museums, libraries, zoological gardens and aquariums.[36]

London was the great centre of journalist activity and by the spring of 1856 Adams had at last secured a permanent printing job: he was "assigned a frame" on the *Illustrated Times* the successful Fleet Street paper of Henry Vizetelly.[37] Adams was well-pleased with himself. Permanent employment now brought for the first time a real possibility of an improvement in living standards which other skilled workers were already enjoying. The different pieces of evidence suggest, for example, that he was able to forget completely about the money Linton owed him for certain Christmas presents and sundry goods required from time to time for the Brantwood household;[38] that he could afford a daily copy of the *Morning Star*, the then leading radical paper in London, which he bought at a news stall near his lodgings in Kennington and had finished reading by the time he had reached work in Fleet Street;[39] and was able to save sufficient from his earnings to contemplate marriage in 1858.[40]

Such a situation also enabled Adams to pass his leisure hours in the pursuits and activities that pleased him. Predictably, these were all of an educational or political kind, or both. To the regular attendance at the family gatherings of the little republican club was added another enjoyable weekly venture: enrolment for classes at the newly opened Working Men's College founded by F.D. Maurice in Great Ormond Street,[41] in order to continue the processes of self and mutual instruction begun at Cheltenham. At the College Adams was inspired by the lectures of Christian Socialists such as Charles Kingsley and Maurice himself; by the Positivists, Godfrey and Vernon Lushington; and by the Pre-Raphaelites, John Ruskin, Ford Madox Brown and Edward Burne Jones.[142] He also continued his study of Latin, English Grammar and love of Chaucer and Shakespeare in English class evenings he remembered as:

> "exquisite ... Part of the time Mr. Furnivall took the words as they followed in the dictionary — dissecting them, showing their origin, and tracing their transformation in sound, meaning, and spelling ... The members of his class were mostly working men ... we sat over biscuits and coffee till an advanced hour of the morning, talking or listening to talk about poets and poetry, and languages and literature, and having such a feast of reason and flow of soul as almost never was since Shakespeare had his bout with Ben Johnson at the Mermaid." [43]

Adams's political horizons were also considerably widened through access to a range of political venues — themselves a magnet for dynamic and distinguished radicals — which few provincial cities could rival. On Sunday mornings, for example, he was often drawn to Ernest Jones's open-air Chartist meetings in the large Copenhagen fields (later the site of Smithfield Market.)[44] The movement was now virtually like Jones's own threadbare clothes on such public occasions: so reduced in circumstances that barely a remnant Chartist Association remained. Nevertheless, political animals like Adams had not lost faith. At the time of the Indian Mutiny in 1857, Adams was present to hear Jones deliver an eloquent speech denouncing the English military machine for its equally barbarous methods in suppressing the Indian insurgents. Few people, of course, were prepared to show any consideration towards the plight of the Sepoys, native Indian soldiers from Bengal who, in revolt, had massacred a large number of Europeans. Adams, however, was one of a handful of radicals courageous enough to express sympathy following Jones's lecture:

> "Well do I recollect the ferocious spirit which took possession of the entire body of our countrymen during the Indian Mutiny. I stood alone in a large workshop in London in appealing for clemancy for the Sepoys."[45]

London in the 1850s was particularly well-known for its popular debating or discussion halls, the "real little images of the British Parliament".[46] They provided a forum for a free interchange of ideas, of all sorts and conditions of thought; although it is clear that in Adams's time amongst the "men of light and leading", Chartist, Radical, Secularist and political refugee orators were predominant on the platforms.

In the Fleet Street neighbourhood there were three such halls: the Cogers Hall, an ancient public speaking institution in Bride Lane; the Discussion Hall, a spacious room in a tavern in Shoe Lane; and the Temple Forum, a meeting place located in the back of the Green Dragon in Fleet Street. Is is difficult to imagine a more lively scene than when the oratorical proceedings and beery atmosphere of these places were joined and in full vigour. Publicans were determined to ply their trade and to this end paid a fee and sufficient beer money for an evening's debating performance from prominent working men. In smoke-filled rooms, amidst animated discussions and debates into the early hours, Adams often heard, for example, a decrepit and dishevelled Bronterre O'Brien, "a tribune of the people in the palmy period of Chartism",[47] make spirited speeches. Sometimes, too, instead of reeling home when the taverns closed their doors, Adams found himself, drawn by the subject of the debates themselves, in the company of revellers adjourning to a "night house" in Farringdon Street; they would also be joined by sober and intelligent press colleagues finishing the early nightshift in Fleet Street; and together they would continue their debates and discussions albeit sometimes in a noisy fashion. But it was not always beery people on the platform, for among the many frequenters Adams met in debates were Thomas Cooper, Joseph Barker, the Holyoake and the Watts brothers, Charles Bradlaugh and Louis Kossuth.[48] Such meetings led to more permanent associations. Adams struck up a close and lasting friendship with the secularists, George and Austin Holyoake; he also became a firm and valued friend of Charles Bradlaugh, who welcomed him into a select circle of republicans and free thinkers that met weekly at his home in Cassland Road, Hackney for some time up until the autumn of 1858.[49]

A popular discussion hall attached to a tavern meant good business for the drink-sellers. Adams, however, was sufficiently open-minded and realistic to appreciate how very difficult it was at that time to break such social connections: the politically conscious working man learnt much about the art of public speaking by performing in the large rooms furnished by or within taverns. Although he was never a member of any official temperance organization, Adams was deeply influenced by it; but it was not in the narrow minded or indignant way which characterised so many middle class temperance campaigners that he took up his own position. Indeed, in his temperance views on club life we see his tolerance and humanity:

> "I saw the orators of the Discussion Hall in what might be called their dishabille, and I am free to confess that the spectacle was not impressive. All the same, the men who contributed to enlighten the London public on the advanced political doctrines of the period, though they did it amidst the fumes of tobacco and beer, were men, many of them, of conspicuous ability, sincere convictions and genuine affection for the people."[50]

Adams was himself a lifetime smoker and not unfamiliar with the smoke-room in the taverns; he also realised from what he witnessed at first hand that drink was not in itself an evil; rather, it was the social pressures which drove men to drunkeness; and the real attraction of the public house was, like that of the debating halls, the warmth, conviviality and companionship it gave to working men who were denied access to, or could not afford, leisure in other public or private places.

It was at the Temple Forum that the question of tyrannicide was announced for debate shortly after the attempt of Felice Orsini on the life of Louis Napoleon on January 14, 1858.[51] The whole of Europe was astonished by the news of a fresh attempt on the Emperor's life as he and the Empress were proceeding in their carriage to an evening at the opera. The chief conspirator was Felice Orsini but two of his accomplices, Dr. Simon Bernard and Thomas Allsop, were alleged to have been principally involved in the manufacture in England of the bombs which were thown at the Emperor's carriages.[52] The latter escaped unscathed but many others in the entourage, as well as innocent bystanders, were killed or wounded. The incident seriously damaged Anglo-French diplomatic relations.[53] England was denounced as a nest of assassins; colonels in a number of French regiments in remonstrations to the Emperor demanded to be led against the country; and Count Walewski, the French Minister of Foreign Affairs, sent despatches to Palmerston charging the government with harbouring murderers and of allowing the question of assassination to be openly preached in the London streets. A startled but compliant Palmerston, it appears, in obedience to the dictates of the French Ministry and to appease Louis Napoleon embarked on yet another reactionary domestic crusade: simultaneously he prepared to introduce a Conspiracy-to-Murder Bill, initiated a campaign of persecution of Radicals and their press, and placed many exiles under police surveillance.[54] By Sunday, February 19 his plans appeared to be well in place. On February 12, at about the time the Orsini band was being indicted in a Paris court, the Conspiracy Bill, whereby political refugees might at any time be described as "suspect" and denied a safe haven in England, passed its first reading. Two days later Dr. Simon Bernard, arrested at his lodgings in London, was charged with conspiracy to assassinate the Emperor and subsequently committed for trial at the Old Bailey on

April 12.[55] In the course of these proceedings a reward of £200 was offered for the capture of Thomas Allsop who had gone to ground; he was also to be charged when apprehended with being an accessary to the assassination attempt in Paris.[56]

Such a range of coercive measures triggered off a storm of protest activity amongst members of radical clubs and circles in London. Two issues now became entwined with important ramifications on national politics. The first was a spirited defence of Orsini through an exposure of the crimes of Napoleon III; the second was a successful campaign by Radical MPs and disaffected Liberals, with considerable extra-parliamentary backing, against the Conspiracy Bill, or French Colonels' Bill as it was now cleverly nicknamed.[57] Adams's pamphlet "Tyrannicide: Is it Justifiable?" was formally published by Edward Truelove at his Strand Offices on Saturday, February 13 1858, the day after the first reading of the Conspiracy Bill. It articulated most effectively and coherently the arguments voiced by radicals since January in support of Orsini at the London debating halls, which the French colonels had truculently demanded to be allowed to root out.[58] Adams endeavoured in dramatic language to redress the "long howl of execration" against the Italian patriot by putting the incident in context: that is of the "Caesaraping, liberty-hater activities"[59] of Napoleon himself. He first offered readers a grim reminder of the bloody events surrounding the notorious Paris Coup of December 1851:

> "With fair pretensions and a seeming justice, a secret pretender obtains the suffrages of his countrymen; he swears to preserve their right; in the dead of a December night his soldiers fill the gaols with the elect of the people; amid the light of a December day his assassins — made drunk that remorse may penetrate their souls — seek their victims in the public streets among unarmed men and harmless women and children. He terrifies the unconscious people by the audacity of his crimes; and in the midst of the blood he has spilt, and the carnage he has occasioned, he erects an empire."[60]

But it was in relationship to the repression of Italy's national aspirations that Adams answered unequivocally in defence of the strategy of tyrannicide. In April 1849 a Roman Republic had been proclaimed by Mazzini and Garibaldi. It proved to be extremely shortlived. In July, Rome was re-captured for the Pope by Napoleon's invading troops; the two popular Italian patriots fled; and under the protection of French bayonets the old Papal absolutism was restored. There was no hope, therefore, for Italy as long as France, misled by the man who had mastered her, remained at the head of a coalition of enemies. Thus it followed for Adams that Orsini was justified because:

> "The doom of Roman liberty was sealed in Paris; it is in Paris, then, that Pianovi, with strictest justice, and Orsini with inexorable logic, strike for the liberation of Rome. Insurrection inevitably causes the shedding of guiltless blood, the flowing of rivers of blood. Tyrannicide, affixing the dagger where crime has affixed the guilt, executes a surer justice."[61]

The pamphlet immediately received considerable publicity[62] not least because, within hours of its availability, Metropolitan police officers, probably under Cabinet orders, arrested Edward Truelove; he was subsequently charged at Bow Street Police Station with publishing a seditious libel on the French Emperor and committed for trial. No warrant was issued for Adams's arrest, as his name was assumed to be fictitious. Protesting in vain to the Trueloves that he should give himself up, external events finally dictated that Adams was to take his first step into public recognition as the accomplice rather than the leader, as was the reality in fact, of a specific cause.

The Truelove prosecution, like that of Bernard and Allsop the week before, created some sensation because it served to fuel concern felt increasingly at Westminster that Palmerston, having got the Conspiracy Bill through on its first reading with a 200 majority, had now become the determined instrument of Napoleon III's interfering demands. It is difficult to explain precisely that great sea-change within one week at Westminster which led to the fall of Palmerston's ministry on the second reading of the Conspiracy Bill on Friday February 19, 1858. Doubtless the government's high-handed actions resulting in police arrests, particularly that of Truelove, and the publicity afforded them "put the English people on their mettle!":[63] a poor publisher had been arrested for printing language "not half so strong as that of all our press some years since".[64] At Westminster, libertarian sentiment also received an important fillip. Liberal members such as Samuel Morley, John Bright, W.J. Fox and Milner Gibson promptly constituted themselves into what turned out to be a powerful Anti-Conspiracy Committee; it also included on its executive seasoned extra-parliamentary radicals as diverse as Holyoake, the ex-Chartist and secularist, and Richard Cobden of Anti-Corn Law League fame.[65]

This little group of practised agitators had less than a week in which to destroy the Conspiracy Bill, and they succeeded brilliantly! A number of meetings were held,[66] resolutions passed and London quickly covered with "a garment of striking placards"[67] condemning the Bill as un-hasty, un-English and un-necessary.[68] Sufficient ground-work was done to point out to the people of London that in the wake of the Truelove prosecution Palmerston was "truckling to the foreigner", one of the seven deadly sins of English political ethics.[69] According to one source, "before the end of the week all

London was discussing the "French Colonels' Bill".[70] The vote on the second reading was taken on the Friday (February 19th). Milner Gibson proposed a resolution which implied censure of the Bill. The House it seems had not been unreceptive to public opinion: others followed Gibson, including Gladstone and Peel, in submitting Palmerston to "deadly jets of hostility": so much subserviency could not be tolerated. At 2 o'clock on Saturday morning, February 20th, on the division being taken in a highly charged atmosphere, Palmerston's majority of 200 vanished, and the Bill was rejected by 234 votes to 215![71] The government resigned the same day, but the agitation the Committee had whipped up was not to be denied its final fling. They had announced a demonstration in Hyde Park for Sunday February 21: although an attempt was made to call it off, some 200,000 people attended and revelled in the delight of the fall of Palmerston.[72]

Radical attention now re-focussed on the Truelove case since Lord Derby's new Conservative Ministry showed, at least for the time being, no sign of abandoning the prosecution. Indeed, whatever hopes of the Derby Cabinet that might have been entertained by those in the country who thought the Conservatives were better than the Whigs, were to be dispelled in the beginning of March, when yet another government prosecution swelled the list of attacks on the liberty of the press. Seditious libel proceedings were commenced against a Polish book-seller in Rupert Street, Stanislaus Tchorzewski, who had published a pamphlet by Felix Pyat and other Frenchmen exiled in Jersey, which was again expressly and stridently anti-Napoleonic.[73]

Adams was now drawn increasingly into the political limelight. The content of the "Tyrannicide" pamphlet raised fundamental issues about the individual's ability to exercise liberty of thought and utterance; and in the prosecution of Truelove could be seen an unconstitutional, unnecessary and pernicious attack on the freedom of the press. Adams himself was particularly incensed by the class nature of the government's attack, for the charge of incitement to murder could easily have been levelled at modern statesmen and poets. Walter Savage Landor, for example, was almost fanatical in his pronouncements. Adams recalled how the poet had written that "tyrannicide is the highest of virtues"; that Disraeli had published a "Revolutionary Epic" in 1834 wherein occurred similar sentiments;[74] and only two weeks before Orsini's attempt a poem of Matthew Arnold's on an incident in Greek history had appeared in which the poet had justified murder:

> "Against a Power exempt from common checks,
> Dangerous to all and in no way but this
> To be annulled — ranks any man an act
> Like this with murder?"[75]

Of course, no prosecutions followed against such influential people.

In the country at large there was much activity amongst working men and women in defence of Adams's right of free discussion. Presses were everywhere at work and vendors active in defiantly selling copies of the proscribed pamphlet;[76] public readings were greatly applauded in Chartist, Secularist and Trade Society meetings;[77] and Radical leaders such as Holyoake and Bradlaugh stoutly defended Adams's arguments for removing tyranny at large funeral orations on Orsini in Newcastle-upon-Tyne, Manchester and at the John Street Institute, London.[78] Significantly, influential members of the radical middle class also rallied to his and Truelove's defence: the issues at stake offered common ground in the radical ideology. Professor Francis Newman of University College, brother of the famous Cardinal, for example, saw more clearly than most the dangers to freedom of discussion inherent in the government's insidious attack. If the prosecutions were successful, he declared, then the right to discussion in a spirit of speculative inquiry of a question which had been an open subject of debate for ages — of "free moral criticism" — would be lost.[79]

The upshot of all this frenetic activity was the formation of a Truelove Defence Committee; and by early April, after a similar fate befell Tchorzewski, it generalised itself into the Press Prosecution Defence Committee in order to defray trial expenses for the two publishers.[80] English liberties now endangered, the Defence Committee attracted both generous and broadly-based support. Charles Bradlaugh was appointed secretary and James Watson, treasurer. A total of £70 was rapidly realised in time for the trial scheduled for April 5th.[81] The subscription list drew impressively on nation-wide support from working men and women:[82] There were also such notable contributors as Joseph Cowen, Harriet Martineau, Professor Newman, W.J. Fox, Edmond Beales, P.A. Taylor and James Stansfeld.[83] John Stuart Mill was particularly concerned: he not only gave £20, but also included a footnote on the incident in Chapter 2 of his latest work, the very influential *On Liberty*; and called the prosecution "that ill-judged interference with the liberty of public discussion".[84]

The legal machinery of the State meanwhile marched on. The trial of Dr. Bernard was arranged for Monday April 12 before a special commission — unprecedented since 1848 — at the Old Bailey a week after the ordinary session of the court;[85] that of Truelove and Tchorzewski was, after further delays, finally fixed for June 22, 1858 in Westminster Hall.[86] "Not since the Irish rebellion of 1848" wrote the *Times* "has there been any State trial approaching in importance the case of Simon Bernard."[87]

The French Emperor looked forward to a successful prosecution as a means of soothing away many diplomatic difficulties. To the Derby Cabinet, which had ousted its opponents for bringing in the Conspiracy Bill, a verdict of "guilty" would have given the opportunity either of proving that no legislation was necessary, or of legislating under the sanction of a judicial decision. In the event, the calculations of statesmen and lawyers were confounded. After a long and wearisome trial of six days, Simon Bernard was acquitted: the jury remained in deliberation only an hour and twenty minutes.[88] The radicals were jubilant; the acquittal was regarded a "a popular triumph".[89] Much of the credit for the victory was due to the skills of Edwin James, a promising young barrister,[90] who was now retained to defend Truelove and Tchorzewski.

Adams re-doubled his efforts to give himself up in place of Truelove, but his offers were again resisted by the Defence Committee.[91] Salutory advice was also offered by his friend and mentor, W.J. Linton, buoyed up by the news of Bernard's acquittal:

> "I think most decidedly, unless Truelove wishes to throw the matter from his shoulders to yours (which I do not believe) that nothing is to be gained by your taking his place. The battle is best fought in his person. I am sure of it. I am sure for you to give yourself up would be every way a blunder. They will not even yet — I think — carry the matter into Court against Truelove. Against you they might; and a special jury would give a verdict against you — if only for your impudence as a working man in doing what the special jury clearly is afraid of."[92]

Linton's prophetic words were ultimately to come true. Their immediate effect on Adams, however, was, as he amusingly noted, to encourage another grave indiscretion: he got married! His bride was Elizabeth Jane Owen Smith who lived in Munster Square off Albany Street, Regent's Park. They were married on May 25 1858 at St. Pancras Church[93] and just two months after Linton himself had wed Eliza Lynn at the same place.[94]

By the time of their return from a short honeymoon on the Isle of Wight, secret moves had been initiated by the Law Officers of the Crown in an attempt to barter Adams for Truelove.[95] The Defence Committee, sensing in these overtures clear evidence of weakness in the prosecution's case, declined to help the "legal advisers of the Crown out of the quagmire".[96] Yet they were to be denied that public form — a court hearing — in which they felt confident the issue of freedom of speech and of the press would be vindicated. Just as proceedings were about to commence at Westminster Hall before a special jury, it was announced that Edwin James had unilaterally reached a compromise with the Crown prosecution: that the defendants had never intended to incite murder and had agreed to discontinue the sale of the offending pamphlets. The Law Officers accordingly withdrew the charges against the two book-sellers forthwith.[97]

Adams and Truelove felt cheated by "the inglorious conclusion";[98] they were also justly indignant with James for denying them the chance of exposing the hollowness of the Crown's legal arguments in what was perceived to be a government show-trial. After paying legal expense, no money was left to compensate Truelove for the serious loss of business he had incurred.[99] Although the victory might have been greater — an acquittal instead of a withdrawal — it was nevertheless a victory. According to one radical supporter, Robert Cooper:

> "The Government are cowed, and will not be so ready, a second time, to tamper with the English press, to propitiate a tyrant and an enemy under the mask of an ally."[100]

In the final analysis, the right to freedom of discussion and the liberty of the press had not been seriously imparied. By the rejection of the Conspiracy Bill, the acquittal of Dr. Bernard and the abandonement of state prosecutions against Truelove and Tchorzewski, Adams could feel well-satisfied, at least for the moment, that arbitrary state power had been emasculated. Leading radicals, such as Charles Bradlaugh, continued to argue the justification of tyrannicide against Louis Napoleon and Adams shared in the martyrdom afforded Truelove.[101] One interesting sequel to the Orsini affair occurred for Adams in November 1862 when he attended the funeral of Dr. Bernard at Kensal Green Cemetery. Amongst the main body of mourners were many revolutionary exiles, including Michael Bakunin, Felix Pyat and Alexander Herzen. After the orations Adams was introduced to Pyat: they shook hands; at which moment the French patriot reverently exclaimed "L'Accomplice!"[102]

Life "in clover" as a labour aristocrat did not last long. A change of editorship in May 1858 brought disastrous results for Adams's usual work routine. The new editor's office policy was splenetic: he would send round great batches of copy to be set only in the early evening period when it was time to go home. Consequently, Adams found himself in a situation of enforced idleness in the day, for he dare not leave his work-place since others would be put in his place; and the kicking of heels was followed by all-out, wearisome activity preparing set late into the night.[103] Such exploitation, the miserable remuneration and his new responsibilities as a married man certainly precipitated a personal crisis outside the scope of his Paineite thinking:

> "I had suffered so much, mentally and bodily from the treatment I had received in common with the rest of our little companionship, that it was no longer a mystery to me why working men hated their employers."[104]

Life for Adams in Manchester, to which place he moved in 1859, proved to be both kind and rewarding. He appears to have remembered the cotton capital less for its reputation as the shock city of the age, the cradle of an exploitative factory system and home to the harsh doctrine of political economy; it was more the font of wider opportunities: of free libraries; Hallé concerts; a Working Men's College; a compositor's place in a small and pleasant jobbing office; a political column on Bradlaugh's *National Reformer* from its inception in April 1860; the birthplace of his first daughters, Gertrude Amy and Florence Annie; and the springboard for family excursions into the surrounding countryside on Sundays during the next three years.[105]

Following his new found fame and conscious of his ability to write lively and politically inspired prose, Adams had hoped for better things. He fancifully confided in Linton that ideally he would like a sub-editor's place, but, knowing this to be most unlikely, hoped for a compositor's position where he would have more time to write.[106] Fortunately, he found what he wanted in his more realistic fall-back option: a situation as reader and compositor for the printing establishment of John Beresford and William Southern at 32, Corporation Street in central Manchester; and, as a denizen of the inner city working class housing district of Hulme,[107] he lived well within walking distance of his work.

Adams's main job was to type-set and print the *Alliance News*, the organ of the Manchester-based teetotal United Kingdom Alliance and his employer's principal customer. The United Kingdom Alliance aimed to promote the legislative prohibition of alcohol through the columns of its paper.[108] Adams, as we have noted, had a strong temperance background but, apart from working on the *Alliance News* as a compositor, does not appear to have contributed to the content of its teetotal journalism. Nevertheless, he was extremely impressed by its quality, tone and appeal; and some of the secret ingredients of its success[109] he took with him to the *Newcastle Weekly Chronicle in 1863*.

In Manchester he was better able than before to continue his self-instruction, attending classes at the Workingmen's College and lectures at the Free Trade Hall; he also became a regular user of the new Free Library.[110] The fruits of such amenities of urban life were remembered as entirely uplifting:

> "Our literary evenings under Mr. Gaskell (husband of the famous novelist) were ambrosial evenings indeed, Mr. Marriott's class was devoted to the History of England. ... his lectures, if they could be called lectures, were notable for their freedom from the least sign of pedantry."[111]

While gratifying his taste for such studies, Adams did not forget "the republican idea".[112] In his spare time and in consultation with Linton to whom he sent earlier drafts[113] he wrote during the winter of 1859 a second pamphlet, "An Argument for Complete Suffrage", which appeared in March 1860; he was also invited to write his own choice of leading articles — "fiery lucubrations" in support of Italian unity[114] — in a weekly holiday paper, the *Buxton Visitor*, for the same kind of unsuspecting élite who fluttered around Hyde Park in the season on Sunday afternoons.[115]

The "Suffrage" pamphlet was a response to the abortive Reform Bills of 1859 and 1860, and in it he put the case opposing the imposition of any kind of property, educational or gender discrimination as a basis for the franchise. Amongst radical leaders, too, it performed a particuarly valuable role: it tried to clarify the true political goal at a time when compromises between working and middle class reformers was very much in vogue. By 1858 when G.J. Holyoake, the ex Chartist, was advocating an intelligence franchise in *The Reasoner*, he had clearly travelled far in the direction of the radical middle class and left many Chartists behind. W.E. Adams in the "Suffrage" pamphlet and through the sharp exchanges which followed in the radical press[116] was voicing the opinion of most working men when he argued unequivocally for manhood suffrage:

> "Well, then Education ... guarantees nothing but educated electors; does not guarantee ability, or worth, or justice. Such a qualification, affirming no right, answering no need, and providing no security, is manifestly as unjust and as unwise as the qualification of property."[117]

Thereafter, most if not all radicals including an energetic Adams campaigned on the platform of manhood suffrage,[118] a goal which was largely achieved only when the agricultural labourer secured the vote in 1884.

In the winter of 1859 Charles Bradlaugh on a visit to Manchester asked Adams to contribute to his Radical and free-thought newspaper, the *National Reformer*, the first number of which appeared on April 14, 1860: it included an article by Adams echoing the manhood suffrage arguments of his "Suffrage" pamphlet. Thereafter, until 1865, he made a regular contribution under the pseudonym of "Caractacus"; it was generally the chief political item in the paper. Most of his writing at this time was suffused with radical republicanism.[119] Whilst Bradlaugh and his co-editor, the mercurial Joseph Barker, devoted their time to debunking the scriptures, Adams censured once again the expansionist policies of Napoleon III and the connivance of Palmerston, championed the Italian cause of Garibaldi, and railed against the privileges and anachronistic power of the House of Lords.[120] There was also a new cause to rally behind. In 1861 the American Civil War broke out: Adams became an active member of the Manchester-based Union and Emancipation Society, which played a central part in the propaganda for the North's arguments on the abolition of slavery; and in the *Reformer* he both eulogised Abraham Lincoln, condemned the slave-owning South and attacked those, such as J.A. Roebuck, the Radical M.P. for Sheffield, for sympathizing with the evil regime of the Confederacy.[121]

In July 1861 the hoary issue of defending freedom of speech surfaced again when Radicals and Secularists discovered the sinister implications of the Offences against the Person Act. The Conspiracy Bill with which Palmerston had sought to appease the French in 1858 was embodied in this harmless-looking measure of 1861: it contained a clause which made it a felony, subject to up to ten years imprisonment, to transmit letters inciting or threatening murder; it was, of course, aimed against activists and refugees whose only means of action was "political" conspiracy. Adams rightly saw in this legerdemain state activity the thin end of the wedge for freedom of expression. Secularists, some of whom like Bradlaugh were known republicans and anti-Napoleonic, were already suffering for their public utterances at the hands of an over-zealous police and religious busy-bodies.[122] Adams, therefore, as one who knew the perils of a government prosecution, took to the Secularist platform in person in an effort to publicize the absolute right of the individual to the utmost liberty of thought, speech and publication. Around the Secularist strongholds of Lancashire he built on Mill's works, advocating freedom of expression and basic civil rights.[123] His stock lecture, "The Province of Authority in Matters of Opinion", argued that fewer restrictive laws were needed, not more; reason was the only sovereign authority; and individual judgement, the touchstone on all matters of opinion. Adams, however, felt unable some years later in 1867 to defy the "Caesarism which had infected the legislation of England"[124] and allowed his second pamphlet justifying tyrannicide to be suppressed.[125]

Work on the *National Reformer* brought with it a widening range of contacts and involvement in Secularist cultural activities, the majority of which were most agreeable.[126] There was, however, one exception: in the prickly character and disposition of Joseph Barker, Adams met one of his few public enemies. All the evidence suggests that the fault was entirely Barker's: he was an egotistical and erratic man given to all kinds of apostasy;[127] and could pick a quarrel with his colleagues, no matter how slight the grounds. Not surprisingly, he quarelled in turn with Bradlaugh, John Watts and Adams before departing the *Reformer* in August 1861. He fell foul of Adams because of his support for Napoleon III and sympathy for the Confederate cause in the American Civil War; but the actual breach came over the initiative Adams took in calling upon all free-thinking men to rally round Bradlaugh and Barker in defence of free speech following the Devonport police case. Barker objected to his name being used.[128] Adams stood his ground arguing that Barker:

> "never seemed to know his mind for longer than a month or two together. Thus it happened that he boxed both the political and theological compass."[129]

In the spring of 1862, the transfer of the *Alliance News* to another office threw Adams out of employment, and he returned with his wife and two daughters (Gertie was born in 1859; Florence in 1860) to unfurnished accommodation in Kennington. Once again he fell upon hard times. Work was almost as scarce in London as it was in Manchester; and his meagre savings soon began to dwindle as "bread had to be bought and rent had to be paid",[130] Fortunately, his old friend Charles Bradlaugh came to the rescue offering the family warm hospitality at his London home and finding Adams employment in a political cause.

Adams was certainly down at heel; it was the most depressing and forlorn period of his life; and his family though small at the time was still "large enough to cause great anxiety".[131] For many months during the summer of 1862 he would resolutely trek to and breakfast at Bradlaugh's house in Tottenham in order to learn what had come of the inquiries which the latter was making day by day on his behalf.[132] Fortune was to smile on Adams once more as he found temporary work in "a service of the highest value",[133] and for which he had, notwithstanding Bradlaugh's help, the appropriate credentials.

When the Polish Revolution broke out in 1862,[134] a committee was formed in London to assist the insurgents. In December 1862, Adams succeeded Linton as Secretary of the Central Committee of the Friends of Poland at its offices in Southampton Street, Strand.[135] Here was brought to bear that valuable administrative experience and internationalist perspective he had gained as a branch level Chartist and Republican activist. Besides his routine secretarial duties in fund-raising, Adams during the short time that he was in post tried several things: to form new branches in support of the Polish insurrection of January 1863 in Manchester and Newcastle;[136] to liaise closely with working class *Beehive* readers, who, like the influential radical middle class members of the Committee, aspired to the establishment of a free and united Poland;[137] and lastly attempted the hazardous task of steering the Committee away from coming under the influence of the more conservative forces of Prince Czartoryski's friends, amidst the welter of conflicting factions that characterized the activities of Polish émigrés at this time in England.[138]

At the end of May 1863 Adams resigned; and it was no coincidence that his departure for Newcastle-upon-Tyne helped precipitate the disastrous collapse of the Committee within one month.[139] The reason for leaving, like the explanation for joining, was largely owing to Bradlaugh. Joseph Cowen, the leading radical and republican in the north of England and proprietor of the *Newcastle Weekly Chronicle*, had been making inquiries about Adams's work on the *National Reformer*. On Bradlaugh's recommendation, Cowen invited Adams to write a weekly political article over the signature of "Ironside", with the prospect of obtaining a permanent position.[140] The first of over five hundred such letters appeared in late December 1862. Within eighteen months Adams was editor and the *Weekly Chronicle*, Cowen let it be known, was entirely "Adams's paper".[141] According to Maurice Milne, a leading authority on North East journalism,

> "Cowen had a genius for singling out men of talent to work for his newspaper: rarely was he to make a happier choice than in his recruitment of Adams."[142]

The mid-Victorian period has traditionally been seen as signalling the political and social incorporation of articulate and highly skilled members of the working class — the so-called labour aristocracy — into the traditions and values of a consciously, hegemonic middle class.[143] Excepting the halcyon times at Manchester in the 1850s and intermittently in the 1860s, Adams found himself repeatedly falling on hard times. At the outset he possessed many of the traits of the respectable, skilled working man: he was industrious, resourceful, sober and self-reliant; but there is very little evidence to suggest that he was in a position to be bought off in the work-place by the material gains which some highly skilled workers were apparently enjoying elsewhere in the country.[144] For Adams, unlike the secure skilled workers in Kentish London, for example, there does not appear to have been in his Fleet Street work stable employment, high earning or the chance of a settled home.

The corollary of this situation was that as yet Adams's sense of political commitment to the new ideals of bourgeois society, under the auspices of Mid-Victorian Liberalism, was extremely problematical. There were, of course, increasingly areas of overlap and cooperation between radical republicans like himself and members of the radical middle class with regard to such issues as internationalism and self-improvement through education. However, Adams still viewed the mid-Victorian state as politically unrepresentative and the liberal consensus, extremely fragile. Successive governments in the 1840s and later had admittedly begun to enact reforms that made it more and more difficult to address the State as an oppressor or tyrant. Adams's great contribution in these years was to test the extent to which the state had shifted away from the coercive strategies employed in 1848. His "Tyrannicide" pamphlet and the Government Press Prosecutions of 1858 drew this illuminating response:

> "A State Trial and a Special Commission are startling and novel matters now-a-days. We recollect them in the height and greatness of the Chartist movement — much reason have we for so doing. We are now to have more experience in these legerdemain proceedings. Dr. Bernard is to be tried by a special commission at the Old Bailey ...Mr. Truelove's trial is not to be distinguished by being put in the same category as Orsini's friend."[145]

Adams's position as a sturdy radical-republican was therefore one that still offered a challenge to bourgeois hegemony on the terrain of the political realities of the day, in particular the issue of freedom of speech and of publication.

In 1861, under the guise of the Offences Against the Person Act, the law was cunningly changed in order to proscribe what behaviour could be construed as constituting political conspiracy. Adams exposed yet again the tyrannical powers of the State in this new and perhaps more sinister way; and six years late he himself fell foul of the Act when his second polemic justifying tyrannicide was suppressed for fear of prosecution. It was perhaps a sign of the times that he did not feel on this occasion confident enough to challenge the formidable powers of the bourgeois State.

Notes

1. W.E. Adams, Memoirs, op.cit., p.281.
2. A. Watson, A Newspaper Man's Memories, London, 1925, pp.52-53.
3. Ibid., p.53.
4. F.B. Smith, Radical Artisan, W.J. Linton, 1812-1898, op.cit., pp.112-120.

5. W.E. Adams, Memoirs, op.cit., pp. 279-287. Chapter XXIX, "Brantwood".

6. Newcastle Weekly Chronicle, Jan. 8, 1898, The Gossip's Bowl.

7. Idem., See also MS Eng 180, W.J. Linton to W.E. Adams, Brantwood, April 17, 1855, and Nov. 19, 1856.

8. W.E. Adams, Memoirs, op.cit., p.264.

9. Ibid., p.288.

10. See Newcastle Weekly Chronicle Nov. 13, 1869, "The Gardener" by James Glover.

11. W.E. Adams, Memoirs, op.cit., p.292.

12. Ibid., p.292.

13. Ibid., pp.290-291.

14. Ibid., p.293.

15. For tramping in the printing trade, see A.E. Musson, The Typographical Association, London, 1954, pp.50-51; J.W. Rounsfell, On the Road: Journeys of a Tramping Printer with Introduction by A.Whitehead, Horsham, 1982, generally.

16. MS Eng 180, W.J. Linton to W.E. Adams Wednesday April 5, 1855 from 6, Lower Calthorpe Street, London, including a testimonial.

17. Idem.,

18. W.E. Adams, Memoirs, op.cit., p.291.

19. Ibid., pp.294-303.

20. Ibid., p.301.

21. Ibid., p.297.

22. Ibid., p.304.

23. D.G. Wright, Popular Radicalism, op.cit., Chapter 7, The Mid-Victorian Consensus 1850-80, particularly pp.152-153.

24. MS Eng 180, W.J. Linton to W.E. Adams, Brantwood, Monday Dec. 15, 1855.

25. For Zabicki, See F.B. Smith, W.J. Linton, Radical Artisan 1812-98, op.cit., pp.135-136.

26. W.E. Adams, Memoirs, op.cit., p.309.

27. Ibid., p.313.

28. For the "Free Sunday Movement", see E. Royle, Victorian Infidels, Manchester, 1974, pp.258-259.

29. MS Eng 180 W.J. Linton to W.E. Adams, Brantwood, Saturday, July 19, 1856.

30. W.E. Adams, Memoirs, op.cit., p.321.

31. E. Royle, Victorian Infidels, op.cit., p.259.

32. W.E. Adams, Memoirs, op.cit., p.327.

33. E. Royle, Victorian Infidels, op.cit., p.258.

34. Newcastle Weekly Chronicle, June 5, 1875, Ironside on the Sabbath Question.

35. Idem.,

36. Idem., For the National Sunday League see B. Harrison, Peaceable Kingdom, Stability and Change in Modern Britain, Oxford, 1982, particularly p.146 of his previously published chapter "Religion and Recreation in Nineteenth Century England".

37. W.E. Adams, Memoirs, op.cit., p.332. He described himself to be "in clover" in securing the post.

38. MS Eng 180 W.J. Linton to W.E. Adams, Brantwood March 7, 1856 and May 29, 1856.

39. W.E. Adams, Memoirs, op.cit., pp.312-313.

40. Adams was married on May 25, 1858 at St. Pancras Church, London.

41. W.E. Adams, Memoirs, op.cit., pp.375-376.

42. Ibid., p.376.

43. Ibid., p.380.

44. Ibid., p.230.

45. Newcastle Weekly Chronicle, Oct. 22, 1881, Ironside.

46. B. Harrison, Drink and The Victorians, London, 1971, p.53.

47. W.E. Adams, Memoirs, op.cit., p.316.

48. Ibid., pp.314-315. See also Newcastle Weekly Chronicle, April 30, 1892, The Gossip's Bowl.

49. Newcastle Weekly Chronicle, Feb. 7, 1891, The Gossip's Bowl. Tribute to Charles Bradlaugh who died Saturday, Jan. 31, 1891.

50. Ibid., March 6, 1897.

51. Idem.,

52. People's Paper, Feb. 27, 1858, "The Napoleon Conspiracy"; and March 20, 1858, "Committal of Bernard".

53. J. Saville, Introduction, Memoirs, op.cit., p.13.

54. Newcastle Weekly Chronicle, Oct. 21 1865. Article on the death of Palmerston. For the activities of the police's "foreign branch", set up directly as a result of the Orsini affair, see B. Porter, Plots and Paranoia, A History of Political Espionage in Britain, 1790-1988, London, 1989, pp.91-93.

55. For the arrest of Bernard and Allsop, See People's Paper, Feb. 20, 1858; Feb. 27, 1858.

56. Allsop was able to make good his escape almost immediately to New York, see People's Paper, April 17, 1858. He was never charged. Later, he was granted a free pardon.

57. J. McCabe, Life and Letters of G.J. Holyoake, London, 1908, Vol.II pp.3-5.

58. Newcastle Weekly Chronicle, March 6, 1897, The Gossip's Bowl.

59. People's Paper, April 10, 1858.

60. W.E. Adams, "Tyrannicide: Is it Justifiable?" London, 1858, p.4.

61. Ibid., p.7.

62. See, for example, People's Paper, Feb. 27, 1858.

63. J.B. Leno, The Aftermath, London, 1892, Reprinted in Chartist Biographies and Autobiographies (ed.) D. Thompson, London, 1986, pp.77-78.

64. People's Paper, April 10, 1858, "The Freedom of the Press", Letter by "Iconoclast". See also, W.E. Adams, Memoirs, op.cit., p.363 where he cites the Times as being particularly outspoken.

65. See, for example, J. McCabe, Life and Letter of G.J. Holyoake, op.cit., pp.3-5 and People's Paper, Feb. 20, 1858.

66. People's Paper, Feb. 20, 1858.

67. J. McCabe, Life and Letters of G.J. Holyoake, op.cit., p.4.

68. People's Paper, Feb.20, 1858.

69. J. McCabe, Life and Letters of G.J. Holyoake, op.cit., p.4.

70. Idem.,

71. Idem.,

72. Ibid., p.5.

73. People's Paper, March 6, 1858.

74. W.E. Adams, Memoirs, op.cit., pp.364-365 for his comments on Landor, Disraeli and Arnold.

75. Ibid., p.365.

76. People's Paper, April 3, 1858.

77. See, for example, reports of meetings in People's Paper, March 13; March 20; March 27; April 3, 1858.

78. Reasoner, March 24, 1858; People's Paper, April 10, 1858.

79. W.E. Adams, Memoirs, op.cit., pp.363-364.

80. E. Royle, Victorian Infidels, op.cit., p.254.

81. People's Paper, April 3, 1858.

82. See, for example, the extensive list of subscriptions in The Reasoner, March 24; March 31; and April 7, 1858.

83. W.E. Adams, Memoirs, op.cit., p.362.

84. John Stuart Mill, On Liberty (1859), Reptd., Middlesex, 1974, op.cit., p.75.

85. People's Paper, April 3, 1858.

86. W.E. Adams, Memoirs, op.cit., p.369.

87. Quoted by the People's Paper, April 24, 1858 "The Verdict on Dr. Bernard". For the "Irish rebellion of 1848" in which the Irish extremists John Mitchel, Devin Reilly and John Martin plotted simultaneous risings in Ireland for June 1848, and for which they were severely sentenced, see J.T. Ward, Chartism, London, 1973, pp.211-212.

88. People's Paper, April 24, 1858.

89. W.E. Adams, Memoirs, op.cit., p.326.

90. Ibid., p.368.

91. The Reasoner, May 26, 1858.

92. MS Eng 180, W.J. Linton to W.E. Adams, Loughton, May 22, 1858.

93. See Marriage Certificate, May 25, 1858, St. Pancras Church, Middlesex, General Register Office, London.

94. F.B. Smith, W.J. Linton, Radical Artisan, 1812-1897, op.cit., p.132. Linton married on March 24, 1858.

95. The Reasoner, May 26, 1858.

96. W.E. Adams, Memoirs, op.cit., p.368.

97. People's Paper, June 26, 1858.

98. W.E. Adams, Memoirs, op.cit., p.369.

99. The Investigator, July 15, 1858. "The Free Press Trials".

100. Idem.,

101. See, for example, People's Paper, Sept. 4, 1858, Bradlaugh on the Press prosecutions at Newcastle-upon-Tyne; The Investigator, Dec.15, 1858, Bradlaugh at the Lecture Hall, Philpot Street, Commercial Road, London.

102. Newcastle Weekly Chronicle, August 10, 1899, The Gossip's Bowl. See also National Reformer, Dec. 6, 1862, "Caractacus" (Adams) on the death of Dr. Bernard.

103. W.E. Adams, Memoirs, op.cit., p.339.

104. Ibid., p.383.

105. Ibid., p.387. See also G.S. Messinger, Manchester in the Victorian Age, Manchester, 1985, p.118.

106. MS Eng 180, W.J. Linton to W.E. Adams, Slattermill, Haslemere, Surrey, Sept. 5, 1858.

107. W.E. Adams, Memoirs, op.cit., p.396.

108. For the Alliance News, see B. Harrison, "A World of Which We had No Conception, Liberalism and the English Temperance Press: 1830-1872", Victorian Studies, Vol.XIII, Dec. 1969, pp.125-158.

109. Ibid., p.139. At the time Adams was working on the Alliance News its circulation had risen to 20,000 per week.

110. W.E. Adams, Memoirs, op.cit., p.384 and 389. The public library was opened in 1852.

111. Ibid., p.391. See also C.D. Legge, "The Manchester Working Man's College", Manchester, circa, 1989, Unpublished paper kindly loaned by the author (formerly Director, Dept. of Adult Education, Manchester University).

112. W.E. Adams, Memoirs, op.cit., p.392.

113. MS Eng 180, W.J. Linton to W.E. Adams, 85, Hatton Garden, Jan. 1860.

114. W.E. Adams, Memoirs, op.cit., p.393.

115. Idem., Adams wrote "At that time I was rejoiced when I could get my opinions before the public, anyhow or anywhere".

116. See The Reasoner, March 4; March 18; April 22 and May 6, 1860. See also National Reformer, April 14, 1860.

117. W.E. Adams, "An Argument for Complete Suffrage", London, Manchester, Newcastle, 1860, p.9.

118. J. McCabe, Life and Letters of G.J. Holyoake., op.cit., p.11.

119. J. Saville and J. Bellamy, (eds.) Dictionary of Labour Biography, Vol. VII, op.cit., p.2. Adams had already made contributions of a similar kind for Bradlaugh when he took over The Investigator in November 1858 from Robert Cooper. See, for example, article by Adams on "Sketches of Commonwealth Men" in The Investigator, Dec.15, 1858.

120. See National Reformer, June 9; June 16; July 14; August 18; Nov. 17, 1860.

121. Ibid., Dec. 15, 1860; August 23, 1862; June 4, 1865.

122. Ibid., August 10, 1861, "The Devonport Police Case" against Bradlaugh.

123. Ibid., March 22, 1862; August 16, 1862; Nov. 1, 1862.

124. Ibid., Nov. 24, 1867, "Bonaparte's Challenge to Tyrannicide".

125. Idem., Adams wrote "That the pamphlet — I am ashamed to say it — is suppressed". He was now unwilling to invite prosecution for a "public that would not, perhaps, appreciate the sacrifice."

126. National Reformer, Jan. 31, 1863. Report of a Secularist Soiree and Ball in the Hall of Science, City Road, London. Among friends present were Mr. Watts, Austin Holyoake, Mrs. Harriet Law and Caractacus.

127. E. Royle, Victorian Infidels, op.cit., p.250.

128. Hypatia Bradlaugh Bonner, Charles Bradlaugh, a Record of his Life and Work, op.cit., pp.124-125.

129. W.E. Adams, Memoirs, op.cit., p.400.

130. Ibid., p.439.

131. Idem.,

132. Hypatia Bradlaugh Bonner, Charles Bradlaugh, A Record of his Life and Work, op.cit., p.110.

133. Idem.,

134. Ibid., p.109.

135. W.E. Adams, op.cit.., p.443.

136. Hypatia Bradlaugh Bonner, Charles Bradlaugh, A Record of his Life and Work, op.cit., p.109.

137. See Beehive, March 21; April 4; April 11, 1863.

138. Cowen Collection, A707, March 9, 1863, W.J. Linton to J. Cowen. See also J.F. Kutolowski, "English Radicals and the Polish Insurrection of 1863-4", Polish Review, XI, 1966, pp.3-28, particularly pp.6-8.

139. J.F. Kutolowski, "Mid-Victorian Public Opinion, Polish Propaganda, and the Uprising of 1863", Journal of British Studies, VIII, May, 1969, pp.86-110, in particular p.104.

140. W.E. Adams, Memoirs, op.cit., p.440.

141. E.R. Jones, The Life and Speeches of Joseph Cowen M.P., London, 1885, p.30.

142. M. Milne, Newspapers of Northumberland and Durham, Newcastle, 1971, pp.65-69.

143. For a recent discussion of the complex character of the Mid-Victorian labour aristocracy, see G. Crossick, An Artisan Elite in Victorian Society, London, 1978, see generally.

144. See T. Matsumura, The Labour Aristocracy Revisited: the Victorian Flint Glass Makers, 1850-80, Manchester, 1983, for his study of the flint glass makers in Stourbridge.

145. People's Paper, April 3, 1858, "Bernard and Truelove".

4 "Ironside": A Radical on the Tyne

Adams came to Newcastle-upon-Tyne, the regional capital of the North-East, at a time when Tyneside was fast becoming one of the foremost industrial workshops of the world and its Great Northern Coal-field, based on the surrounding pit-villages of the two counties of Northumberland and Durham, poised for a period of unprecedented expansion that was to last until World War I. For the next forty years his readership was to be drawn principally from those men and women who sold their labour in the heavy capital goods industries of coal, iron and steel, their related or ancillary manufacturing concerns, and in servicing trades, all of which were essential for sustaining an increasingly complex phase of economic growth in the course of Britain's nineteenth century industrial revolution.

Remarkable economic growth on Tyneside (followed by that on neighbouring Wearside) in the second half of the nineteenth century had been made possible by steady developments in coal-mining.[1] Easily accessible river-side coal-seams, a mass inflow of workers into mining employment and the proximity of the River Tyne — down which some four million tons of coal were shipped by 1850 — provided the conditions for the development of other important industries. These included glass, brick, paper, glue and iron manufacture. An incipient engineering industry was also established: the two engineering and locomotive works of Robert Stephenson & Co. (fd. 1823) and R. & W. Hawthorn and Co. (fd. 1817) were joined in 1847 by the establishment of a third, W.G. Armstrong and Co.,at the giant Elswick Works in West Newcastle; and together they began to create the basis of an engineering centre along the Tyne world-renowned for the manufacture of ships, armaments and locomotives.

Adams arrived in Newcastle in 1863 when the main lines of development of the city as a modern and thriving economic centre had virtually been established. Indeed, the general feeling of optimism that Novocastrians felt about the possibilities of the industrial age was captured in William Bell Scott's painting "Iron and Coal" (c. 1855-60) when he was master of the Newcastle School of Art and Design. According to Asa Briggs, it is "one of the few Victorian paintings glorifying the industrial revolution".[2] Newcastle was an ancient town: it had a strong, pre-industrial sense of community having grown slowly in previous centuries and within fairly precise geographical limits. However its city fathers in the early nineteenth century, at a time when the coal trade was developing, had the foresight, enterprise and an emergent civic consciousness sufficient to anticipate the requirements of an expanding Victorian city in the fast-moving railway age. By the time Adams first had the pleasure of admiring Newcastle's stately streets, both ancient and modern, Richard Grainger, the builder,

John Dobson, the architect and John Clayton, a town clerk with striking business acumen, had completed their city centre development plans; and they deservedly ensured Newcastle's hegemony as the premier financial, commercial, administrative, cultural and consular centre between the Tweed and Tees until well into the twentieth century. The Central Exchange, for example, with its domed, colonnaded and rounded corners was as fine an edifice as any town hall; and Grey Street, where Adams first went to work in the *Chronicle's* office, was described by Gladstone in 1862 as "the best modern street in Britain".[3]

Almost immediately Adams was to witness the old community of the "canny toon" take on a new and more dynamic topography. Elswick and Scotswood on the west had virtually been swallowed up on his arrival by the impact of the mushrooming Armstrong engineering works. Byker, described by Adams in 1863 as little more "than a row of old-fashioned cottages", and Heaton, as "all fields and farmsteads",[4] both on the eastern side of the city, were soon to be transformed by the building of workshops, shipyards, single storey terraced cottages and thousands of terraced flats; and in the case of the suburban morphology of Heaton, expansion well beyond the smoky pall which had long hung over the industrious banks of the "coaly Tyne". According to N. McCord, a leading historian of the North East, the building of terraced flats was the region's "distinctive solution to the problems of housing the swollen numbers serving the local industries".[5] Fortunately, the city fathers had the good sense to preserve for its urban dwellers the large Town Moor before other industrial cities lost their "green lungs".

Underlining Newcastle's golden age was an enormous increase in population. Shortly before Adams started writing in the *Weekly Chronicle*, the Census Return of 1861 recorded the city's population to be 111,151;[6] by the end of the century just before his death in 1906 the figure had nearly doubled to stand at 215,000.[7] Four-fifths of this democratic surge resulted from natural increase and internal migration; the remainder, of which Adams and his family were a tiny statistical element, were immigrants. To the steady inflow of Irish and Scottish settlers was also added, as early as the 1860s, the ethnic diversity represented by such disparate elements as a sprinkling of black workers and a select band of foreign diplomats: together, they helped give Newcastle a distinct cosmopolitan flavour in the second half of the nineteenth century.[8]

The continued expansion of the coal and iron trade and the completion of a navigable channel on the Tyne in 1862 resulted in further economic diversification. By 1874 a chemical industry in Newcastle, including the large Losh and Bell's Alkali works, was arguably one of the biggest concentrations of its kind in the country. Like the giant engineering works in the city, it gave employment to many although by the end of the nineteenth century it was the former which had the most spectacular concentrations in percentage terms of unionised labour, particularly craftsmen, unrivalled elsewhere in Britain.[9]

The main beneficiary of growth after 1860 was almost certainly ship-building; it was an industry which Adams quickly appreciated was to transform the urban character and role of Newcastle; henceforward it was to stand pre-eminent in the sprawling conurbation known internationally as Industrial Tyneside. South of Newcastle on the other side of theTyne in modern diversified, industrial centres, like Gateshead, or further along the river in virtual company and single industry towns like Jarrow and Wallsend, dominated respectively by entrepeneurs, Sir Charles Mark Palmer and John Wigham Richardson, great ship-building communities emerged. The industry responded positively and imaginatively to the mid-century transition from an era of wood and sail to the historic dawning of an age of iron-built, stream-driven vessels. Larger and larger iron ships were constructed in order to satisfy, for example, the increasing demands of the coal trade, an indigenous fishing industry and the complexities of government defence procurement.[10] In their wake, too, developed an extensive marine engineering and ship-repair sector; they fuelled still further the process of urban infill as they required large tracts of land for the production or refurbishment of certain capital goods. By the 1880s the North East, including Wearside, was responsible for satisfying nearly three quarters of the world's shipping demands. The thriving shipping and related trades in turn gave the opportunity of greater prosperity to the commercial and financial interests established on Newcastle's Quayside. By 1900, industrial Tyneside represented a major spatial phenomenon in the modern English landscape. From roughly Blaydon in the west, where Joseph Cowen, Adams's employer, had the largest brick and retort works in Europe, to the ship-building, repair and nearby coal-mining activities at the Shields near the mouth of the Tyne, the population had risen steadily. At the beginning of the nineteenth century it was 80,000, by the end of the century about 800,000.[11]

The full impact of economic change on the North East is perhaps only best appreciated when placed in the context of the continuing expansion of its staple industry, the mining of the Great Northern Coalfield. By mid-century, the markets for coal, particularly the steam variety, had expanded and the seams near the Tyne became exhausted. Powerful coal-owning families such as the Strakers and Love, the Joiceys, Lambs and Londonderrys, led the more expensive initiative of sinking deeper shafts for mining rich and extensive seams away from the river and across much of Northumberland and Durham. As a result new colliery or pit villages were built and existing small communities enlarged in such places as Choppington, Seaham, Cowpen, Seaton Delaval, Cramlington, Brancepeth, Burradon and Birtley. These villages, often isolated, inhospitable and exhibiting something of a frontier mentality, were the harsh and striking realities behind the dramatic rise in coal production. By 1871 the tonnage of coal raised in the Northern Coalfield was 27 million tons; in 1911 it peaked at 56½ million tons.[12] Mining employment also represented a powerful factor behind the enormous population increase for Northumberland and Durham as a whole in the Victorian age: between 1861 and 1901 it doubled from 885,000 to 1.8 million.[13]

Industrial Newcastle had long exhibited many of the more traumatic features of a society in transition. It had, for example, in the 1840s and 1850s its fair share of harsh working conditions, industrial and class conflicts, racial tensions, drunkeness, mean streets, overcrowded tenements, cyclical unemployment, pawn-brokers and second-hand shops. Many of these problems were to persist, often in an acute form. Although, for example, organised Dissent was strong and many Nonconformist ministers extremely active in the temperance campaigns, they continued to despair at the drunkeness, particularly on the Scotswood Road, which brought a seemingly endless trail of disorderly working men before the Newcastle bench.[14] Colour prejudice and anti-Irish hostility also continued to be a feature of host and minorities relationships.[15] Yet by the time Adams had crossed that spectacular urban landmark, Robert Stephenson's High Level Bridge, he entered a society which was in many ways less volatile than was the case in the 1840s; it was a period when the language and machinery of conciliation was gaining more ground in many spheres of every day life and work.

For one thing, whilst the Nonconformist conscience was noticeably vociferous, it displayed in the 1860s and 1870s a new spirit of tolerance: secular propaganda was now allowed a hearing and platform without fear of persecution.[16] For another, if violence and brutality still persisted to some degree it is also possible to detect from Adams's first-hand experiences, new and more civilized activities in the cultural life of its inhabitants. Drama of various kinds was flourishing at the Theatre Royal.[17] A new popular urban-based culture was also being created in novel concert halls. Foremost of the five in Newcastle in the 1860s was the Tyne Concert Hall on Neville Street. Here Adams soaked up the atmosphere created on stage by Joe Wilson, a popular dialect poet, and Ned Corvan, the doyen of the halls and arguably the leading Tyneside poet of the day. Their renditions of such local dialect songs as "Canny Newcassel", "Geordy, Haud the Bairn" and "Geordie, the Keelman" enshrined the men, memories, manners and customs of the North East.[18] Significantly, the halls offered, too, a distinctly cosmopolitan flavour in their entertainment. Adams remembered Tom Handforth, "a negro minstrel who called himself the Black Diamond";[19] but there were many other performers including Harry Baker, the Irish comic artist, and "The Real Blacks", one of a number of Christy Minstrels sets and black dancing troupes who regularly toured the North East in the 1860s.[20] Their visits sometimes coincided with the arrival of George Sanger's spectacular circus which, given its international flavour, completed the range of such fascinating attractions.[21] Elsewhere, amongst the most popular of summertime sporting activities, the perceptive Adams observed the age-old game of bowls, wrestling, cricket and horse-racing.[22] Athletic sports at the Victoria and Fenham Park Grounds were also coming into vogue, facilitated by the increasing availability of free time on Saturday afternoons as some enlightened employers allowed their skilled workers to leave early.[23] But the sport which commanded the greatest amount of attention and generated mass gatherings reminiscent of Chartist meetings was boat-rowing. Aquatic sports on the Tyne in the 1860s was, as Adams witnessed, synonymous with the physique and prowess of several outstanding local rowers: Harry Clasper, his son J. Hawks Clasper and Robert Chambers were the North East's undisputed sporting heroes; they were so lionised and venerated that one might amusingly speculate how in the imagination of some followers they might even have floated on water! Adams nostalgically recalled:

> "When a great race was to be rowed, the banks of the Tyne from the High Level to Scotswood Suspension Bridge were crowded with spectators. Indeed, the factories along the route were all laid idle till the contest was over. The popularity of the sport continued till the district ceased to produce great rowers."[24]

Unquestionably the most significant and probably the most important indicator of a shift in public mood in the mid 1860s was to be found in the changed perceptions surrounding and the codes of conduct determining trade union-employer relationships, both in and outside the work-place. Confrontation and outright hostility between, on the one hand, engineering and mining trade-unions and, on the other, that concentration of control which resulted in the formation of both the powerful Engineering Employers' Association and the Northern Coal-Owners Association, was replaced by formal recognition, however grudgingly at times, of each other's role and importance. In its wake followed a new spirit of moderation and restraint: there was a new willingness to negotiate, compromise and, in the case of awkward issues in the process of industrial bargaining, to set up formal machinery — conciliation and arbitration boards or joint committees — in order to settle outstanding differences and avoid strikes. In such ways passions were often allayed, mistrust and bitterness eased and stability restored; the ultimate aim of both sides was now to make the existing system of industrial production work more efficiently.

A number of important and inter-connected assumptions lay behind the new consensual view between labour and capital. At the outset, a buoyant economy in the mid-Victorian years had allowed larger numbers of working men to improve their material standards; and it induced a general atmosphere of social optimism and expansion which in turn presaged an apparent acceptance of an industrial way of life consonant with liberal values about the efficacy of a laissez-faire based society. Secondly, there was both a decline of a body of ideas representing alternatives to the classical free market and political economy, and a narrowing of economic discussion to the liberal common sense view that accepted free trade as an ineluctable truth. Trade union leaders in the North East, like Robert Knight of the Boilermakers and Thomas Burt of the Miners, came to assume that wages were directly tied to the level of economic activity and their trade's prosperity. [25] The market forces of supply and demand, they believed, helped directly to regulate the wages of their members. This was particularly the case in the mining industry of the North East where both sides agreed "sliding scales": a device by which wages varied according to the price of the goods that were sold.[26]

Alongside Burt and Knight can be placed a small band of like-minded leaders in the North East — John Kane of the Iron-workers, John Burnett of the Engineers, Alexander Wilkie of the Shipwrights, and Charles Fenwick, William Crawford and John Wilson of the Northumberland and Durham Miners — whose perceptions also changed in other, equally vital, ways. They saw that the realistic way forward for themselves was through piecemeal, gradual improvement embracing teetotalism, education schemes and co-operation. In turn, they held these ideas up as a model for the rest of their class. Not surprisingly, we find that in the second half of the nineteenth century all over the region coteries of men and their families were actively involved in temperance societies, co-operative organizations and friendly benefit or self-improvement clubs.

In response to this new mood of restraint and moderation, the employers, too, made important concessions. Many of them came, according to C. Godfrey, to look on the workers "as junior partners in moral progress, rather than misfits to be forcibly reformed".[27] The mellowing of attitude the employers displayed in the workplace took on the form of reasserting the role of "gentlemen" within the notion of paternalism. As both disciplinarians and providers they showed a new sense of responsibility by responding to the unions' demands for what constituted a fair wage for different types of work; by abolishing the Master and Servant philosophy and treating employees equitably — not least in the interests of efficiency; and gaining worker loyalty by the generous provision of works outings, dinners, seasonal benevolence and endowments. In Newcastle, for example, employer paternalism and worker deference was common place: industrialists like William Armstrong, George Stephenson and Joseph Cowen senior, and coal-owners, like George S. Storey, gave money to the Eye Infirmary, endowed the building of a new mechanics' institute or funded a colliery band. In return, they were pleased to receive glowing testimonials of gratitude from their employees.[28]

Undoubtedly, the most symbolic expression of such tokens of reciprocity took place in the world of parliamentary political representation. From Adams's time and down to World War I, despite a distinct Conservative incursion on occasions into Newcastle itself, the politics of North East England were dominated by the Liberal Party.[29] According to A.W. Purdue:

> "A major factor underlying the Liberal Party's success was an alliance between capital and labour which was itself underpinned by a consensual view of the common benefits to be derived from the success of industrial-capitalist enterprises.[30]

We should not, of course, infer from this view that industrial conflicts had all but disappeared — far from it. Just as in the earlier period there had been unrest on the coalfields, similarly there were major strikes and lock-outs in the mid-1860s, in 1878 and 1879, in 1887 and in 1892. The challenges the miners leaders faced on such occasions varied from the punitive evictions in the 1860s of the pitmen by the coal-owners' bailiffs or "candymen" supported by the police and militia, and their importation of scab labour,[31] to the unsuccessful bid for power and changes of policy mounted by socialist trade union elements in the late 1880s and 1890s coal disputes, in relation to the aggressive stance of the nationally-orientated Miners Federation of Great Britain.[32] The most important confrontation between capital and labour was however the protracted 1871 Engineers' Strike which achieved a national significance and heralded a nine-hour day for the rest of the country. Opposition from the employers, particularly Armstrong and Hawthorn, was at first total and uncompromising; but after a four month war of attrition in which public opinion was mobilized behind the engineers' cause, the latter secured a major victory.[33] Scarcity and insecurity in Tyneside engineering and ship-building resulting from rapid booms and then major slumps, and compounded by the intrusion of demarcation disputes, also increased the penchant for lengthy strikes and much class bitterness in, for example, 1886 and 1894.[34] In the final analysis, we should remember that such industrial conflicts operated within the context of a conditional acceptance of the capitalist system.

Political changes amongst the expanded electorate could work to off-set these difficulties. The unique feature about the Liberal ascendancy in the North East in the last quarter of the nineteenth century was that whilst industrial magnates dominated political representation, they did not have a monopoly; power was shared with those miners' leaders who were overwhelmingly returned as M.P.'s in the interest and influence of Liberal-Labourism. Accommodation, however, between capital and labour was not difficult. Although Burt (Morpeth), Fenwick (Wansbeck), Crawford (Mid Durham) and Wilson (Houghton-le-Spring) were always conscious of the need to protect the special interests of labour, their Gladstonian Liberalism and radical-nonconformist, self-improving backgrounds meant that they shared many of the ideals and assumptions of mainstream entrepreneur Liberal M.P.'s like Charles Palmer or industrialists such as Wigham Richardson. Eschewing Socialism and New Unionism, they were concerned rather with such great moral issues as arose from defending or extending individual liberty and freedom of conscience at home, or supporting the struggles of oppressed nationalities abroad. Indeed, so tenacious was the Liberal-Labour sympathy amongst working-class electors for pre-Socialist traditions across the Northern Coalfield, that the infant Labour Party scarcely challenged Liberal hegemony before 1914.[35]

Adams's employer in Newcastle was cast firmly in that mould which displayed the very best traditions of the new spirit of middle class compromise and conciliation. Joseph Cowen jr., brick-manufacturer, coal-owner, newspaper proprietor and advanced Radical-Liberal, had long staked out a position on the far left of middle class radicalism and became a commanding figure in the public life of Newcastle; he still awaits his twentieth century biographer;[36] but for one leading historian at least, Cowen has been justly seen as in the vanguard of that mid-century reconciliation process labelled "the mellowing of middle class liberalism".[37]

Born in 1829, the son of a prosperous, self-made industrialist, Joseph Cowen, the younger, was sent to Edinburgh University. He left without taking a degree, but not before distinguishing himself as a great political debater and inspired, like Adams, by Mazzinian republicanism. He entered his father's business at Blaydon in the 1850s where he followed a somewhat unorthodox career route: he was made to work manually in the smithy before gradually taking over the reigns of power. Cowen became a successful businessman, rapidly expanding the family's brick and retort works and adjoining collieries at Garesfield and Rowlands Gill; his brother, Colonel J.A. Cowen, assumed control of the dynasty's agricultural interests farming 800 acres of land at Barlow and Ryton Grange.[38]

Joseph Cowen jr. was in no sense a typical representative of the provincial middle classes and radicals of the Manchester School. He believed that "Capital had its duties as well as its rights, and there ought to be closer than a mere money-bond between masters and men".[39] Such moralism was translated into aid for working class self-improvement activities. At his own works he was a model employer: the firm recognised trade unions, ran sick benefits, widows pensions, annual outings and made endowments. Company paternalism of this kind earned Cowen the gratitude of his men: at the nearby Blaydon Young Men's General Debating Society in 1863 a bust of Cowen, alongside that of Garibaldi and John Bright, graced the furnishings of the main room.[40] In Newcastle, he was extremely active in the temperance movement, became president of both the Northern Union of Mechanics' Institutes and of the Co-operative Stores, a councillor for the Westgate ward and a Poor Law Guardian for Gateshead.

Cowen broke new ground of course in relation to contemporary employers' views by his outspoken support for universal suffrage in Britain and freedom for oppressed nationalities in Europe. As the radical "Tribune of the North",[41] he first toyed with Chartist-Republicanism in the mid 1850s founding a local club and newspaper, *The Northern Tribune*, to further the cause of Mazzinian-inspired, democratic principles; he also funded W.J. Linton's Brantwood republican activities where Adams, as we have seen, was an important activist. In 1858, he set up the first effective radical organization of the North East: the Northern Reform Union; it was a radical middle class-working class alliance whose objective was the cause of manhood suffrage, a secret ballot, and the ending of aristocratic political rule. During the time the Union lasted — until 1862 — hundreds of meetings were held throughout the North East: small shop-keepers, radical non-conformist ministers, pit-men, ironworkers and agricultural labourers were thus instructed and immersed in popular politics;[42] and Peter Taylor, the future radical-Liberal M.P. for Nottingham, was brought to Newcastle in 1859 on the Radical ticket, but failed to win the Seat from the ruling Whig-Liberal clique.[43] Electoral reform was needed before a Cowen-inspired radical Liberalism could win Newcastle.

Mazzini's ideas on liberty also attracted Cowen to foreign affairs in a substantive way. As I. Waitt has shown, he was a close friend of Garibaldi, Mazzini, Kossuth, and Orsini; and foreign political refugees of every description were harboured at Stella Hall, the family seat near Blaydon.[44] Through his relief work for refugees of all nationalities, arms smuggling campaigns for Polish freedom and conspirational activities on behalf of Orsini and Garibaldi, Cowen soon brought himself under the surveillance of the agents of European despots;[45] it served only to breed a deep and abiding Russophobia since he saw in the Czarist regime the colossos of tyranny and crime across Europe.[46]

To obtain greater publicity for the Northern Reform Union and to augment the cause of oppressed nationalities, Cowen purchased the *Newcastle Chronicle* in 1858/59. The paper had been published weekly in the city for almost a hundred years. The abolition of the newspaper stamp duty in 1855 had made it possible to venture on a daily issue in 1858, but M.W. Lambert and his partners did not feel equal to the task of daily journalism.[47] Joseph Cowen became the sole proprietor by the end of 1859 and within four years had, having sunk the princely sum of £40,000 into his beloved schemes, also launched its stable-mate, the *Newcastle Weekly Chronicle*.[48] Henceforward these two newspapers and Cowen's supremacy over his rivals in North East journalism were "the main preposession of his life ... the commercial venture he valued above all others".[49]
According to R.B. Reed, Cowen's general manager at the *Daily Chronicle*, the latter was determined that the *Chronicle* should become the "*Times* of the North".[50] Otherwise a man of simple tastes and somewhat parsimonious towards his journalist staff,[51] Cowen spared no expense to develop his papers: literary men of the highest calibre were recruited and rotary-web presses, the latest marvel in printing machinery, installed; a London office was opened in 1871 and two years later the *Chronicle* offices became the first English provincial establishment of its kind to possess a private telegraph system.[52] In a dozen years, from obscure and struggling journals with a purely local circulation of 2,500 copies in the case of the *Daily* and 2,000 for the *Weekly*,[53] they were transformed: by 1873, the former was claiming 40,000 daily sales, the largest circulation in the North East; the *Weekly*, with an average of 31,500 copies, the largest in the North of England.[54]

Undoubtedly, the radicalism of the two papers provided Cowen both with a personal political megaphone and a solid and influential power base from which to sustain his parliamentary career after 1874. He was known as a provincial, political leader in the forefront of reform, innovation and agitation;[55] Tyneside, because of him, became for a while the focal point of English agitation on behalf of freedom from tyranny for dispossessed people in Europe and the USA;[56] and his *Chronicles* had an influence which transcended the North East, their views carrying weight "in other newspaper offices and among politicians everywhere, not least in London".[57]

For the accolade and influence accorded Cowen in the golden age of provincialism, W.E. Adams could justifiably take some of the credit. Cowen had systematically gathered around him journalists of distinction. These included Sidney Milnes Hawkes, a republican barrister and friend of Mazzini; Aaron Watson, who later worked on the *Pall Mall Gazette;* James Annand of the *Newcastle Daily Leader* and later a Liberal

M.P. and J.L. Garvin of the *Observer*. However, there was little room for editorial freedom on the *Daily Chronicle*: Cowen allowed his pressmen to possess opinions different from his own, but if they were flaunted considered himself justified in dismissing the offender;[58] and the dramatic clash over the issue of the Eastern Question in 1876 between Cowen the proprietor and Annand, who felt forced to resign as his editor on the *Daily Chronicle*, is well-known in press history.[59] By contrast, Adams was in total control as editor in chief of the *Weekly Chronicle*. For reasons of personal friendship, shared passions about Mazzinian republicanism and not least the supremely successful nature of the *Weekly* as a highly profitable business venture, Cowen left the work to him. The leopard, of course, did not exactly change his spots: notwithstanding an occasional but unsuccessful attempt by Cowen to interfere with the *Weekly's* editorial freedom, Adams resolutely pursued an independent policy; and the former referred, as we have noted, to the *Weekly Chronicle* as "Adams's paper".

Cowen brought Adams to Newcastle as a weekly political columnist writing under the pseudonym of "Ironside" in the *Weekly Chronicle*. The choice of this pseudonym was a brilliant move in that it identified Adams with the enterprise and economy of the region. In return, Adams invested the term with a political meaning: he was a man of sterling independence, robust intellect and unbending in his devotion to a range of views which were at the cutting edge of the North East's much acclaimed tradition of political Radicalism.

It is crucial to bear in mind that, as Adams stood on the threshold of an outstanding career in journalism, the British press had just entered a new era of greater freedom unprecedented in its history. Doubtless Adams himself was extremely conscious of the profound nature of and significance surrounding the mellowing of state attitude and practice towards the "Fourth Estate"; and in responding to the toasts of freedom for the press at the historic centenary celebrations of the founding of the *Chronicle* in April 1864, he made these very perceptive comments about its emancipation and future role:

> "The penny stamp, the duty on advertisements, and the tax on paper, after a struggle prolonged but never doubtful, ingenious and intrepid by turns, were one by one abolished ... And the power and value of the press has increased pretty much in proportion to its development in cheapness and extent ... The press — which represents opinion more or less clearly — is however stronger than armies among ourselves, because no armies of our own could destroy it ... Without the aid of the press, it is not too much to say that not a tithe of the changes wrought within our century could possibly have been accomplished. ... The mission of the press as a political instructor, as one of the moral forces of the world, is distinctly

> defined. Civilization has no nobler produce — than a free, pure and enlightened press."[60]

If Adams was conscious of himself as the standard bearer of a free press, he was also acutely aware of its enlarged place and importance in extra-parliamentary agitation. In the second half of the nineteenth century there was, as K. McClelland points out:

> "... a move away from physical force methods, exclusive dealing and the political strike as potential or actual methods into those governed by a relatively narrowly defined notion of politics: the rhythms of political agitation were largely determined by the focus upon Parliament and the political nation."[61]

It would be an oversimplification to regard "public opinion" and "newspaper opinion" as synonymous:[62] the pulpit, the placard and popular song were other important means of expression; but Adams, the propagandist, was under no illusions of the new found power of the newspaper when he wrote shortly, after arriving in Newcastle, "the press became the adjunct of the platform".[63] For the next forty years, Adams was uniquely placed: he was to expend much effort and energy moulding and influencing the opinions and affairs of Tyneside and beyond to current issues or new crusades.

In the words of Aaron Watson, Adams's assistant editor until 1880, 'W.E.' "was a marvel of industry".[64] The breadth of his interests can best be shown by listing some of the many causes he fought for: the co-operative movement, temperance; trade union rights; national compulsory but unsectarian education; a Channel Tunnel; the ship-wrecked Mariners' Society; and the abolition of all penalties on opinion and association, as symbolized in the struggles of his friend, Charles Bradlaugh. A representative sample can best be explored however under four over-lapping headings: freedom campaigns against what Adams frequently referred to as "the poison of Slavery"; the struggles of oppressed nationalities in Europe; Republicanism and franchise reform in England; and the cause of Ireland and eschewal of Empire in British foreign policy. In all of this activity, of course, we see Adams imbued by a great and life-long adherence to the basic principal of Radicalism: "As I understand it", he wrote, "that love of liberty and right — as much liberty for all as is consistent with regard for the rights of each".[65]

Between 1863-1865, Adams responded in the *Weekly Chronicle* to three great crises in foreign affairs: the American Civil War 1861-65, the Polish Revolt of 1863 and the cause of Garibaldi in the work of Italian Unification, 1864-65; and ultimately each in turn was, as we shall note, linked by Adams in some way to the progress of manhood suffrage at home. Recent re-interpretations of English attitudes towards the American

Civil War have called into question the long-held view that the war placed the aristocracy and establishment press on the side of the South, and the manufacturers, a tiny minority of the press and working class sentiments on the side of the North.[66] In fact, the issue was far more complex. Certainly the aristocracy were pro-South, but both they and the *Times* cheered those ship-builders, like the Conservative, John Laird on Merseyside, where the blockade runner Alabama was built, and the Liberal, William Lindsay on Wearside, who, Adams recalled:

> "cared nothing for the honour of the interests of their country so long as they could make a profit of the nefarious work in which they were engaged."[67]

Similarly, working class opinion was divided, not least in Lancashire by the "sophisms" of James Spence of Liverpool a Southern agent, Joseph Barker, Adams's old adversary at the *National Reformer* and William Aitken, an ex-Chartist. Amidst the misery of the Cotton famine, factory workers were informed by these kindred spirits that the cause of the conflict was oppressive tariffs which, following a Southern victory, would ensure free trade, a resumption of cotton imports and prosperity for the beleagured industry.[68]

By the time Adams commenced his "Ironside" column specifically on the subject of the American Civil War in December 20, 1862,[69] he had been extremely active in countering the falsehoods of Barker and the mendacity of the *Times*. His carefully researched articles in support of the North in the *National Reformer* in 1861/2 on the real nature of the conflict as a struggle by the South to establish a slave empire had been recognised as crucial to the strategy of the Union and Emancipation Society, the influential organ of radical middle class Abolitionists in their moral crusade against slavery. Shortly after the publication by them in March 1863 of his "Slaveholders' War: An Argument for the North and the Negro",[70] two further honours befell Adams: he was appointed a vice-president, alongside such distinguished men as John Stuart Mill and Professor Beesly, to the Union and Emancipation Society; and his well-seasoned pamphlet was translated into Gujratee, one of the languages of India.[71] Living in London, too, until the Spring of 1863 also gave Adams something of a metropolitan perspective on English attitudes to the Civil War. For example, he attended the two great mass meetings — the one in Exeter Hall on January 29 and the other of the organised Trades in St. James's Hall on March 23[72] — which, given the presence of John Bright, were seen as landmarks in fusing the support of British workers and middle class Radicals for the Northern democracy.[73]

On Tyneside, Adams initially faced an uphill struggle. Newcastle had been curiously identified with a number of famous utterances by leading members of the governing classes. In October 1861 at a banquet in the Town Hall, Earl Russell declared that the North was fighting for empire and the South for independence; and a year later, in the same place and on a like occasion, Gladstone expressed his belief that Jefferson Davis had made an army, was making a navy and would make a nation. According to the radical and miner's leader, Edward Rymer, working at this time at Thornley Colliery, Co. Durham, Gladstone's speech influenced "not a few in favour of the South",[74] while at Jarrow the ship-yard workers, engaged on Confederacy Naval orders, were equally enthusiastic for the South.[75]

Adams quickly embarked on the campaign initially launched by Cowen and Radical Nonconformist ministers to rally solidarity with the Northern cause. A number of features distinguished his particular contribution. Firstly, he was instrumental in helping to found a Newcastle branch for Aid to the Emancipation of Slaves, which raised over £100 for freed slaves within a year of its inception.[76] Secondly, he took to the platform speaking at meetings of craft workers in Newcastle, North and South Shields, and in the colliery villages of West Cramlington and Dudley. The same message was hammered home at each: slavery, as both an economic system and a moral symbol, was the cause of the war; and in turn resolutions were passed and memorials despatched to the American Ambassador expressive of sympathy with the emancipation policy of President Lincoln.[77] Thirdly, through his ready command of the pen he made great play of an attack on some of the country's intellectual elite by way of an incident which occurred when William Craft, an ex-slave, brushed aside attempts by the British Association for the Advancement of Science to prevent him from speaking at their gathering in Newcastle during August 1863.[78] Craft, who was an accomplished debater and respected Radical, made a considerable impact: he carefully and humorously destroyed the arguments of Dr. J. Hunt and Mr. Carter Blake, two learned defenders of the Confederate cause, in debates following on their papers in the Ethnology section, which had argued for in-born, Black inferiority. Adams turned Craft into a star attraction: the former took great delight in describing at length to his readers how, in what he dubbed "Wise Week", the latter had not only humbled the theories of two eminent philosophers by the mastery of his arguments and the dignity of his presentation, but also drawn standing ovations from distinguished members in the audience.[79] The *Chronicle* also rebuked the two academics "not to try it on in Newcastle where a Negro is treated as a man and a brother".[80] It was Adams's good fortune to befriend Craft, about whom he wrote: "A finer gentleman in every respect I think I never met".[81]

Undoubtedly, the most important aspect of Adams's anti-slavery fight was the way in which he drove home the message to the working men and women of the North East that the War was not simply about justice and freedom for Black people in the Deep South; it was about the rights of labour all over the world. In an "Ironside" letter to this effect, entitled "The Solidarity of Labour", he reminded readers:

> "The confederate States are not likely to limit themselves in the matter of slavery to a mere question of colour. People who tell you that they would rather five thousand negroes were enslaved than a single white man, forget that it is not a question of white or black slavery, but a question of white and black ... slavery is not now confined to the black race, since all the shades of colour between black and white are found among the slaves of the South."[82]

Judging by the many reports of large and enthusiastic meetings at which trade union leaders like John Kane and William Crawford were present,[83] the round of popular concerts held at theTyne Concert Hall in aid of the freed slaves[84] and the widely supported Memorials to President Lincoln,[85] large sections of the North East's population became inspired by the *Daily* and *Weekly Chronicle's* campaign for the Federal cause. As a tribute, too, for that support and loyalty, a steady stream of eminent Abolitionist Americans including William Lloyd Garrison, Frederick Douglass, Reverdy Johnson and ex-President Grant himself paid courtesy visits, before crowds of up to 80,000, between the end of the war and 1877.[86]

If Adams despaired over the Southern slave-owners' attempt to preserve and perpetuate tyranny, he was, by contrast, delighted when, in 1863, the Poles revolted against Russian oppression; and the effect of alternating between writings on Poland and the Civil War in his "Ironside" column was to interlink them in the public mind. As we have already seen, Adams was intimately associated with the affairs of Polish revolutionaries whilst in London. On Tyneside, he continued to urge organized public demonstrations of sympathy, the setting up of Relief Committees to help Konstanty Lekawski, the leader of the Newcastle group of Polish refugees, return to fight, and demanded that the English Government should materially aid the Poles.[87] Later in the year when Russia rejected an armistice, he urged Britain should go to war because

> "it would be the most just and honourable ... the most disinterested and humane, of all the wars in which England had been engaged."[88]

At the same time he did not disguise his continuing sympathies for the republican faction, as opposed to the monarchists, within the Polish movement; and urged the Government to recognise the radical Joseph Cwierczakiewicz, the official representative of the Central National Committee of Warsaw, who had become responsible for the disposal of money collected from sympathisers in England.[89] Ultimately, of course, there was little that public opinion could achieve. Russell, the Foreign Secretary in the Whig-Liberal ministry, sympathised with the Poles, but was emphatic on the impossibility of England rendering any material assistance. By August 1863, the Russians had ruthlessly crushed the Uprising. Adams however could draw some comfort from the fact that a year later the issue of Poland was drawn into the debate about Parliamentary reform and the state of representation in Newcastle. Radical supporters — shop-keepers, a few artisans, Nonconformist ministers, small businessmen and solicitors — imbued by Cowenite radicalism had become extremely dissatisfied with the local Whig clique and their Whig-Liberal M.P.'s: T.E. Headlam and S.A. Beaumont; the latter were disinclined to reform and rarely prominent on key issues at Westminster. Public awareness in Newcastle was such that at a series of large public meetings specifically organised in April and August 1864 to scrutinize their members' Parliamentary work, Beaumont's do-nothing policy over Poland became a major issue of debate and consternation.[90] The upshot was the mobilization of an advanced Liberal challenge which, when it came at the next General election in 1865, resulted in Joseph Cowen senior topping the poll; Beaumont, who was defeated by Headlam into third place, lost his seat.[91]

Adams was also kept extremely busy through the early part of 1864 because of the prominent part he played as a joint secretary on the Reception Committee set up, under Joseph Cowen jr's chairmanship, to welcome Garibaldi to Newcastle. The cause of Italy and the part Garibaldi had played in its heroic struggle for liberty was a dear one to many working class men and middle class radicals in all parts of the country, not least on Tyneside. Only ten years before, Newcastle had been the only city in England to recognise the heroism of Garibaldi after the memorable defence of Rome.[92] On that occasion in 1854, his friend Joseph Cowen had presented him with a sword and telescope as a token of the high esteem in which he was held in the North East. Adams was not to be outdone either by the knowledge of that event or the great welcome now being afforded Garibaldi after travelling from Southampton to the capital. From the offices of the old Northern Reform Union in Newcastle, he launched testimonial funds not only for Garibaldi himself, but also for his two sons, Menotti and Riccotti, and a number of close advisers.[93] Adams also chaired a sub-committee of local trade unionists, including the iron-workers leader John Kane, drawn from every conceivable engineering works in Newcastle in order to arrange a grand procession of the trades and their banners as a colourful prelude to the formal presentation of the Testimonials at the Town Hall.[94] All these plans were dashed at an advanced stage however by the sudden news that Garibaldi was cutting short his English tour, ostensibly on health grounds, in order to return to Italy. Not to be outdone, the Mayor's party, headed by Thomas Headley, went forthwith to London in order to present the Testimonial; they also learnt here the real reasons for Garibaldi's premature departure. Louis Napoleon of France and Francis Joseph of Austria had taken umbrage at the enthusiastic receptions the Italian patriot had received in England. Palmerston's Government also felt pressurised into asking Garibaldi to leave because if political demonstrations on the scale of that in London were to be repeated all over the North, "a democratic force might be created that would render impossible the maintenance of the political equilibrium".[95]

The indignation felt in Newcastle was considerable. By such undue pressure on Garibaldi, Adams saw Palmerston's Government following up the policy of his degraded Conspiracy Bill.[96] The Town Council also passed a resolution deeply regretting his untimely departure.[97] Although Newcastle was deprived of the opportunity of once more demonstrating its attachment to the cause of oppressed people, the Testimonial Committee for Garibaldi maintained its existence indefinitely, in the hope that Garibaldi might yet return.[98] This was not to be and the Committee evolved in a different but not entirely unconnected way. Comprised as it was of local Radical middle class elements and of trade unionists from amongst the engineering works, united in the cause of freedom, it became essentially the parent by September 1866 of the movement for universal suffrage in Newcastle and district, the Northern Reform League.[99]

The movement for political reform had steadily gathered momentum after the death of Palmerston in October 1865. By the end of 1866, in the wake of Radical disappointments over Gladstone's limited Reform Bill in March, his subsequent defeat in June and the mounting pressure exerted by the Reform League on the new Conservative ministry of Disraeli to concede manhood suffrage, Adams uninhibitedly linked the state of British politics with those struggles across the Atlantic for which his working class readers had given so much both morally and financially:

> "The negroes have got the suffrage ... The emancipated slave has outstripped the English artizan; but the patient workers of this country will not brook another year's delay. The year 1866 has seen the beginning of the enfranchisement of the negro, and the year 1867 must not close before the English artisan shows the new energy divine of Toil's enfranchised glance."[100]

Newcastle had certainly begun to mirror some of the changes nationally. The Cowens, father and son, both councillors by 1866, had galvanised the discontent within the

Liberal hegemonic bloc in an attempt to democratize local government and wrest Parliamentary representation from Whiggish-Liberals.[101] The balance of power on the Council and in the local Liberal group came to be held by such Radical-Liberals as the influential Rev. J.C. Rutherford, the ex-Chartist shopkeeper Thomas Gregson, the temperance advocate Ralph Dodds, the radical solicitor, William Lockey Harle and the free library campaigner, Dr. Henry William Newton. These men successfully mobilized the discontent of upward of 2,000 of the 7,000 electorate,[102] who had requested Joseph Cowen senior to contest the borough into his victorious return in 1865; it was a seat he was to retain until his son succeeded him at the bye-election after his death in January 1874.

The key issue for Adams however was the need to persuade many local Liberals of the need for universal suffrage; they had elected an M.P. whose Radicalism was somewhat diluted by the fact that he stood only for household suffrage.[103] Fortunately, Adams's employer felt differently to his father on this issue: Joseph Cowen jr. had been moving steadily leftwards to embrace the democratic republicanism of Mazzini; and he was now an unwavering supporter of manhood suffrage.[104]

Following its preliminary meeting in September, the Northern Reform League was formally constituted on November 6, 1866 with the object of attaining manhood suffrage and the secret ballot. Joseph Cowen was its chairman; but Adams, alongside another ex-Chartist Robert Gammage, was a member of its otherwise trades' dominated council.[105] Adams's role was very much that of its publicity officer. He aided the developing political consciousness of the Tyneside working classes by his extensive and detailed reporting of the movement's progress beyond Newcastle and into the Northern Coalfield;[106] caught in his writings the mood and sense of occasion which accompanied the visit of Ernest Jones and Lord Teynham, two of the League's national leaders, to the great mass demonstration organised on the Town Moor in January 1867;[107] and paid glowing tributes to the peaceful nature of the crowds and well-ordered conduct of the men in organising this new phase of extra-parliamentary agitation.[108] Certainly on Tyneside Adams's journalism did much to prove that the aspersions cast on the artisans by the Liberal reactionary, Robert Lowe, justifying their continued exclusion from the franchise, were entirely groundless. According to one Newcastle contemporary:

> "When the Liberal Party took up the question of Parliamentary Reform, there was no part of England better prepared, from knowledge of the question and interest in its settlement.[109]

Adams and his colleagues in the Northern Reform League were in no doubt about the merits of Disraeli's Reform Bill when it came in March 1867. As a householder suffrage, yet again, it was

> "both a delusion and a snare. What he offered the country was a feast of Dead Sea apples — fair to look upon, but ashes in the mouth."[110]

By this time, although it was no longer possible for the government to ignore the popular clamour in favour of reform, the shape of the Act was largely determined by parliamentary manoeuverings between Disraeli and the Radicals. The major victory for the Radicals, amongst whom Joseph Cowen senior was prominent, was the achievement by May 1867 of household suffrage, which added a million new, mainly urban, voters to the electoral list. In Newcastle the electorate grew dramatically from 7,500 to 18,600.[111]

To Adams, the manhood suffrage pamphleteer, the Act was only a partial victory. Joseph Cowen senior was again returned at the top of the poll at the general election in November 1868;[112] but in such boroughs as Morpeth nearby in the Coalfield, it rapidly became apparent that the miners were still excluded from the franchise on account of the peculiar tenure on which they held their houses.[113] Of the thousands of miners in Northumberland and Durham by 1873,[114] only a few hundred had become eligible for the vote under the provisions of the Second Reform Act.[115] The miners or pit-men as they were more usually referred to in the North East were in an anomalous and inequitable position in two respects. Firstly, many of them lived in colliery villages in the counties where the minimum property qualification for the vote under the 1867 Act was virtually prohibitive; and, secondly, in those colliery settlements which had become part of enlarged parliamentary boroughs, like Morpeth, they found themselves excluded from the vote, because the act did not enfranchise employees, who, in occupying premises — in this case the colliery owners' houses — as a necessary condition of their employment, did not pay rates. Adams considered this clause to be a gross injustice. Consequently, throughout the franchise agitation which began in Choppington and surrounding pit villages in 1871 and ended in the famous election victory of Thomas Burt at Morpeth in 1874, the first working man to be returned to Parliament, Adams and his *Weekly Chronicle* gave both unswerving support and complete endorsement. He gave full coverage to their meetings and rallies, publicized their grievances and, in the wake of the Agricultural Labourer's strike of 1872, encouraged the pit-men to see themselves as "pioneers of political progress".[116]

In his leader columns and as "Ironside", Adams was arguably the campaign's best image-builder. Between September 1872 and February 1874, as part of a strategy to influence public opinion in the pit-men's favour, the *Weekly Chronicle* carried long and detailed articles describing the living conditions and social life of over seventy local colliery villages. Their impact as a piece of investigative journalism in pursuit of the dignity of mining life was all the more effective because they followed a series of blistering attacks by Adams against an expensive aristocracy and an extravagant royalty in the summer of 1871,[117] when Bradlaugh's Republican movement was gaining ground.[118] His readers came to appreciate how he had gained his knowledge of the pit-men's culture at first hand not only by meeting them out of working hours in their clubs, institutes and on colourful picnics complete with brass bands, but also by visiting and seeing for himself the skilled nature of their work in "the gloomy recesses of the mine". What emerges is a clear picture of individual self-help and community responsibility particularly through the role of co-operative stores, of sobriety, inventiveness, thrift and stoicism in the face of danger and harsh working conditions. Adams also considered the role of Primitive Methodism in pacifying the Coalfield and fusing with an emergent class consciousness; and of a responsible trade union leadership whose policies were realistic, responsible and non-violent. By the time the Revision Court at Morpeth had recognised the miners' right in September 1873 "to become a power in the State", Adams had also concluded that:

> "The common notion of a pitman as ... a rough, uncouth, aggressive person, about equally addicted to oaths and dogs ... is altogether false."[119]

In return, Adams and his wife were amongst the honoured guests invited to celebrate at a temperance banquet the historic victory of Thomas Burt as M.P. for Morpeth in March 1874.[120] Thereafter he was often referred to as the miner's friend[121] and his *Weekly Chronicle* became known in the Coalfield as "the Pit-man's Bible".[122]

In respect of Ireland Adams was also no mere theorist. His knowledge of the workings of repressive legislation in England's first colony was based on personal observation and careful enquiries during his visit to "the most disturbed districts of that unhappy country" in September 1875.[123] His solutions, however, before becoming convinced of the necessity of Home Rule for Ireland in the mid 1880s, were very much in the radical mould. He followed Bright, for example, in arguing that the tyranny of the landlords would be removed by comprehensive land reform in favour of an Irish tenantry:

> "I have over and over again contended in these letters that the establishment of a system of peasant proprietors, such as that which prevails in Norway and other parts of the Continent would go a great way to solve the Irish difficulty."[124]

Nor did the power of the Catholic Church escape the scathing criticism of his pen:

> "... the tyranny of priests is worse. The one affects the material circumstances of the vote; but the other invades his mind, corrupts his conscience, terrifies his very soul. There is no such despotic machinery in the world as that controlled by the Catholic Church."[125]

Like Cowen, he called upon Gladstone not to shut his eyes to the power of the Catholic hierarchy, but otherwise offered nothing concrete on this vexed question. At the same time he was allied with those radicals displaying a continued and spirited opposition to the Liberal's policy of coercion in the Emerald Isle.[126] Such a position, of course, found considerable favour with Irish readers among both *Chronicles;* it also helped ensure their electoral loyalty to Joseph Cowen jr. on more than one occasion in the 1870s.[127]

Adams's sympathies towards Ireland must also be set in a broader framework of an antipathy towards an enlargement of the British Empire, poised as it was in 1880 for a period of considerable expansion in parts of Africa, Afghanistan and Burma.[128] At root, Adams does reveal a fundamental acceptance of the Englishmen's civilizing mission and duty to rule over an Empire:

> "The honour of our country, it seems to me, depends less upon the extent of our possessions than upon the manner in which we rule them."[129]

Perhaps naively he felt, like other Radicals, that the power of Empire would be used for the advancement of freedom throughout the globe. However, he had become seriously alarmed by Disraeli's plans for imperialist ventures, particularly when, in 1876, "the tawdry title of Empress was conferred upon the Queen".[130] Such titles he believed were associated with "the most odious race of rulers that ever disgraced the world".[131] His objections to imperialism after 1880 were both moral and economic:

> "What comfort or advantage can it be to the English people to oppress the people of a distant country? Besides, adventures of this description cannot be undertaken without cost — cost of money and cost of blood."[132]

He condemned unequivocally therefore the British invasion of Afghanistan and the Zulu War of 1879, exposed the hypocrisy of the English clergy who were trying to justify intervention as "missionary enterprises",[133] and opposed the annexation of Cyprus in the same year on the grounds that it constituted a reversal of the Gladstonian policy recognising her long-standing aspirations to union with Greece.[134]

The bedrock of Adams's opposition to Colonial domination continued to hinge around the issue of racism. The old divisions over colour prejudice and Negro inferiority had again surfaced towards the close of the American Civil War when a fatal riot in October 1865 was made the pretext by the governor, Edward Eyre, of a frightful massacre of over 450 of the coloured population.[135] Adams firmly allied the *Weekly Chronicle* behind John Stuart Mill's campaign, albeit unsuccessful, to prosecute Eyre following the Government's muted response. Elsewhere, he drew attention to a new kind of slave trade in 1869 between the British colony of Queensland and the islands of the South Seas over the forced employment of over 3,000 Polynesians on the Australian sugar plantations;[136] and cast Emilio Castelar, the Spanish Republican politician, in the mould of liberator in his work during the 1870s against slavery in the country's colony of Cuba.[137].

Two final questions need to be addressed in respect of "Ironside's" role: firstly, how much of an impact did his political correspondence in the *Weekly Chronicle* have on public opinion in the North East; and secondly, to what extent had Adams become by his social and occupational mobility 'incorporated' into the political values and assumptions of Newcastle's middle class liberalism. While there is no disputing the hegemony of the *Daily* and its stable-mate the *Weekly* in the region's newspaper circulation at this time,[138] it is extremely difficult to assess with any precision the impact of "Ironside's" political column because, other than the evidence of a continued rise in circulation figures, there are no opinion polls or independent surveys in existence to suggest what the readership thought of the content. Such evidence as we have in terms of the impact of the leading articles is largely impressionistic: we need to explore, for example, the opinions of contemporaries and rely on methods of inference; and A.J. Lee, a leading authority on the history of the Victorian provincial press, has offered cautious advice in respect of what might be found:

> "newspapers, when they did preach, almost always did so to the converted (the adherents), for it is usually only the converted who will abide being preached too."[139]

By way of a general commentary on the *Weekly's* value George Julian Harney, the ex-Chartist, writing to Adams in 1873 from distant Boston where he was a reader, complemented the paper on the fact that:

> "There is always something in the shape of political action going on in Newcastle ... industrial struggles ... are ably and successfully conducted on Tyneside."[140]

Political elections represent one yardstick by which we might test the importance of the *Weekly's* editorial opinion in rallying the fair-weather birds or the unconverted. In the 1874 General Election, Joseph Cowen jr. was returned at the top of the poll, but Newcastle was politically divided against itself for the first time in many years by the election of a popular local Conservative, C.F. Hamond, who took the second seat.[141] As for the wider campaign waged by the *Chronicles* in defence of the Liberal cause, one contemporary, G. Hodgson, the biographer of James Annand, wrote:

> "It was unquestionably due in no small part to the influence of the '*Newcastle Chronicle*' that, while in many parts of England the Liberal Party in that election were overwhelmingly defeated, the representatives of the Counties of Northumberland and Durham remained almost wholly Liberal."[142]

Obviously we must take into account additional variables: the existence of special local issues, the efficiency of the rival party organisations and the personal standing of the candidates. Cowen's personal popularity amongst the working classes of Byker, Westgate and Elswick was still supreme.[143] However, in 1880 and 1885 he had to contest the Parliamentary elections without the assistance of the local Liberal party organization because of protracted infighting.[144] The fact that he headed the poll on both occasions is ample testimony again to the role of both *Chronicles* in his campaigns.[145] In industrial matters, too, editorial support was viewed by trade union leaders as a valuable political asset. While John Burnett, leader of the successful North East Engineers' Strike in 1871, appreciated the vigorous support offered to his men by the *Daily Chronicle*,[146] Thomas Burt, the long-serving Northumberland Miners' leader, was equally fulsome in his praise of the *Weekly Chronicle*:

> "a powerful organ of public opinion ... [which] in its leading columns boldly champions the cause of labour, and stoutly vindicates the rights of combination."[147]

Working for Cowen gave Adams a natural entry into provincial Liberal politics and a ladder of opportunity that permitted upward social mobility. Within a year of his appointment as leader writer — a position in terms of pay and status between that of editor and sub-editor[148] — he was preferred by Cowen to G.J. Holyoake as the new editor in chief of the *Weekly Chronicle.*[149] Unfortunately, no evidence exists with regard to what Adams earned. The average rates in the provinces which, according to A.J. Lee, varied between £150 and £300, put them on a level with the experienced bank or insurance clerk.[150] Shortly after his appointment Adams let it be known to close friends that he was both happy and settled: he had attended the Paris Exhibition of 1867 and been financially rewarded with a pay rise, albeit after some prompting on his part.[151] His remarkable talents as a journalist also brought job security to the extent that he felt confident enough to take out a mortgage in 1877 with the Northern Counties Building Society on his beloved house at 32, Holly Avenue in the leafy suburb of Jesmond.[152]

Did such changes suggest new meanings and perspectives to Adams that were fundamentally different from his Chartist days? In political terms the answer must surely be no. Adams was not 'incorporated' because he belonged from the beginning to a political tradition which encompassed both Chartism and Liberalism. He had been attracted to the Chartist movement in Cheltenham by a radicalism which saw privilege and political inequality as the root of many social evils. Moreover, in the continuing campaign for Parliamentary reform, the abolition of primogeniture, the game laws, the power of the Anglican Church, the freedom of the individual both home and abroad, and the ethic of self-improvement, it was possible, after the repressive spirit of 1840s bourgeois liberalism had given way to the genial optimism of the 1850s,[153] for members of the radical middle class with similar perspectives to cohere with the politically conscious working class.

Adams was particularly fortunate in finding a congenial political atmosphere of this kind in the North East. Newcastle Liberalism by the mid-1860s had become a fairly broad church movement; it was also being shifted to a position "on the far left of middle-class radicalism and won a great deal of working class support"[154] by the policies, personality and press power of Joseph Cowen jr. As we have seen, by his unequivocal support for manhood suffrage, freedom for oppressed people and numerous self-help activities, Cowen projected the Liberal Party in Newcastle as "the organ of the people, the true embodiment of progress and enlightenment".[155] For Adams, of course, there was the added knowledge that Cowen had become, like himself, thoroughly imbued with Mazzinian ideals about devotion to duty and service to the community. His radicalism thus reinforced, Adams became the consistent and life-long defender of democracy, education, freedom of conscience and self-improvement; he was in no way compromised by his new found respectability or creature comforts which were increasingly available to him at his Jesmond retreat.

In the final analysis, however inappropriate the notion of 'incorporation', there cannot be any doubt that in Newcastle Adams no longer stood outside the middle class dominated political and economic system. By entering Cowen's payroll and selling his labour in such a key way, Adams was at the very least consenting to an ordered relationship in which his powerful employer, a self-made member of the dominant class, held to middle class assumptions not only about the creed of laissez-faire and what might sell, but also displayed very definite views on what constituted a journalist's acceptable political loyalty to the party line on his two radical newspapers. In the work-place this could mean staff who did not agree with Cowen were, as we have noted, either removed or transferred to another job. Given his acknowledged independence of mind and integrity of character, Adams's long editorial reign was therefore a remarkable achievement by any standard. He was not, of course, to be spared the unenviable clash with or occasional reprimand from the pen of Cowen; but their mutual respect was sufficient to ensure that whatever their differences they were negotiated or buried in the long term interests of the *Weekly Chronicle*; and perhaps the greatest testimony to their enduring friendship was Cowen's approval of Adams's son, Ernest Welles, as his successor at the *Weekly* in 1898.

Notes

1. N. McCord, "Some Aspects of North-East England in the Nineteenth Century", Northern History, Vol.VII, 1972, pp.73-88, in particular pp.74-76.

2. A. Briggs, A Social History of England, Middlesex, 1983, p.200.

3. A. Briggs, Victorian Cities, Middlesex, 1968, pp.366-367.

4. W.E. Adams, Memoirs, op.cit., p.459.

5. N. McCord, "Some Aspects of North-East England in the Nienteenth Century", op.cit., p.74.

6. Newcastle Chronicle, May 10, 1862, Report on Census Returns. The paper became known as the Newcastle Weekly Chronicle by June 1864.

7. E. Allen, J.F. Clarke, N. McCord and D.J. Rowe, The North East Engineers' Strikes of 1871, Newcastle, 1971, p.13.

8. See, for example D.J. Rowe, "The Population of Nineteenth Century Tyneside", pp.1-24 and T.P. MacDermott, "Irish Workers on Tyneside in the Nineteenth Century" pp.154-77 in N. McCord (ed.), Essays in Tyneside Labour History, Newcastle, 1977. See also N. Todd, "Black-On-Tyne: The Black Presence on Tyneside in the 1860s", Bulletin of North East Labour History Society, No.21, 1987, pp.17-27.

9. E. Allen, J.F. Clarke, N. McCord and D.J. Rowe, The North-East Engineers' Strikes of 1871, op.cit., p.19. The agreement in 1867 between W.G. Armstrong and C.W. Mitchell & Co. Shipbuilders at Low Walker to develop naval work jointly anticipated their amalgamation in 1884. A new shipyard at Elswick, which was capable of building warships from start to finish, employed in excess of 20,000 workers, many of them highly skilled engineers, boilermakers and ironfounders, by 1901.

10. N. McCord, "Some Aspects of North-East England in the Nineteenth Century", op.cit.; p.76. McCord notes that success in industrial enterprise saw, for example, 90 warships launched on the Tyne in 1893-94; Armstrong's build 62 and Palmer's, 28.

11. E. Allen, J.F. Clarke, N. McCord and D.J. Rowe, The North-East Engineers' Strike of 1871, op.cit., p.13.

12. Ibid., p.10.

13. T.J. Nossiter, Influence, Opinion and Political Idioms in Reformed England, 1823-74, Brighton, 1975, p.15.

14. Newcastle Chronicle, Sept. 13, 1862. The Rev. J.H. Rutherford, the leading Radical Nonconformist minister in Newcastle, was highly critical of the city's "Licensing System". Strategically placed next to this report are those relating to the numerous cases brought before the Police Courts. See also N. McCord, North East England, London, 1979, pp.127-128 for the wide-ranging interests of Rutherford.

15. N. Todd, "Black-On-Tyne: The Black Presence on Tyneside in the 1860s", op.cit., pp.20-21; and N. McCord, "Some Aspects of North-East England inthe Nineteenth Century", op.cit., pp.85-86.

16. E.I. Waitt, "John Morley, Joseph Cowen and R. Spence Watson : Liberal Divisions in Newcastle Politics, 1873-95", op.cit., p.2.

17. W.E. Adams, Memoirs, op.cit., p.474.

18. Ibid., p.475.

19. Idem.,

20. Newcastle Chronicle, June 14; Oct. 4, 1862.

21. Ibid., May 17, 1862.

22. W.E. Adams, Memoirs, op.cit., pp.468-472.

23. Newcastle Chronicle, Aug. 23; Oct. 18, 1862.

24. W.E. Adams, Memoirs, op.cit., p.471. See also N. McCord, North East England, op.cit., pp.188-189 for the immense amount of popular enthusiasm for competitive rowing.

25. L.J. Satre, "Thomas Burt and the Crisis of Late-Victorian Liberalism in the North-East", Northern History, Vol.XXIII, 1987, pp.174-193, in particular p.174; and J.F. Clarke, "Workers in the Tyneside Ship-Yards in the

Nineteenth Century", pp.109-131, in particular pp.127-128, in N. McCord, Essays in Tyneside Labour History, op.cit.

26. W.R. Garside, "Wage Determination and the Miners' Lock-Out of 1892", pp.132-153, in particular pp.143-44 in N. McCord, Essays in Tyneside Labour History, op.cit. "Sliding Scale" agreements turned out to be tactical and unstable concessions in the history of industrial relations between pit-men and coal-owners.

27. C. Godfrey, Chartist Lives — The Anatomy of a Working Class Movement, op.cit., p.332.

28. See, for example, Newcastle Chronicle, Jan 18; Feb. 8; April 5 and May 17, 1862 for examples of paternalism respectively by Joseph Cowen and Co.; William G. Armstrong; G.R. Stephenson and G.S. Storey.

29. A.W, Purdue, "Jarrow Politics, 1885-1914: The Challenge to Liberal Hegemony", Northern History, Vol. XVIII, 1982, pp.182-198, in particular p.182.

30. Idem.,

31. Benwell Community Project, Final Report Series No.6, The Making of a Ruling Class, Newcastle, 1978, p.40.

32. L.J. Satre, "Thomas Burt and the Crisis of Late-Victorian Liberalism in the North-East", op.cit., pp. 180-181.

33. E. Allen, J.F. Clarke, N. McCord and D.J. Rowe, The North-East Engineers' Strikes of 1871, op.cit., particularly pp.98-188.

34. J.F. Clarke, "Engineering Workers on Tyneside" pp.88-108, particularly pp.102-1-3 and his "Workers in the Tyneside Shipyards in the Nineteenth Century" pp.109-131, particularly p.119 in N. McCord, "Essays in Tyneside Labour History", op.cit.

35. A.W. Purdue, "The Liberal and Labour Parties in North-East Politics, 1900-14: The Struggle for Supremacy", International Review of Social History, Vol.XXVI, 1981, Part 1, pp.1-24, particularly pp.3-6.

36. Apart from Dr. Waitt's critical and scholarly analysis of Joseph Cowen's political life between 1873-95, there are only two highly, hagiographical late nineteenth century biographies: E.R. Jones, The Life and Speeches of Joseph Cowen, M.P. op.cit., and W. Duncan, The Life of Joseph Cowen, London and Newcastle, 1904. The late Keith Harris, formerly historian of Newcastle Polytechnic, began a full length biography, which, hopefully, will now be completed by the Newcastle historian, Nigel Todd.

37. T. Tholfsen, Working Class Radicalism in Mid-Victorian England, London, 1976, particularly pp.124-154.

38. E.R. Jones, The Life and Speeches of Joseph Cowen, M.P. op.cit., p.14.

39. A.R. Schoyen, The Chartist Challenge: a Portrait of George Julian Harney, op.cit., p.236.

40. Newcastle Chronicle, Feb. 21, 1863.

41. K. Harris, "Joseph Cowen — The Northern Tribune", Bulletin of the North East Group for the Study of Labour History, No.5. 1971, pp.1-7. See also W.E. Adams, Memoirs, op.cit., p.495.

42. W. Duncan, The Life of Joseph Cowen, op.cit., p.24.

43. T.J. Nossiter, Influence, Opinion and Political Idioms in Reformed England, 1832-74, op.cit., pp.159-160.

44. E.I. Waitt, "John Morley, Joseph Cowen and R. Spence Watson: Liberal Divisions in Newcastle Politics, 1873-95", op.cit., pp.4-6.

45. P. Brock, "Joseph Cowen and the Polish Exiles", Slavonic and East European Review, Vol.XXXII, 1953, pp.52-69, particularly pp.55-56 and pp.65-66. See also K. Harris, "Joseph Cowen — The Northern Tribune", Bulletin of the North East Group for the Study of Labour History, op.cit., p.1.

46. J. Saville and J. Bellamy (eds.), Dictionary of Labour Biography, Vol.1, 1972, pp.81-86, contribution by the late Keith Harris, particularly p.84.

47. M. Milne, The Newspapers of Northumberland and Durham, op.cit., p.41.

48. J. Saville and J. Bellamy (eds.), Dictionary of Labour Biography, Vol.1, op.cit., pp.82-83.

49. A. Watson, A Newspaper Man's Memories, op.cit., p.31.

50. J. Dellow, Memoirs of An Old Stager, Newcastle, 1928, p.11.

51. See, for example, G. Hodgson, From Smithy to Senate: The Life Story of James Annand, Journalist and Politician, London, 1908, p.194, and A. Watson, A Newspaper Man's Memories, op.cit., p.49.

52. M. Milne, The Newspapers of Northumberland and Durham, op.cit., p.71. Milne devotes a Chapter to "Joseph Cowen and the Newcastle Chronicle", pp.63-83.

53. A. Watson, A Newspaper Man's Memories, op.cit., p.31.

54. E.I. Waitt, "John Morley, Joseph Cowen and R. Spence Watson: Liberal Divisions in Newcastle Politics, 1877-95", op.cit., p.6. For comparison with a number of other provincial newspapers, see L. Brown, Victorian News and Newspapers, Oxford, 1985, p.32. The Manchester Guardian's circulation in 1870 was said to be 30,000 and that of the Yorkshire Post, 16,000.

55. J.M. Bourne, Patronage and Society in Nineteenth Century England, London, 1986, p.131.

56. A.R. Schoyen, The Chartist Challenge: a Portrait of George Julian Harney, op.cit., p.234.

57. A. Watson, A Newspaper Man's Memories, op.cit., p.29.

58. Ibid., p.45.

59. A.J. Lee, The Origins of the Popular Press in England, 1855-1914, London, 1976, p.174.

60. Newcastle Chronicle, April 2, 1864, Gratis Supplement to celebrate the centenary of the Newcastle Chronicle. The Advertising Duty was repealed in 1853; that on excise in 1855; and on paper in 1861.

61. K. McClelland, "A Politics of the Labour Aristocracy ? Skilled Workers and Radical Politics on Tyneside, c.1850-74." Bulletin of the Society for the Study of Labour History, Conference Report, No.40, 1980, pp.8-9.

62. M. Milne, "Strikes and Strike-Breaking in North-East England, 1815-1844: The Attitude of the Local Press", International Review of Social History, 22(2), 1977, pp.226-40, particularly p.226.

63. W.E. Adams, Memoirs, op.cit., pp.494-495.

64. A. Watson, A Newspaper Man's Memories, op.cit., p55.

65. Newcastle Weekly Chronicle, Dec.2, 1876. Radical Policy by "Ironside".

66. See M. Ellison, Support for Secession, Chicago, 1972 whose study of the Lancashire working classes suggested pro-Confederate feeling was strong; and P.S. Foner, British Labour and the American Civil War, New York, 1981, who argues that British labour sentiment in general was strongly pro-Northern.

67. Newcastle Weekly Chronicle, May 15, 1869, "Ironside" on The Alabama Question. See also Newcastle Chronicle, March 28, 1863, "Ironside" on English Help to American Slavery.

68. See, for example, W.E. Adams, Memoirs, op.cit., p.420 for Spence's; Beehive, June 6, 1863 for Barker's and C. Godfrey, Chartist Lives — The Anatomy of a Working Class Movement, op.cit., p.429 for Aitken's pro-Confederate campaigns.

69. Newcastle Chronicle, Dec. 20, 1862, "Ironside" on Public Feeling in England and America.

70. See the announcement for the pamphlet in the National Reformer, March, 21, 1863.

71. W.E. Adams, Memoirs, op.cit.., pp.423-424.

72. Newcastle Weekly Chronicle, May 15, 1869, "Ironside" on The Alabama Question. Adams referred that these were "Two of the most crowded and enthusiastic meetings I ever attended".

73. P. Adelman, Victorian Radicalism, The Middle-Class Experience, 1830-1914, London, 1984, p.38.

74. E. Rymer, "The Martyrdom of the Mine", History Workshop Journal, No.1, Spring, 1976, Introduction by R. Neville, pp.220-244. See text, pp.8-9.

75. Newcastle Chronicle, Oct. 8, 1862.

76. Newcastle Chronicle, April 2, 1864.

77. See, for example, Newcastle Weekly Chronicle, Oct.1; Oct.15; Oct. 29; Nov. 12; and Dec. 10, 1864 for reports of Adams's lecturing activities and the fruits of his labour.

78. N. Todd, "Black-On-Tyne: The Black Presence on Tyneside in the 1860s", op.cit., pp.22-23. See also W.E. Adams, Memoirs, op.cit., pp.424-426.

79. See, for example, Newcastle Chronicle, Sept. 5, 1863; Jan.16; Jan 23, 1864. Adams also recalled the incident in The Gossip's Bowl, Newcastle Weekly Chronicle, Feb. 27, 1895.

80. N. Todd, 'Black-On-Tyne: The Black Presence on Tyneside in the 1860s", op.cit., p.23.

81. W.E. Adams, Memoirs, op.cit., p.426.

82. Newcastle Chronicle, April 11, 1863, "Ironside" on The Solidarity of Labour.

83. Ibid., Feb. 21, 1863; Nov. 12, 1864.

84. Ibid., Dec. 31, 1864.

85. Ibid., May 30, 1863.

86. Newcastle Weekly Chronicle, Aug. 25, 1877. "Ironside" on the approaching visit of General Grant, who came at the end of September. Garrison came in 1867, Douglass in 1868 and Reverdy Johnson, the American Ambassador to Britain, in April 1869. See also W.E. Adams, Memoirs, op.cit., pp.528-530 for the remarkable reception afforded Grant.

87. See Newcastle Chronicle, March 7; March 14; 1863, "Ironside" on English Help for Poland.

88. Ibid., August 1, 1863.

89. Ibid., March 7, 1864. Adams referred to him as "A delegate from the Warsaw Provisional Government". See also P. Brock, "Joseph Cowen and the Polish Exiles", op.cit., pp.63-64.

90. Newcastle Chronicle, April 2; Aug. 20, 1864. Public meetings on Parliamentary Reform in Newcastle.

91. Newcastle Weekly Chronicle, July 15, 1865. Election Result: Joseph Cowen, senior — 2, 941 votes; T.E. Headlam — 2,477 votes; S.A. Beaumont — 2,060.

92. W.E. Adams, Memoirs, op.cit., p.526.

93. Newcastle Chronicle, April 16, 1864.

94. Idem.,

95. F.E. Gillespie, Labor and Politics in England, 1850-1867, op.cit., p.218. See also Newcastle Chronicle, May 28, 1864, "The Departure of Garibaldi".

96. Newcastle Chronicle, April 23, 1864.

97. Idem.,

98. Ibid., May 14, 1864. Adams regularly included pieces thereafter on Garibaldi's brave campaigns against the Papacy, supported by Napoleon III's French troops, to complete the unification of Italy. See, for example, Newcastle

Weekly Chronicle, Nov.9, 1867 (after his defeat at Mentana), "The End of the Roman Insurrection — who has Gained by it?"; and for Adams's open delight at the ending of Napoleon's interference in Italy in 1870 by way of the "Collapse of the French Empire" at the hands of Russia, see Newcastle Weekly Chronicle, Aug. 20, 1870, "Ironside" column.

99. Newcastle Weekly Chronicle, Sept. 15, 1866. Preliminary meeting of the Northern Reform League at the Adelphi Hotel, Clayton Street, Newcastle.

100. Ibid., Dec. 29, 1866, "The Year and Its Events".

101. T.J. Nossiter, Influence, Opinion and Political Idioms in Reformed England, 1832-74, op.cit.., p.37 and pp.157-160.

102. Newcastle Weekly Chronicle, Feb. 18, 1865, "The Representation of Newcastle".

103. Ibid., July 8, 1865 Election speech by Joseph Cowen senior.

104. T. Tholfsen, Working Class Radicalism in Mid Victorian England, op.cit. p.323.

105. Newcastle Weekly Chronicle, Nov.10, 1866. The Rev. J.H. Rutherford and Rev. J.C. Street, a leading Unitarian in Newcastle, were also on the Council. Thomas Doubleday, a veteran Chartist in the North East, was another influential member; he could trace a direct line of political agitation back to the 1830s.

106. See, for example, Newcastle Weekly Chronicle, Dec. 15; Jan. 19 and Jan. 26, 1867.

107. Ibid., Feb. 2, 1867. Great Reform Demonstration on the Town Moor and in the new Town Hall, The crowd was estimated to be 50,00.

108. Idem.,

109. E.R. Jones, The Life and Speeches of Joseph Cowen M.P. op.cit., p.25.

110. W.E. Adams, Memoirs, op.cit., p.533.

111. T.J. Nossiter, Influence, Opinion and Political Idioms in Reformed England, 1832-74, op.cit., p.39.

112. Ibid., p.160.

113. For the history of the Miners' campaign see W.H. Maehl, "The North-Eastern Miners' Struggle for the Franchise, 1872-74", International Review of Social History, Vol.XX, 1975, Part 2, pp.198-219.

114. R. Fynes, The Miners of Northumberland and Durham, Blyth, 1873, Reptd. Sunderland, 1923, p.261. There were in Fynes's estimation at this time, 16,000 members of the Northumberland Miners' Mutual Association under Burt's leadership, and 35,000 in the Durham Miners' Association under William Crawford and John Wilson.

115. W.E. Adams, Memoirs, op.cit., p.537.

116. Newcastle Weekly Chronicle, June 21, 1873, "Ironside" on The Miners' Demonstration. See also, for example, Newcastle Weekly Chronicle, Aug.30;

Sept.28; Oct.5 1872; and Feb.8; March 22; April 12, April 19, 1873 for Adams's support for the Miners' cause.

117. Ibid., July 29, 1871, "Ironside" on The New Royal Pension.

118. Ibid., Feb. 25, 1871. Charles Bradlaugh lecturing in Newcastle on "The Possibility of an English Republic". A Republican Club was formed shortly afterwards and Joseph Cowen jr. was elected president. For the nature and significance of Republicanism see F.A. D'Arcy, "Charles Bradlaugh and The English Republican Movement, 1868-1878", Historical Journal, 25 (2), June 1982, pp.367-84.

119. Newcastle Weekly Chronicle, Oct. 25, 1873, 'Ironside" on Morpeth Radicalism.

120. Ibid., March 7, 1874.

121. Newcastle Daily Chronicle, May 15, 1906, Letter by Thomas Burt on the death of W.E. Adams.

122. Newcastle Weekly Chronicle, Dec. 21, 1940, Presentation article to Ernest Welles Adams (Adams's son) on his retirement as editor from the paper.

123. Ibid., Sept. 18, 1875, "Ironside" on Impressions of Ireland.

124. Ibid., April 16, 1881, "Ironside" on The Land Bill.

125. Ibid., June 1, 1872, "Ironside" on Priestly Tyranny in Ireland.

126. Ibid., Feb. 25, 1882, "Ironside" on Home Rule.

127. E.I. Waitt, "John Morley, Joseph Cowen and R. Spence Watson: Liberal Divisions in Newcastle Politics, 1873-1895", op.cit. p.23.

128. Newcastle Weekly Chronicle, Oct. 13, 1879, "Ironside" on The British Empire.

129. Idem.,

130. Idem.,

131. Ibid., March 18, 1876, "Ironside" on The Queen's Title.

132. Ibid., Oct. 13, 1879, "Ironside" on The British Empire.

133. Ibid., Feb. 22, 1879, "Ironside" on How We Treat Our Enemies.

134. Ibid., March 29, 1879, "Ironside" on Cyprus.

135. Ibid., Dec. 9, 1865, The Jamaica Butcheries. For their wider significance see E.J. Feuchtwanger, Democracy and Empire, Britain 1865-1914, London, 1985, pp.30-31.

136. Newcastle Weekly Chronicle, July 3, 1869, "Ironside" on Queensland Slavery; and Jan. 29, 1870, "Ironside" on The Slave Trade in the South Seas.

137. Ibid., Feb. 22, 1873, "Ironside" on Position and Prospects of the Spanish Republic.

138. K. Robbins, Nineteenth Century Britain. England, Scotland, Wales. The Making of a Nation, Oxford, 1989, p.159. The Chronicle, Robbins notes, was also able to flourish in Middlesborough, Stockton and Darlington because it arrived in these towns by an earlier train than that from London.

139. A.J. Lee, The Origins of the Popular Press in England, 1855-1914, op.cit., p.188.

140. Newcastle Weekly Chronicle, April 12, 1873. Letter from G.J. Harney, Boston. March 29, 1873.

141. M. Milne, Newspapers of Northumberland and Durham, op.cit., p.83. According to Milne the Cowenites had not had time to forget, or forgive, these supporters of T.E. Headlam, the Whiggish-Liberal member, who had supported Hamond in the by-election only three weeks before on January 17, 1874. The Chronicle voiced, Milne notes, "embittered suspicions that the Headlamites might not split their votes fairly with Cowen. In reality, it was the Cowenite Liberals who plumped for their hero, leaving Headlam in third place."

142. G. Hodgson, From Smithy To Senate: The Life Story of James Annand, op.cit., pp.64-65. Hodgson does not distinguish between the two papers in his Chapter entitled "The Newcastle Chronicle".

143. E.R. Jones, The Life and Speeches of Joseph Cowen, M.P. op.cit., p.33.

144. See E.I. Waitt, "John Morley, Joseph Cowen and R. Spence Watson: Liberal Divisions in Newcastle Politics 1873-95", op.cit., see generally. Adams steered well clear of the disputes between Cowen and the Newcastle Liberal Association, which Spence Watson had founded in 1874. Cowen saw the Association as a threat and sought to preserve his power from interference. The differences became even more pronounced in the late 1870s when Cowen's Russophobia, strongly awakened by the Eastern Question, saw him vigorously supporting Disraeli's foreign policy. Estrangement continued in the 1880s when Cowen would have nothing to do with John Morley, the other Liberal M.P., and continued to show support for imperialist policies.

145. M. Milne, Newspapers of Northumberland and Durham, op.cit., p.212. See for example, Newcastle Weekly Chronicle, March 27, 1880 and Nov. 7, 1885. Although offering support, Adams was increasingly pre-occupied from the early 1880s with conservation schemes and in 1885 was busy launching the innovative 'Literary supplement' of the Weekly Chronicle. See below, Chapter 5.

146. E. Allan, J.F. Clarke, N. McCord and D.J. Rowe, The North-East Engineers' Strikes of 1871, op.cit. pp.116-117.

147. Newcastle Daily Chronicle, May 18, 1906. Letter by T. Burt on the death of W.E. Adams.

148. A.J. Lee, The Origins of the Popular Press in England, 1855-1914, op.cit., p.110.

149. Holyoake Papers, Microfilm Edition, Introduction by E. Royle, Cambridge 1969. Co-operative Library, Manchester Collection, MM/96636/4. Letter 1,560, J. Cowen to G.J. Holyoake, Sept. 21, 1864 advising Holyoake not to give up the Leader as it was uncertain that he would get the editorship of the Chronicle.

150. A.J. Lee, The Origins of the Popular Press in England, 1855-1914, op.cit., p.110.

151. Ms Eng 180, Letter from James Glover to W.E. Adams, 53, Wells Lane, Streatham, October 8, 1867.

152. I am particularly grateful to Miss Audrey Dalby, the present owner of 32, Holly Avenue and herself a distant relative of W.E. Adams, for providing me with details from the house deeds.

153. T. Tholfsen, Working Class Radicalism in Mid Victorian England, op.cit., p.124.

154. Ibid., p.149.

155. N. Kirk, The Growth of Working Class Reformism in Mid-Victorian England, London, 1985, p.153.

5 Editor in Chief and Homely Reforms

From 1864 until virtually the end of the nineteenth century Adams's life was inseparable from the affairs of the *Weekly Chronicle*. Confirmed in the position of editor in chief in June 1864, he began almost immediately the task of turning a two-penny publication of no particular account into one of the most popular and widely read of all weekly newspapers published outside London.[1] Adams had an intuitive feeling about what a popular newspaper should be: the formula for the *Weekly's* commercial success came to lie in combining a remarkable diversity of reading material with the preservation of literary taste and standards, and a forthrightness in the content, tone and quality of its advanced radicalism.

Beneath a new and eye-catching flowing scroll on which was inscribed the newspaper's title, the front page of the first edition under his control on June 18, 1864 offered readers that standard diet of private and public advertisements carried by nearly all provincial papers; but as an inducement to better sales and business, the print was now copied off a bolder type face, with clearer headings and a neater layout. Inside, the seven pages contained an astonishing variety of reading material. There were the familiar features of earlier years: a couple of pages devoted to local, domestic, foreign,industrial, commercial and Parliamentary news; the familiar back-page reporting of aquatic, athletic and equestrian sports; and the interstices filled with the movements in local agricultural markets, theatrical events, the licensing decisions of the Brewster Sessions, Police and Court reports, and the notification of births, marriages and deaths. Adams now introduced a good deal more politics, with his own "Ironside" column taking a prominent place. Whilst there was always to be at least one full page given to international and national news with verbatim reports on political speeches, he perceived that the future of a weekly newspaper lay in "concentrating on achieving a distinctive type of journalism rather than merely producing a potted version of the daily news of the previous week".[2] In effect, he aimed to create a family newspaper and magazine in one.

The first of the new features in pursuit of such a goal included "Notices to Correspondents", "Events of the Week", "Travel Tips", and "American Items"; there were also two novel pieces with catchy titles — "The Tatler Column by One of the Mob" and "Scissors and Paste"— respectively dealing with topical events and offering historical information on issues of interest. The magazine elements were steadily expanded in the 1870s to include such topics as natural history, popular science, topographical descriptions, local anecdotes, "Notes and Queries", North East folk lore, legend and curiosities, biographies, genealogies, serialised fiction and a range of home-centred amusements like illustrated puzzles, games of chess and draughts. There were a number of other, regular features which added considerably to the colour, variety and attractiveness of the paper. One pioneering feature, begun in 1880, was a weekly "Ladies Column": as one of the first of its kind in British journalism[3] it dealt with all matters affecting women; and it was from here that the campaign against the Crinoline was launched when women were threatened with a resurrection of "one of the most absurd follies of fashion";[4] and the appearance of a weekly letter in 1889[5] from "Geraldine", Adams's talented daughter Ada Eveline, also gave female readers a more personalised touch as she too covered the world of fashion, motherhood, cookery, household management and mildly feminist issues from the perspective of a young woman growing up on Tyneside. Another was the "Gossip's Bowl" by Robin Goodfellow. Here, Adams mixed local chitchat from the Northern Counties with a unique, personalized political commentary of his own: it attempted to relate the ongoing concerns of the "Ironside" column to the achievements of an heroic past as revealed in printed reminiscences in the *Weekly* of those Chartist survivors like R. Gammage, G.J. Harney, J. West and E. Jones, and co-operative pioneers, G.J. Holyoake and Lloyd Jones with whom he could closely identify. Judging by the scores of letters Adams received on Chartist or radical nostalgia over the years, this unique device re-awakened the consciousness of many readers, whose collective traditions of political struggle and involvement stretched back to 1839. Finally, there was a "Household Corner" offering tips and advice on running the home; a "Doctor's Department" which prided itself on "how health is to be preserved rather than how disease is to be cured";[6] a "Lawyer's Corner" operating on the same principle in respect of litigation; and an "Open Council" which, in offering a platform to all kinds of 'advanced' political opinion, testified to the liberality of Adams as editor.

Sales of the *Weekly* rose steadily: it had a distribution network with sixty eight agents nation-wide and was readily available in New York, Paris and Antwerp; by December 1875 its circulation was reported to have passed the 45,000 figure;[7] and judging by the appeal to which the advertisements were directed, the readership now embraced not only its traditional supporters amongst Tyneside artisans and Coalfield pit-men, but also a growing army of lower middle class clerks and small businessmen. Such was its success that by 1885 Adams was able to realise his ambition: the "Literary Supplement" was introduced as a separate section; it was devoted entirely to literary, historical, antiquarian and artistic features relating both to the North East and the country as a whole.[8] According to M. Milne, this innovation was "an early example of the format that weekly publications have increasingly adopted during the twentieth century".[9] The final thrust in the *Chronicle* office's late nineteenth century reorganization was made later in the year when the half-penny *Evening Chronicle* was launched.[10] This low cost publication led the field in local and commercial news; it also built on the *Weekly's* reputation for reporting organized sport in the coalfield[11] by catering expressly for that explosion of interest in professional football which gripped the region from the late 1880s.[12]

Adams's success stemmed from a number of inter-connected factors. Firstly, he made the *Weekly Chronicle* a focus for community consciousness by promoting a number of distinct features which transcended the contradictions of everyday life. One of these was the "Notes and Queries" column: it bound newspaper and reader in a close two-way relationship concerning the exchange of miscellaneous information and knowledge; and for their participation up to four hundred readers at a time from widely differing backgrounds were invited to unique contributers' gatherings or 'conversaziones' at the *Chronicle's* expense in Newcastle in the 1890s.[13] Adams was shrewd enough to realise that as journalism was becoming big business, the mass reading public no longer formed an identifying relationship with the editor. There was a touch of old-world charm in his speech when he told the assembled that:

> "Gatherings of this kind would not have been possible except for the peculiar relationship that exists between the readers of the 'Weekly Chronicle' and those who are concerned in its production. That relationship is not a mere trading relationship ...We are friends of fellow-workers rather than mere buyers and sellers."[14]

"Notes and Queries" was the storehouse for Adams's next community based venture — the collection of material on local history and legend, tradition and story. This came to fruition with the publication by him of the *Monthly Chronicle of North Country Lore and Legend*, which lasted from 1887 until 1892. The context for this local antiquarianism is also interesting. At a time when there was a growing intensification of interest in what constituted the national or dominant sense of Englishness,[15] Adams was reasserting a provincial cultural identity. His avowed intention was to preserve for posterity the great wealth of history and tradition, legend and story, poetry and song, dialect and folk-lore which abounded in Northumberland and Durham. Readers were given a foretaste in the *Weekly* of their findings, which were later to appear in the more durable and illustrated *Monthly* magazine and for which leather binding was also available at the end of a twelve monthly run.[16] Amongst the two thousand odd subjects covered by 1892 were such fascinating pieces as "Men of Mark 'twixt Tyne and Tweed"; "North Country Slogans and Songs"; "Wit and Humour"; "Oliver Goldsmith on the Tyne and Wear"; "Willie Carr, the Strong Man of Blyth"; "Jean Paul Marat in Newcastle"; "Blaydon Races"; "Coal in the North"; and "Pitmen's Songs".

It is virtually impossible to assess how far the authenticity of such material had been compromised by the collectors or mediated by Adams's and his friend's — the Tyneside merchant Richard Welford — co-editorial work before entering print. One historian of folk song has strongly argued that nineteenth century collectors were prone to removing erotic references, excluded songs with drink and minimised those dealing with struggle.[17] Notwithstanding these kind of doubts, Adams helped bring together, via the platform of the *Chronicle*, the celebratory display of local cultural diversity and antiquity in such a way as to project a regional identity and unity amongst an urban-based readership that was keen on nostalgia and curious about its pre-industrial ways of life.

A sense of community was also cemented by Adams's ongoing policy of inviting readers to enter competitions of various kinds. Prize essay competitions were run for such features as the best literary essays and poetical compositions, and, as the paper spoke the language of co-operatives and trade unionism, for prize pieces which furthered the aims and objectives of these forms of collective working class self-help; it also offered challenge cups in rowing, cycling, bowls and chess; and, in competition with the *London Graphic*, provided all readers with a free coloured picture in the late 1880s. These were of a distinctive type. Adams, remembering how great a part the artisan, pit-man and fisherman played in developing the industry of the North, was able to reproduce on single-sheet form those paintings of his friend, the artist Ralph Hedley (1848-1913), a frequent exhibitor at the Royal Academy, in which he had sympathetically depicted various aspects of the dignity of nineteenth century labouring life in the North East.[18]

A second major factor explaining Adams's editorial success can be found in the way in which he preserved literary taste and standards, firstly in relation to the demand for serialised fiction in the post 1870 period and secondly in the way he responded to the arrival of a different style in press reporting, the so-called 'new journalism'. Following the creation of W.F. Tillotson's 'fiction bureau' in 1873, the first systematic attempt was made to syndicate new fiction in newspapers. Syndication was the serial publication of a novel simultaneously in a number of different provincial or local papers. The *Weekly Chronicle* was one of the first journals to get involved with this practice in 1873 when it serialised the novel "Taken at the Flood" written by Miss Braddon, a leading Victorian fiction writer. There followed a virtual army of novelists — sixty two in all by 1893 — offering serialised fiction, some of whom were or became household names; these included H. Rider Haggard, Thomas Hardy, Conan Doyle, Florence Marryat, Hall Caine, Captain Mayne Reid, Wilkie Collins and Jules Verne.[19]

In his dealings both with these and lesser known Victorian novelists Adams's policy remained the same: to provide the public with the best, wholesome fiction in the market, "quite regardless of the expenditure necessary to procure it".[20] Fortunately, there is still in print a series of letters that passed between Adams and Captain Mayne Reid, a best-seller of adventure stories for boys, in which we catch a glimpse of Adams' steadfast adherence to the preservation of taste when assessing a number of variables.[21]

Between 1876-79, Reid tried to syndicate three of his novels in the *Weekly Chronicle.* These were "Gwen Wynn, A Romance of the Wye (1876)"; "The Free Lances, A Romance of the Mexican Valley" (1879); and "No Quarter! A Cromwellian Novel" (1879). In their negotiations over the first, Reid had to assure Adams that:

> "I can promise that the tale will be of a pure morality and not tainted with disgusting murders, seductions, and elopments with other men's wives — incidents which seem to be the staple of interest in most modern novels, to the disgrace of our English Literature."[22]

Adams was interested, but they could not agree over precisely when it should appear in the *Weekly*; the latter's "legitimate exclusive district" of influence was defined as "Cumberland, Northumberland, Westmorland and Durham", yet Reid, who was under financial pressure, was not prepared to guarantee against any other Northern-based provincial newspapers having use of the story at this time. A similar fate befell "The Free Lances". However, in the case of the third, "No Quarter", the assurance Adams received over its quality outweighed all other factors. The reasons for this are revealed by Reid himself when first assessing whether the novel would be acceptable to Adams:

> "I frankly told you it would be very radical in tone, taking the Cromwellian side, and bitterly hostile to Toryism, and the Charles's. You gave me gratification by saying, that this tone, so far from being offensive to you, would be exactly what the *Newcastle Chronicle* would wish."[23]

Adams promptly paid Reid £50 in advance for twenty-six weeks' instalments, which appeared in the *Weekly Chronicle* from April 3, 1880.[24]

While always full of enterprise and quick to avail himself of every new development which would enable the *Weekly* to keep fully abreast of the times, Adams relied for success upon the accuracy of the news he purveyed, and the vigour and sound reasoning of his leading articles, rather than upon the snippety sensationalism of the 'new journalism'.[25] In Adams's mind this was but a passing phase of journalism, but he warned that:

> "If the 'new journalism' should find a foothold in this country, our newspapers will become as useless for historic purposes as the newspapers of the United States. The object of the people who conduct the 'new journals' is not so much to record occurrences as to make use of occurrences for the purpose of tickling the taste of the vulgar."[26]

Although of course Adams's son, Ernest Welles, found himself having to adjust the paper to the needs of the twentieth century, which he did so successfully until the exigencies of the time forced its closure in 1940, the old formula of combining instruction with amusement, entertainment with usefulness was largely retained.

For upholding taste and editing a remarkably stimulating newspaper Adams won considerable praise, most noticeably from across the Atlantic. One competent American critic, Paul Carus, the editor in the 1890s of the *Open Court,* a Chicago journal with a high intellectual standard, described the *Weekly* as the "best paper in the world".[27] A similar tribute has been made by the twentieth century American historian, A.R. Schoyen:

> "its foreign and domestic news-coverage, special features, and correspondence page ... make a modern reader aware of the disastrous inverted alchemy Alfred Harmsworth and others worked on the British press."[28]

Unlike Harmsworth Adams was concerned to treat his readers both with respect and to impart knowledge at every available opportunity. Such an ethos reflected his long-standing belief in the value of education for citizenship, duty and progress.

The final factor explaining the success story of W.E. Adams's journalism must be sought by reference to Adams's genius for independent editorial authority and an ability to work with and inspire those under his particular management. By the early 1870s the whole *Chronicle* operation was virtually big business. Considerable expansion necessitated two moves before the *Chronicle* found a suitable home in the commodious offices on Westgate Street, opposite the Stephenson Memorial. Here, by 1869 in excess of one hundred staff were employed in what the *Weekly Chronicle* referred to as its "literary, commercial and mechanical departments".[29] By the late 1880s in response to increasing demand for the *Daily*, *Evening* and *Weekly Chronicles*, Joseph Cowen purchased new double web printing machines and ordered the state of the art in printing, the Linotype, of which twenty six were operational by 1898.[30] No evidence has been unearthed to suggest that printing staff were put out of work because of these innovations.

By virtue of his skill as a compositor Adams appears from what little we know to have enjoyed a good relationship with the printing staff, being a frequent guest of their annual 'Chapel' dinners and social gatherings.[31] More revealing are the comments of his literary colleagues. Aaron Watson, his assistant editor for about eleven years, said that his work had "many fine qualities of style";[32] William Longstaffe, who moved to the *Chronicle's* London Office, said "he was one of the nicest and fairest men I ever met";[33] John Bell, one of Adams's sub-editor's, wrote "I owed a great deal to the example he set before me and to the encouragment he was always ready to give;[34] and I. Mitchinson, another colleague, paid this glowing tribute:

> "The late Mr. Adams lived a noble, unostentatious life, a very pattern of kindness and fidelity to truth, whilst his tolerance, love of fair play and desire to assist others were beyond praise; he was one of 'nature's true gentlemen'".[35]

Adams's ability to exercise editorial power in relation to Joseph Cowen, the *Weekly's* proprietor and his employer, was more problematic. Cowen ran his newspapers, as he did his works, on paternalistic lines; and there was on occasions direct interference if he judged the subject to be unsuitable or impolitic. Certainly Adams was a man who must have benefitted from his own discretion; but it would be totally unrealistic to think that he was in any way tied to the coat-tails of Cowen the press baron.

Two incidents serve to illustrate his independence of mind and integrity of character in the editorial chair of the *Weekly Chronicle*. The first of these occurred over policy with regard to the Eastern Question between 1876 and 1877. In May 1876 about 12,000 Bulgarians were massacred after rebelling against the Sultan of Turkey. On September 6 Gladstone added to the mood of widespread indignation when be brought out his pamphlet, "The Bulgarian Horrors and the Question of the East." His twin aims were to see Turkey punished and then removed from European influence; and to allow Bulgaria, Bosnia and Herzegovina the right to become independent states. At first Cowen, James Annand (the editor of the *Daily*) and Adams displayed a united front in support of Gladstone. However, when Russia, the ostensible protector of Bulgarian Christians, invaded Turkey in April 1877 it reawakened Cowen's deep-seated Russophobia; he could not share the enthusiasm of other Radical Liberals for Russia's new defensive role. Instead he increasingly allied himself in Parliament with Disraeli and the Conservatives, who saw in the Russo-Turkish war and the subsequent Treaty of San Stefano of March 1878, dictated by Russia to a prostrate foe, yet another phase of Czarist expansionism at Britain's expense.

At the *Daily* and *Weekly*, there followed a running battle through 1877 as both Annand and Adams openly opposed their proprietor's Disraelian line. Indeed, as I. Waitt has suggested, "the *Chronicle* was at war with itself".[36] In Adams's case, it is important to realise that he was not in any sense pro-Russian; but he did believe Alexander II's (1818-81) public assurances given in November 1876 that he had no war aims in Turkey or India; and he was particularly encouraged by the Czar's position on the emancipation of the serfs[37] vis à vis Turkish attrocities against the Bulgars.[38] Both Adams and Annand were also at pains to point out to Cowen that Gladstone's policies did not favour Russia: they argued forcefully that what was being sought was independence for the Balkan States, not the supplanting of one foreign oppressor by another. To protest about British interests, as Cowen was doing publicly and in print, in such a context appeared to Adams to be "mean and selfish and contemptible".[39]

Cowen made no attempt to dismiss his out of line editors, but when Annand fell ill in the Autumn of 1877 the *Daily* reverted to a Cowenite stance. On his recovery, Cowen suggested to Annand that the post placed too great a strain on him and that perhaps he should resign from the editorship.[40] Annand took the hint and resigned at the end of 1877. By contrast, Cowen appears to have allowed Adams a completely free editorial hand. In turn, Adams did not flinch from upholding the Gladstonian line until the Eastern Question no longer warranted public consideration.[41]

The second incident which severely strained their relationship occurred two years later when Cowen, clearly still smarting from the rebuffs of the Eastern Question, took Adams to task over matters relating to his reporting of Liberal members' views on coercion policy in Ireland. Albert Grey, the Liberal M.P. for South Northumberland and later a Liberal Unionist, had become the specific target of Adams's acerbic comments because the former had demanded more vigorous coercion measures from Gladstone's Liberal Ministry.[42] Grey had evidently complained to Cowen in private about Adams's censures and while Cowen was no friend of Irish coercion, he used the incident as a pretext for rounding on Adams's editorial conduct in no uncertain terms:

> "As you know, although I have disapproved of the general tone, and a good deal of what has been written in the *Weekly* for some time, I have never interfered with it. But I would like you to bear in mind in anything you say about Mr. Grey and almost any other Liberal member, that whoever else advocates an unqualified support of any ministry, it is scarcely the part of a paper professing to be radical to do this ... I will have a conversation with you on

> various matters that I think require revision in connection with the paper. I think its contents are becoming too antiquarian."[43]

Judging by the unchanged tone and stridency of the leader columns when the occasion demanded, Cowen, short of dismissing a recalcitrant employee, was unsuccessful over the years in his attempts at curtailing Adams's freedom and independence in editorial matters on the *Weekly Chronicle.*

There is no doubt that Cowen had a deep and abiding respect for Adams's conduct as a journalist. In conversation with Thomas Burt, the miners' leader, Cowen is reported to have said:

> "There's your friend, Adams, nothing on earth would ever induce him to write a line contrary to his convictions, or that he did not honestly believe to be true and right."[44]

His friendship for Adams aside, Cowen probably did not wish to disrupt a paper which was successful in the way it remained representative of the wide spectrum of Radical opinion;[45] he also did not allow personal feelings "to interfere with good business even if they did interfere with his politics".[46]

From the mid 1870s Adams increasingly used editorial power to promote the *Weekly* as a vehicle of propaganda for a number of 'homely' reforms or causes which progressively filled his time and preoccupied his thoughts. As a young compositor in a literate occupation growing up in Cheltenham, Adams had become conscious of his unique identity at the interface between a traditionally oral and a new print-based literate society and culture.[47] In his working class district of the Spa, where the main forms of discourse for transmitting political ideas were the spoken words from platform speeches, personal canvassing, songs and day to day conversations, Adams was able to record of himself:

> "To be able to read and write was a distinction then. Anybody who could do more was almost accounted a phenomenon."[48]

The regular Sunday morning Chartist gathering of illiterates, which included the crippled shoemaker Larry, at Adams's household must surely have made him conscious of what influence the tools of literacy could bring as he enthusiastically read aloud and interpreted events reported in the *Northern Star*. By the late 1850s, following his first flush of personal satisfaction in preparing a well-received piece of propaganda on behalf of Polish refugees in the *Cheltenham Free Press* and imbued with the ideas of Linton on the transforming power of the printed word over the lives and minds of the people, Adams became more than ever convinced of Ernest Jones's ringing remark in the *People's Paper* that:

> "A movement that has not the mighty organ of the press at its command is but half a movement."[49]

Adams picked up on this tradition of press power used by the Chartists, but his campaign to influence readers' children's minds into joining an army of kindness towards animals, begun in the *Weekly* in 1876, depended very much on their ability to read and write. Fortunately, great strides had already been made in the removal of illiteracy.[50] Sunday Schools, Church of England and Nonconformist day schools, Ragged Schools, mutual instructuion groups and not least the influence of the home supplied a demand for reading skills.[51] The real benefit therefore of the Forster Education Act in 1870 was not so much in increasing the onset of literacy, as in maintaining the momentum just when the formidable obstacle of urban slums were coming to the forefront of educational campaigns.[52]

Adams, the innovative editor,[53] believed in a system of morality which embraced an unconditional responsibility to animals:

> "Nature is not a dead hourse beneath a living rider; but one thought, one idea, proceeding from higher to lower animates both."[54]

The spectacle of animal cruelty began to loom large in the public persona at this time, not least because of the debasing impact of the "penny dreadfuls" literature on young minds. These were alleged to have encouraged widespread anti-social attitudes, unrestrained cruelty and criminal behaviour in an adolescent working class,[55] which was increasingly identified as a distinct sociological phenomenon growing up devoid of community spirit in the first mass society in modern history.[56] Adams's revulsion against cruelty to animals led him to initiate a propaganda campaign aimed at instilling in children the idea of kindness and compassion to all living things; he wanted to foster at an impressionable age a new benevolence, respect and responsibility towards the "brute creation" which he hoped would also be translated by the onset of adulthood into humanitarian acts of public duty, citizenship and community responsibility.[57] In essence, he believed that human nature was inherently good and that when kindness was stimulated, its gentle influence would generate a new respect for, and understanding of, humanity.

As the genial old gentleman, "Uncle Toby" (a name taken from the good deeds of an important character in Lawrence Sterne's, "Tristram Shandy"), Adams founded the Dicky Bird Society in October 1876;[58] he devoted two columns entirely to the

Children's Corner in the *Weekly*; and under a wood-cut depicting an old man in an arm-chair, surrounded by small children and accompanied by a guiding spirit, his feathered friend "Father Chirpie", wrote stories about kindness to animals in language they could understand, printed tales and poems, and entered into extensive correspondence with young readers on how to cultivate the sentiments of compassion to all living things.

The Dicky Bird Society allowed a unique interaction between the *Weekly* and its young readers. Children were encouraged to join by taking a pledge of kindness; in return Adams printed every name first in the *Weekly Chronicle* and then felicitously recorded the increase in membership in what children came to understand was Uncle Toby's special but very real "Big Book". The Society could boast a number of attractions. Firstly, it was gender free: to encourage propagandism, successful canvassers of new members obtained honours according to the number of recruits they introduced; and when they had brought in fifty co-workers they were called captains or companions. The Society received a great impulse from the new schools: masters and mistresses became important proselytizers in the cause and hundreds of village schools signed the pledge together.[59] Secondly, it was a classless campaign. Adams was as anxious to attract what he called the "Street Arabs of London, Newcastle, Liverpool and Manchester"[60] as he was to reproach those whose parents were guilty of succumbing to such trends in personal fashion which involved the destruction of thousands of birds, in order to use their spectacular plumage to decorate ladies' bonnets, fancy articles of dress or even Valentine cards.[61]

The Society enjoyed extraordinary success. From very small beginnings the number of members steadily rose to 100,000 in ten years; and when the membership reached 250,000 in July 1894 a great demonstration was held on the Town Moor recreation ground in Newcastle, where 30,000 children of successive generations of the Dicky Bird Society gathered to take part in the day-long festival of celebrations. As the membership rose, others imitated its example. Bands of Mercy and Humane Societies of a similar kind appeared in connection with such provisional newspapers as the *Leigh Chronicle*, *Huddersfield Examiner*, *Preston Guardian*, *North Cheshire Herald* and Cassell's children's publication, *Little Folks*.[62] Several of the London journals — notably the *Daily News*, the *Standard* and the *Pall Mall Gazette* — devoted leading articles to the subject, all of them extolling the objects and principles of the Society.[63] In August 1879 a great and special honour befell Adams: he was awarded a diploma by the R.S.P.C.A. in recognition of his sterling work.[64] By 1898, at the time of his retirement, the membership world-wide had risen to 300,000 with special branches in Norway, Australia, Canada, Portugal and the U.S.A.; and it had some famous people as honorary members, including Florence Nightingale, Rev. Dr. Westcott, Bishop of Durham, John Ruskin, Sir Henry Irving, Baroness Burdett-Coutts and H.M. Stanley, the explorer.[65]

The indefatigable Adams also extended the nature of the Society's work in the late 1880s. To encourage kindness to animals amongst the pit-men and hauliers, the *Weekly Chronicle* offered prizes from 1882, in connection with the May Day Procession of Horses, to the drivers of pit-ponies and coal cart horses which showed the best condition and treatment.[66] By 1885 Adams was offering prizes for the best essays on kindness to animals, through the Newcastle Branch of the R.S.F.C.A.[67] The most ambitious move, launched in 1890 and in keeping with the spirit of the age, was his Christmas Charity Toy Scheme.[68] Society members were asked to make or collect toys for distribution among the sick in hospital, or for the inmates of work-houses and orphans in asylums. By 1898, when Adams could proudly claim that

> "upwards of 100,000 toys have helped to gladden the hearts of the victims of poverty and misfortune,"[69]

the scheme had virtually become a civic occasion in the Yuletide activities of Newcastle and Gateshead.[70]

It is virtually impossible to measure the effectiveness of such a scheme on the minds and manners of young children and adolescents. We have no real way of calculating how much cruelty had thus been prevented. The Newcastle branch of the R.S.P.C.A. introduced a note of realism in its assessment of the influence of the "D.B.S." in promoting kindness to animals at the annual general meeting of 1882. According to one spokesman:

> "Although he was not sanguine enough to believe that all those who took the pledge kept it, still if even half of that number did, it was a matter of great congratulation."[71]

Significantly, the R.S.P.C.A. nationally continued to attach considerable importance to the educational work which Adams had initiated in the *Weekly*. By 1892, it had over eight hundred "Bands of Mercy" committed to recruiting "the younger generation for humanity".[72] Perhaps one sign of the success of the Dicky Bird Society was the correspondence the *Weekly Chronicle* received from the troubled minds of former members fighting in the Boer War between 1899-1902. The British Army was chiefly dependent on animal transport; but animal casualties, particularly horses and mules, became something of a national disgrace;[73] and the *Weekly* became a platform for exposing their suffering as ex-members wrote home in anguish about the scenes of lingering death from injury, thirst or starvation resulting from want of proper care.[74] Public opinion was outraged in Britain. Adams must have been well-pleased to learn how, within two years of exposing such animal cruelty, the Conservative Government had been moved to set up the Royal Army Veterinary Corps.[75]

Adams further exploited his editorial visibility to direct public attention towards the pressing need for a free Public Library service in Newcastle-upon-Tyne.[76] In 1874, after the public resolution to adopt the Public Libraries Act had been passed, W.E. Adams was one of only two co-opted members on the Borough Council's influential and founding Library Committee. In the long contest between the opponents and advocates of the Public Library over financial and siting issues which followed the appointment of the Committee, Adams was a staunch and resourceful ally of Alderman Dr. Henry Newton, the Committee's chairman. By means of letters and articles in the *Weekly* (often under the pseudonym of "Ironside"), and by various manifestoes, Adams managed "adroitly to keep the library question before the public without the subject ever palling".[77] Undoubtedly, he helped to create that climate of public opinion in the city which ensured a successful vote at Council meetings and the opening finally in 1880 of Newcastle's first Public Library in part of the old Mechanics' Institute in New Bridge Street.[78]

Adams was also instrumental in building up the Library stock. In 1880 when it opened the lending department could boast a total of 19,783 volumes, but the collection of material had been going on for some time. In 1876, for example, Adams had, on behalf of the Committee, personally received both a fine collection of books and documents, a gift from the "Commonwealth of Massachusetts",[79] and also a parcel of publications from the Cobden Club which had been sent by T.B. Potter, the Manchester reformer and Liberal M.P.[80] The process of book collecting for juvenile needs and the work of the Dicky Bird Society in fostering the reading habit were also symbolically brought together in 1880: Adams was honoured with an invitation by the Council to write a "Preface to the Juvenile Catalogue", which, when the Library first opened, already contained entries for over a thousand children's books.[81] In the 1890s, it is clear that Adams's scheme of teaching children to be kind to animals led directly to an even greater demand for books on animals and nature study.[82] The new building, adjoining the Mechanics' Institute, was finally opened in 1882 and the Library steadily expanded. Shortly before his death in 1906, Adams made a final presentation of over 200 volumes and pamphlets to the Library.[83] Amongst these were works by Charles Bradlaugh, George Julian Harney, W.J. Linton and George J.

Holyoake; it also included such writings as the *Red Republican, British Controversialist, Cooper's Journal* and *Friend of the People.*

The constant growth of Newcastle from the late 1870s also led Adams to direct public attention to an overlapping concern: the provision of drink-free recreational facilities for its toiling inhabitants in the form of the preservation of open spaces or commons, the creation of parks for the people and, more generally, in ornamenting the streets and open spaces of the city with trees.[84] As early as 1867 Adams, following his visit to the Paris Exhibition, was commentating favourably on how the work of Baron Haussmann was improving the French capital through, amongst other things, the provision of parks and tree-lined boulevards.[85] In Newcastle, he urged the Council and the freemen of the borough not only to preserve its two large open spaces — the Town Moor and the Leazes — from urban encroachment, but also to turn them into "People's Parks" with walks and arbors. A scheme for such improvements covering thirty-five acres in the city was finally realised in December 1873.[86] Later, in 1879, its Parks' Committee purchased Heaton Park in the east end of the borough.[87]

Fortunately for Newcastle, too, it had a powerful private benefactor: through the generosity of the wealthy industrialist, Sir William Armstrong, head of the giant Elswick engineering firm, twenty-six acres were added in 1880 at Heaton in what was henceforth called Armstrong Park; and by 1884 his beautiful grounds, banquetting hall and walks at Jesmond Dene had also become the property of the public.[88] From the 1860s on industrial Tyneside, there was also a ferocious debate, as Tony Seaton has explored, about environmental pollution and conservation led by George Clayton Atkinson (1808-77) on behalf of what might be considered as "the first Green Lobby movement in the North East", the Tyneside Naturalists' Field Club.[89] It played a big part in Parliament passing the Alkali Act of 1863 in an attempt to reduce atmospheric pollution through acid discharges; but it failed to control the harmful effects created by others such as the copper, iron and coal industries. Undeterred, Atkinson commissioned a five-year Northumberland Tree Survey in 1873 in order to document and photograph the extent of the existing damage to trees by atmospheric contamination. In so doing, he continued to draw attention to an industrial scandal which had reached crisis proportions. Such activities helped persuade the Government to amend the Alkali Act in 1874 and set up a Royal Commission in 1876.

Adams's particular contribution to the urban conservation debate in Newcastle, albeit modest, took two forms. Firstly, he was actively involved in the late 1870s in the development of Portland Park, Jesmond, as a bowling green.[90] Initially, it had an exclusive list of subscribers, but under his presidency it was turned by 1880 into a popular, public club run for the purposes of "wholesome amusement and healthy recreation".[91] Secondly, Adams was the founder of the celebrated "Newcastle Tree Planting Society".[92] Like-minded naturalists and environmentalists followed Adams's lead in his "Arbor" campaigns, advertised through the *Weekly*, of making Newcastle a pleasanter and healthier place in which to live.[93] To this end, the Town Moor and Leazes were planted with clumps of trees following the Council's Parks initiative in 1879, and the monotony of the main streets, (particularly the North Road), suburban thoroughfares and avenues of the city relieved by the planting of trees, shrubs and flowers.[94] The Council was also approached to make its contribution over areas in which it had a vested interest,[95] and local employers were asked to consider ways in which the smoke nuisance could be alleviated so as to lessen the possibilities of defoliation.[96] In 1893, for financial reasons, the Tree Planting Society was disbanded and its work transferred into the care of the Council.[97] However, in a quiet way — Adams's initimable style — much had been achieved: the tree-lined city avenues and magnificent plantations surrounding the Town Moor, like the Public Library, stand as the most enduring testimonies to his contribution to the public life of late nineteenth century Newcastle.

On the face of it these small pieces of assorted reforms appear unconnected. They were however all inspired by Mazzinian notions about what constituted public duty and citizenship. So far as the absorbing pursuit of running a flourishing newspaper business could be reconciled with promoting homely reforms, Adams's concern for animal rights, the moral and mental training of children, the inter-dependency between humanity and nature and the need to preserve or maintain a healthy balance between these forces in the artificial urban context, were all part of a pattern of thought which derived from ideas about service to and respect for the chain of life activity of all living things in the community. In the final analysis, they represent Adams's propagandist attempts in the late nineteenth century world to move one step nearer to realising the goals of the "Republic as a system of morals, a creed, a faith, a new and benign gospel".[98] Perhaps it was as a fitting tribute to his belief in progress through reason, that on his tombstone in Jesmond Cemetery should be inscribed this apt and rhyming couplet:

> "Each kindness shown to birds and men
> is sure to flutter back again."

Notes

1. A. Watson, A Newspaper Man's Memories, op.cit., p.27.

2. M. Milne, Newspapers of Northumberland and Durham, op.cit., p.65.

3. J. Saville, Introduction, Memoirs, op.cit., pp.18-19.

4. Newcastle Weekly Chronicle, Dec. 18, 1880, "The Ladies Corner".

5. Ibid., Feb. 23, 1889. It ran until the mid-1890s.

6. Ibid., Feb. 22, 1879.

7. Ibid., Dec. 25 1875. At this time the Newcastle Daily Chronicle had a circulation of 30,900 per day.

8. Ibid., Oct. 3, 1885. The price of the Weekly and its 'Literary Supplement' together was two-pence; sold separately, the Weekly, which continued with political matters and news of the week, cost one penny.

9. M. Milne, Newspapers of Northumberland and Durham, op.cit., p.211.

10. Newcastle Weekly Chronicle, Oct. 3, 1885. The Evening was launched in November.

11. A. Metcalfe, "Organised Sport in the Mining Communities of South Northumberland, 1880-1889", Victorian Studies, Summer, 1982, Vol. 25, No.4, pp.469-495, in particular pp.469-470.

12. W.E. Adams, Memoirs, op.cit., p.600.

13. Newcastle Weekly Chronicle, May 23, 1891, "Conversazione at the new Assembly Rooms".

14. Ibid., Jan. 1, 1898, "Our Contributors' Gathering".

15. See, for example, R. Colls and P.Dodd, (eds.), Englishness: Politics and Culture, 1880-1920, London, 1986. See generally.

16. Newcastle Weekly Chronicle, Jan. 16, 1892.

17. D. Harker, Fakesong: The Manufacture of British 'Folk Song', 1700 to the Present Day, Milton Keynes, 1985. p.122.

18. Newcastle Weekly Chronicle, Feb. 23, 1889 for a feature on Hedley's life and work. The scheme beginning in December 1889 lasted several years. For an assessment of Hedley's place in modern British art see C. Wood (ed.), The Dictionary of Victorian Painters, Woodbridge, 1978, Rept. 1981, p.216 and J. Trenherz, Hard Times, Social Realism in Victorian Art, London, 1987, pp.117-118; and J. Millard, Ralph Hedley, Tyneside Painter, Newcastle, 1990. Some of the works Adams utilized included "Going Home" (a painting of two stalwart miners, father and son, returning home from the mine), "The Fishermen's Sunday" and "The Market Morning".

19. Newcastle Weekly Chronicle, Jan. 28, 1893. For a complete list of the novelists.

20. Idem.,

21. G. Pollard, "Novels in Newspapers: Some Unpublished Letters of Captain Mayne Reid", Review of English Studies, Vol.XVI, Part II, 1942, pp.72-85.

22. Ibid., p.74.

23. Ibid., p.80.

24. Ibid., p.83.

25. For the 'new journalism' see S. Koss, The Rise and Fall of the Political Press in Britain, Vol.I, London, 1981, pp.343-346.

26. Newcastle Weekly Chronicle, Nov. 30, 1889, The Gossip's Bowl. See also Feb. 22, 1890 for another outburst of hostility: "'New Journalism' is everything that panders in the form of news to the coarser appetites of the people. It comprises the scum of sensation and the essence of vulgarity, and it is composed of paragraphs which give distorted ideas of life."

27. A.R. Schoyen, The Chartist Challenge, op.cit., p.275.

28. Idem.,

29. Newcastle Weekly Chronicle, April 3, 1869.

30. Ibid., Jan. 1, 1898.

31. Ibid., Jan. 31, 1880; Jan. 28, 1882.

32. A. Watson, A Newspaper Man's Memories, op.cit., p.55.

33. Memorial to W.E. Adams, Newspaper Cuttings L920 A219 op.cit. p.103. Letter from W. Longstaffe, Chronicle Offices 84, Fleet Street, Aug. 15, 1906.

34. Ibid., p.85. Letter from John Bell, 50, The Chase, Clapham Common, London, July 29, 1906.

35. Ibid., p.106. Letter from I. Mitchinson, 16, Albert Road, Stockton-on-Tees, May 7, 1907.

36. E.I. Waitt, "John Morley, Joseph Cowen and R. Spence Watson: Liberal Divisions in Newcastle Politics, 1873-95", op.cit., p.87.

37. Newcastle Weekly Chronicle, May 16, 1874, "Ironside" on the Czar.

38. Ibid., Aug. 26, 1876, "Ironside" on The Horrors of Ottoman Rule; see also Nov. 25, 1876, The Eastern Question.

39. J.O. Baylen and N.J. Gossman (eds.), Biographical Dictionary of Modern British Radicals, Vol.III, op.cit., Maurice Milne's contribution on W.E. Adams p.16.

40. E.I. Waitt, 'John Morley, Joseph Cowen and Robert Spence Watson: Liberal Divisions in Newcastle Politics, 1873-95", op.cit., pp.88-89.

41. Newcastle Weekly Chronicle, March 15, 1879. Adams was reviewing Cowen's Parliamentary activity.

42. Cowen Collection, B415, 1881 pp.27-29. Undated letter by Joseph Cowen to W.E. Adams.

43. Idem.,

44. Newcastle Daily Chronicle, May 18, 1906, Letter to the paper from Thomas Burt on the death of W.E. Adams.

45. J. Saville, Introduction, Memoirs, op.cit., p.23.

46. E.I. Waitt, "John Morley, Joseph Cowen and R. Spence Watson: Liberal Divisions in Newcastle Politics, 1873-95", op.cit., p.89. It is important to remember, too, that as the Newcastle Daily Chronicle veered increasingly towards Unionism, the Gladstonians in Newcastle were left without a journal until the Newcastle Daily Leader appeared, under Annand's editorship, in September, 1885.

47. For an appreciation of the transition from orality to literacy in the nineteenth century see D. Vincent, Literacy and Popular Culture, England, 1750-1914, Cambridge, 1989. See generally. For Adams's role as a kind of "earnest worker" in the reciprocal relationship between the printed and spoken word, and the ability to influence others, see p.264.

48. W.E. Adams, Memoirs, op.cit., p.70.

49. S. Harrison, Poor Men's Guardians, London, 1974, p.138.

50. D. Vincent, Literacy and Popular Culture, England, 1750-1914, op.cit., p.53.

51. L. James, Print and the People, 1819-1851, London, 1987, p.17. See also R.D. Altick, The English Common Reader, 1800-1900, Chicago, 1957 p.171. Quoting the Registrar-General's returns from the signing of marriage registers, Altick calculated that seventy-five per cent of all men could read in 1861, and eighty per cent in 1871.

52. M. Milne, Newspapers of Northumberland and Durham, op.cit., p.30. See also Newcastle Weekly Chronicle, Dec. 7, 1878, Progress in Newcastle: Education. According to the report "at present the average number of children attending the public elementary school is 13,473, with 2,002 in attendance at other elementary schools, so that since the establishment of the School Board the attendance has been considerably more than doubled".

53. For a discussion of the Victorian editor see J.H. Wiener (ed.), Innovators and Preachers, The Role of the Editor in Victorian England, Westport, 1985, Introduction XI-XIX.

54. Newcastle Weekly Chronicle, May 27 1876, Vivisection.

55. P.A. Dunae, "Penny Dreadfuls : Late Nineteenth Century Boys' Literature and Crime", Victorian Studies, Vol.22, No.2, Winter, 1979, pp.133-150.

56. S. Humphries, Hooligans or Rebels? An Oral History of Working-Class Childhood and Youth 1889-1939, Oxford, 1981, pp.3-5.

57. Newcastle Weekly Chronicle, June 11, 1898. Speech by W.E. Adams at his Presentation gathering.

58. W.E. Adams, History of the Dicky Bird Society, Newcastle, 1887, Newcastle Central Library L179.3. See generally. The "Big Book" is in Newcastle Central Reference Library.

59. Newcastle Weekly Chronicle, April 12, 1879; Animal World, Sept. 1 1886.

60. Ibid., August 11, 1877.

61. Ibid., Feb. 15, 1879. See also Animal World June 1, 1886 and E.S. Turner, All Heaven in a Rage, London, 1964, pp.172-192 for the specific campaign against cruelty to birds.

62. Newcastle Weekly Chronicle, March 1, 1884.

63. Ibid., Oct. 20, 1883.

64. W.E. Adams, History of the Dicky Bird Society, op.cit.., p.7.

65. Newcastle Weekly Chronicle, July 28, 1894.

66. Ibid., May 5, 1883.

67. W.E. Adams, History of the Dicky Bird Society, op.cit., p.10.

68. Newcastle Weekly Chronicle, Dec. 20, 1890.

69. Ibid., Jan. 1, 1898.

70. Idem.,

71. Ibid., July 29, 1882.

72. B. Harrison, Peaceable Kingdom, Stability and Change in Modern Britain, op.cit., "Religion and Recreation", pp.123-156; in particular p.129.

73. J. Cooper, Animals in War, London, 1983, p.27. Out of the 520,000 remounts supplied, an appalling 326,073 horses died.

74. Animal World, Jan 1, 1901, "Animals Suffering in the War": Reports from Newcastle Dicky Bird Society.

75. A.W. Moss, Valiant Crusade, The History of the R.S.P.C.A., London, 1961, p.122.

76. J. Knott, The First Hundred Years, Newcastle Upon Tyne City Libraries, Newcastle Polytechnic School of Librarianship, Occasional Papers, No.3, 1980, particularly pp.7-13.

77. Ibid., p.13.

78. Newcastle Weekly Chronicle, Sept. 18, 1880.

79. Ibid., Jan. 15, 1876.

80. W.E. Adams, The Struggle for a Free Library in Newcastle Upon Tyne, 1870-1880, Ms Notes and Newspaper Cuttings, LO27,4N536, p.47 Gift of Books by T.B. Potter, Oct. 7 1876.

81. Newcastle Weekly Chronicle, Oct. 2, 1880, "A Public Library for Young People" featured in The Children's Corner.

82. J. Knott, The First Hundred Years, Newcastle Upon Tyne City Libraries, op.cit., p.19.

83. Newcastle Daily Chronicle, May 16, 1906, Letter from B. Anderton, Librarian of the Public Library on Adams's contribution to the Public Library. Adams had a complete gift set of Linton's English Republic, See MS Eng 180, Letter from W.J. Linton to W.E. Adams, 32 Keppel Street, Russell Square, May 27, 1884.

84. Newcastle Weekly Chronicle, Dec. 1, 1866, The Gossip's Bowl; June 11, 1898, Presentation Address to W.E. Adams.

85. Ibid., Dec. 14, 1867.

86. Ibid., Nov. 30, 1878, Progress in Newcastle : Public Parks.

87. Idem., See also T.W.P. Taylder, History of the Rise and Progress of Teetotalism in Newcastle Upon Tyne, Newcastle, 1886, p.3 for the benefit of Parks for the Newcastle artisan.

88. Ibid., Dec. 29, 1900. Lord Armstrong's Obituary.

89. G.C. Atkinson, Journal Of An Expedition to the Feroe and Westman Islands and Iceland, 1833, Edited and Introduced by A.V. Seaton, Newcastle, 1989, particularly pp.xviii-xxv.

90. Ibid., July 29, 1899, Portland Park Bowling Club.

91. Ibid., June 11, 1898. Presentation Address to W.E. Adams.

92. Idem.,

93. Ibid., March 22, 1884, The Gossip's Bowl; June 16, 1888; Aug. 4, 1888; Aug. 11, 1888.

94. Ibid., Dec. 7, 1878; June 11, 1898, Presentation Address to W.E. Adams.

95. Ibid., June 16, 1888.

96. Idem., June 28, 1888, The importance of smoke abatement.

97. Ibid., March 11, 1893.

98. W.E. Adams, Memoirs, op.cit., p.266. According to Adams, Mazzini's Republicanism was the "exposition of the greatest democratic document of the century".

6 Private and Family Life

As a successful, salaried journalist and newspaper editor, Adams's career path from humble origins in Cheltenham to a prestigious position in the social and political life of North East England showed a striking example of both social and geographic mobility. What did such changes in life-style mean? Did he become vulnerable to accepting or emulating middle class values and ideals, particularly the concept of 'respectability'? Was he ultimately absorbed by the dominant bourgeois culture? Such questions need to be addressed here.

From rented accommodation first at 5, Lawson Street, Ryehill in Elswick,[1] he moved for a time to 18, Chester Street in the municipal ward of North St. Andrew;[2] then finally in April 1877, through a building society mortgage, purchased the family home, a new three storey property in a terraced row at 32, Holly Avenue, Jesmond from the Newcastle builder, William Temple.[3] Holly Avenue was a far cry from the gregarious and often rough street life of the narrow little alleys which Adams had known and enjoyed in the working class district of Cheltenham Spa. His new neighbours were employed in bourgeois-waged occupations that have been described, broadly speaking, as lower middle class.[4] On one side according to the Census of 1881 lived an "export merchant"; on the other a "foregeman" in a business employing twenty six men and six boys; and further along on either side were a sprinkling of white collar commercial clerks, accountants, a horse agent and a mining engineer.[5]

Adams's life-style on the face of it accorded well with middle class ideas about domesticity and the integrity of family life. He was able to support his family without sending his wife out to work; they employed by 1881 a sixteen year old general servant, a maid of all work who hailed from Yorkshire;[6] and the children were encouraged to spend their spare time outside school hours in such home-centered activities as reading, music and the care of many household pets rather than, as young Adams did, larking about or playing football in the street.

Outside the home his editorial position, breadth of interests and radical affinities placed him in a talented and often cultivated circle of literary, political and artistic figures. He was a close friend of the novelists, Mayne Reid and Mrs. Stannard; the Lib-Lab leaders, Thomas Burt and George Howell; the trade union leader, Robert Knight, secretary of the Boilermakers; the artist, Ralph Hedley; and the celebrated Victorian actors, Sir Henry Irving and J.R. Anderson.[7] On occasions too he was invited to the London Hotspur Club, a literary gathering of exiled Tynesiders;[8] and nearer to home, an honoured guest of the Newcastle Bewick Club, which was dedicated to perpetuating the memory and work of the famous wood-engraver and artist Thomas Bewick (1753-1828) of Newcastle.[9]

As and when time allowed Adams's hobbies were of a wholesome or self-improving kind. He was an omniverous reader, a member of the Newcastle Burns Club, played chess and during the summer months was a keen bowler at Portland Green. His horizons were broadened, too, by a number of touring holidays in the late 1870s and early 1880s first to Norway,[10] then Germany[11] and finally to North America in 1882, about which he wrote and published in his travelogue, *Our American Cousins.*[12] Music was also a major source of enjoyment. Adams was a fairly regular attender at the People's Promenade Concerts at the Town Hall run by Dr. William Rea, a leading musical director in the North East who liked to promote Beethoven, Mozart and Mendelssohn nights.[13] Adams's musical tastes were fairly wide-ranging: he was a lover of folk songs and joined the Northumberland Small Pipes Society, having as its object the preservation of Border Counties music and ballad literature.[14]

The concept of 'respectability' is "a particularly slippery one",[15] and life-styles of 'respectability' and independence (freedom of action and the ability to make choices) are often wrongly equated with middle class values. Repectability was certainly as central a value to skilled artisans like Adams as it was to the middle classes. As a compositor in Cheltenham, London and Manchester, Adams's respectability owed little if anything to bourgeois initiatives and exhortations: rather it arose out of the realities of working class mutual experiences and commitments as a highly skilled and politically conscious artisan. Adams always valued such qualities as self-respect, self-reliance, emancipation from poverty, illiteracy and drunkeness for their own sake; they helped realise a decent standard of living in Newcastle and a recognition of his claim to citizenship; but they were not viewed in changed circumstances either as tools for social ascent or as a means of emulating the middle class attitudes and norms of those influential people with whom his work brought him into contact.

A number of personal characteristics also underline Adams's life-long humility. One of the most distinctive things that struck Thomas Burt about Adams after thirty years of friendship was "the grand simplicity of the man".[16] As we have seen, Adams led an unostentatious and unobtrusive life, had a reputation at work for fairness and impartiality, displayed a genial spirit and was a delightful companion; he was not easily impressed; nor could he be bought. Above all else, beneath his artisanal aspirations still lay a distinctive radical ideology, which drew on Paineite and Mazzinian traditions and thinking. Although sobered by a clear understanding of what could and what could not be done by political action, Adams's radicalism remained as keen and robust in the

1880s as it did in the 1840s. Thus far from signifying a surrender to bourgeois individualism, what Adams displayed was great individuality. Although his interests did take him away from many aspects of working class life, he was nevertheless equally at home in the company of literati and those of social standing as he was with his friend Thomas Burt and at the galas, concerts and social gatherings of the Northumberland pit-men.[17] In Holly Avenue, too, neighbours may well have despaired at the fact that amongst a collection of feathered friends were his sons' homing pigeons[18] which, if perched on the roof-top or wherever conspicuous, may well have seen the house resemble more the abode of a pigeon-fancier than that of a 'respectable' editor in chief of a powerful provincial newspaper. In the final analysis, bourgeois hegemony was negotiated rather than given in Adams's life and work.

Adams's autobiography, like so many of its genre, is virtually silent about all aspects of family life and such emotional experiences as love and death.[19] This is very misleading because the family was far from being of marginal importance in Adams's life; and it is essential that we place him in the domestic context in order to get a more rounded picture of his illustrious career.

Adams married, as we have already noted, Elizabeth Jane Owen Smith in London in 1858. We know nothing about their courtship or her family, except for the fact that she had one sister, a deceased father and, according to Peg Adams, had come from a Quaker family.[20] Such influences as that religious creed might have had terminated on marriage; the Adams household was in no way steeped in any kind of religious tradition or cultural practice.

The marriage, which appears to have been a long and happy one, produced six children: two boys and four girls. In the *Memoirs* Adams hints at the fact that his first two children, Gertrude Amy and Florence Annie, were born in Manchester in 1860 and 1861 respectively. The first son, Ernest Welles, was born in Newcastle in 1866. The spelling of his middle name is interesting: it reflected Adams's Cheltenham roots on his mother's side, but also incorporated the name of Gideon Welles, an American whom Adams greatly admired. Welles was Secretary of the United States Navy under Presidents Lincoln and Johnson (1861-69); and during the Civil War, long before the army acted, Welles ordered naval commanders to give protection to runaway slaves and then issued orders to enlist them in the service.[21] The second Newcastle son, Horace Owen, was born in 1873. Of the remaining Newcastle-born daughters, Ada Eveline was born in 1868; Minnie Blanche in 1870; and Hilda Kate in 1878.[22]

In the raising of his children Adams appears to have had considerable influence. Unfortunately, excepting Ada Eveline, we know next to nothing about their elementary or secondary schooling in Newcastle. In Ada's case, she attended the Bath Lane School, founded by the Radical-Liberal the Rev. Dr. J.H. Rutherford, which was known for its broadly-based progressive curriculum in the humanities, sciences and modern languages.[23] In keeping with Rutherford's style, the children were encouraged to be socially responsible citizens. For example, in October 1883,when Ada was a thirteen year old pupil, major gales along the North East coast caused the loss through drowning of the Eyemouth fishing fleet of over one hundred and sixty seven men. At the school, collections were made for the fishermen's widows and orphans, and children encouraged to give as much as possible, rather than spending their money in the school tuck-shop.[24]

Adams's wide-ranging reading experiences, even indirectly his radical beliefs, brushed off on the books his children were encouraged to read. They were introduced, for example, to Shakespeare and also read the historian Henry Hallam's authoritative *Constitutional History of England* (1827) and *The View of the State of Europe During the Middle Ages* (1818, Reptd. 1848).[25] Adams enjoyed Hallam because of his conscientious handling of historical evidence; he was also, like Adams, an advocate of the abolition of all forms of Negro Slavery. In keeping with their father's love for animals, the children read Cassell's illustrated *Little Folks*, a popular nature story series for young people; they also enjoyed W.J. Linton's *Wild Flowers for Children* and *The Flower and the Star, or the Course of the Stream* (with twenty-five engravings); both were much prized gifts donated to the household by the author in August 1873.[26] Adams was always interested in education. Late in life, whilst in Madeira, he was still counselling his grandson, Alfred Edwin Adams, (Ernest Welles's son) about the importance of lessons following the little boy's success in winning a school prize:

> "keep on being attentive to your lessons. But don't forget Alfie, that the lessons you learn are much more precious than prizes."[27]

Two subjects dominated the children's domestic spare time: music and love of animals. Although Adams himself loved music, he could not play a musical instrument. All the children, it appears, were successfully encouraged to play the piano; some were even sufficiently competent to be able to give public pianoforte recitals at Christmas concerts in the 1890s.

Like his old home in Cheltenham, Adams's house in Holly Avenue became a virtual menagerie: feathered friends (canaries and pigeons) lived uncomfortably under the same roof as pet cats, kittens and dogs (one of which was known as Jowler). The children naturally became active members of their father's Dicky Bird Society; but only

Ernest and Ada managed to be promoted to the rank of captain and companion respectively. They were all regular contributors to Uncle Toby's letter-bag in the Children's Corner. Sometimes their precociousness found expression in the Corner with little poems on birds and nature. One such simple verse written by his eight year old, Minnie Blanche read thus:

> "Who taught the birds to build her nest
> Of wool and hay and moss?
> Who taught her how to weave it best
> And lay the twigs across?[28]

The relaxed nature of the children's upbringing did not of course prevent problems. Not surprisingly, Ada's cats and Horace's and Ernest's pigeons were often a source of sibling friction as the former were always out to try and trap the latter![29] Adams inevitably attempted to arbitrate in a way which placated the situation, until the next incident of its kind occurred; their pets were never removed from the house.

As they grew older the children took part, as did Adams's wife Lizzie, in the public affairs of the Dicky Bird Society. For example, at the annual Christmas Exhibitions of Toys on display at the Academy of Arts in Blackett Street, Ada Eveline, Minnie Blanche and Hilda Kate gave piano recitals to the public viewing of the toys;[30] and by the early 1890s they were joined by Adams's first grandchildren, Amy and Florence Smith, the offspring of his eldest daughter Gertrude Amy.[31] Adams must have taken great joy in elderly life from these occasions knowing that his grandchildren, having themselves joined the Dicky Bird Society, could express such opinions as the following:

> "I am glad that it is not fashionable to wear birds in hats and bonnets, because I think it is very cruel to kill them for that purpose."[32]

Adams also experienced moments of great sadness. Two months after the birth of their last child, Hilda Kate, in June 1877 joy and grief were cruelly mixed when the second daughter, Florence Annie, died tragically on August 16,[33] possibly from an outbreak of the deadly disease of typhoid which was fairly rife in Newcastle at this time. Adams's grief was rationalised by reference to lines from Tennyson's "In Memoriam". In reply to the bereaved parents of a little girl member of the Dicky Bird Society who had died at the same time, Adams attempted to console them and himself with these words written in his correspondence column of the "Children's Corner":

> "Uncle Toby feels with them in their loss. He, too, in his time, has known what it is to have seen dear faces fade from him ... He can only, in thought,

> silently shake hands with those upon whom the shadow of so great a loss has fallen and wish them some relief from their burden of grief, in the thought that "it is better to have loved and lost than never to have loved at all".[34]

Health problems continued to beset the family. Hilda Kate was a sickly child. She was seriously ill with scarlet fever for eight weeks in the autumn of 1888.[35] Two years later she was confined to her bed for a second time;[36] and the following year, partly to recuperate, was sent for a time to a school in the countryside near Redditch.[37] Adams's own health began to suffer from the early 1880s. From evidence suggested in the *Memoirs* his health was:

> "permanently injured, and my life was nearly lost, through the conduct of workmen who deliberately mislaid the drains in a new house."[38]

The most likely cause of the problem Adams encountered was a back-fall on the domestic sewerage drains which allowed stagnant water, poisonous fumes and harmful gases to build up over time in his home. Blood-poisoning from foul washing water was the first and most serious manifestation of ill-health; but given the fact that Adams was already an inveterate smoker, it is just possible that his chest was also particularly sensitive to this unsuspecting kind of pollution; and when his personal fitness finally appears to have been imperilled in 1882 — only five years after purchasing 32, Holly Avenue — Adams gives as one of the reasons for his trip to North America, the need to get away and restore his "broken health".[39] Alas, such attempts were only partially successful. Adams continued to be bedevilled by poor health in the late 1880s and early 1890s. Advancing years did not help his situation. By 1893 he was complaining to Linton about the onset of sciatica;[40] nor were his bouts of asthma and bronchitis making life any easier. At the same time, his wife's health began to break, although we do not know the cause. In typical self-help fashion, Adams resolved to do what he could to alleviate his health problems and chose the warm climes of Madeira to get over the English winters. The financial burden of these journeys was undoubtedly eased from 1898 by the public gift of £450 guineas kindly donated by Novocastrians. According to Peg Adams, his eldest daughter, Gertrude Amy, invariably accompanied Adams on his sojourns; the mother's poor health made it unsafe for her to travel with them.[41]

Adams's literary talents rubbed off onto his children: three of them became journalists. Ernest Welles began work as a fifteen year old consul's clerk in the American Consulate in Grey Street, He then served "an apprenticeship of four years to the wholesale drapery trade"[42] with a firm in Newcastle before joining the staff of the new

Evening Chronicle in 1885. During his long association with the *Chronicle* offices Ernest worked for a time alongside the distinguished journalist J.L. Garvin, who subsequently became editor of the *Observer*. Within seven years of becoming a sub-editor on the *Weekly*[43] he effectively took over from his father by the end of 1898; and for the next forty two years ran the paper as a Liberal-based, popular and commercially successful venture. By 1900 he had the *Weekly* carrying front page news and eye-catching headlines; but it also continued many of its traditional features such as "The Gossip's Bowl", "Nature Notes", "Local Anecdotes" and "The Children's Corner"; he also succeeded his father as the genial Uncle Toby, who by 1940 had signed a further 110,000 children into the "Big Book" pledged to be kind to all living things.[44] Occasionally, the ghost of Joseph Cowen appeared in the guise of his interfering daughter, Jane Cowen, who took control of her father's empire on his death in 1900;[45] but Ernest inherited the same spirit of independence in the twentieth century as his father had displayed in the nineteenth. Unlike his brother and most of his sisters, Ernest spent all his life in Newcastle, living first in Heaton and then in Gosforth, where he was an extremely keen supporter of Gosforth Bowling Club and Gosforth Rugby Club until his death after a short illness in 1946.[46]

Ada Eveline was arguably the most talented of the daughters. After leaving school at Bath Lane she too joined the *Weekly Chronicle* staff in 1889, writing under the pseudonym of "Geraldine" in the Ladies Corner. One of the distinguishing features of her journalism was the vigour of her campaigning work against the cruelty of fashion. She called upon readers not to purchase sealskin jackets because of the brutality involved in the seal kill;[47] encouraged women to join the Plumage League which campaigned against the use by humans of birds' feathers;[48] and urged women everywhere "to prove that they were not slaves to fashion".[49] Elsewhere in her writings she supported the Rational Dress Society, campaigned against food adulteration and the exploitation of shop-girls; she was also a seasoned traveller in Europe.[50] In 1896 she married a Wesleyan Methodist minister, the Rev. Leonard B. Dalby of Whitley.[51] Adams must have been well-pleased. Dalby was known for his progressive thinking: his special interests were history, travel, unemployment and the colour bar.[52] For a time her column continued, but when Dalby's work took him away from Gosforth on the Methodist Circuit first to Exeter and then Bristol, it had to be terminated.[53] After spending some time on ministry work in Auckland, New Zealand, they finally retired to Plymouth, although interestingly a grand niece by marriage to Ada, Helen Audrey Dalby, is now in possession of the old family home at 32, Holly Avenue.

Horace Owen, like Adams's own father, appears to have been a bit of a wanderer. In 1898 he is known to have been working in Edinburgh; by 1900 in Hanley, and in 1907, shortly after his father's death, was in lodgings at Honor Oak Park, London.[54] By 1919 he had become a sub-editor of *The World's Paper Trade Review*, a specialist weekly, international journal for paper-makers and paper-mill engineers; he was also a member of the National Union of Journalists.[55] Ironically, Horace came to work within a stone's throw of where his father had laboured in political debates at the tavern-based, Discussion Hall seventy years previously: *World's Paper* was published in Shoe Lane, Holborn Viaduct. Horace finally settled with his wife at Beckenham, Kent; they had two children, one of whom was named William Edwyn Adams.[56]

The three remaining daughters Gertrude Amy, Minnie Blanche and Hilda Kate also travelled considerable social distance in relation to their father's humble background. Gertie married a chartered accountant, Richard Smith, from Redruth in Cornwall. They lived first at Grosvenor Road, then with their three children in Lily Crescent, Jesmond and finally settled in Oakfield Terrace, Gosforth.[57] Minnie Blanche married a leading Newcastle photographer, Robert Barrass, who had an office, the Rembrandt Studio, at 180, Westgate Road.[58] Hilda Kate married a London clerk, Herbert Bodger in 1905 and then went to live in Sydenham.[59]

Adams's family were lively, energetic and talented. Although they did not share the same kind of political awareness as their father, the children blossomed through the freedoms and causes which men like W.E. Adams toiled to achieve. He reared or influenced in many ways a family of activists. They became involved in public charitable work particularly over the care of animals, were accomplished musicians and teachers, enjoyed literature and the performing arts.[60] Surviving descendants, too, exhibit similar traits of character and interests. One great, great, grand-daughter, Gerda Karina Dahlin (born 1952, and Anglo-Danish) perpetuates the family tradition of journalism, working in public life as a press officer for the University of Toronto.[61] Another, David Dalby (born, 1925) is the Secretary of Kent County Cricket Club.[62]

Notes

1. Newcastle Weekly Chronicle, Feb. 24 1866 Births column: Ernest Welles Adams on 21 Feb. at 5, Lawson Street.

2. Census Returns, 1871 North St. Andrew.

3. Details from Schedule of Deeds and Documents on 32, Holly Avenue, kindly loaned by Audrey Dalby. See also Census Returns, 1881. ED31 Reel C53, R.S.D. Byker.

4. G. Crossick (ed.), The Lower Middle Class in Britain, London, 1977, pp.11-60.

5. Census Returns, 1881, op.cit., See also G. Crossick (ed.), The Lower Middle Class in Britain, op.cit., pp.19-20. According to Crossick's calculations, the commercially important city of Newcastle in the late nineteenth century had 8% of its workforce in white collar lower middle class occupations. (Bristol's was 8.3%).

6. Census Returns, 1881, op.cit., Her name was Agnes A. Holmes.

7. All these individuals, excepting Anderson, were also subscribers to the Presentation gifts for W.E.and Elizabeth Owen Adams on June 6, 1898. Adams wrote the Introduction to J.R. Anderson's, An Actor's Life, London, 1902.

8. See, for example, Newcastle Weekly Chronicle, April 5, 1890, The Hotspur Club.

9. Ibid., Jan.22, 1887.

10. Ibid., Sept.6, 1879. He told readers that he was going to Norway "to enjoy the natural beauty of the county between Bergen and Christiania".

11. Ibid., Nov.12, 1881. He toured near Altona on the River Elbe.

12. Our American Cousins was first published in September 1883, price 3/6. According to the Newcastle Weekly Chronicle, Sept. 24 1887, it was "re-issued in a cheap form for railway reading, price 1/-".

13. Newcastle Weekly Chronicle, March 5, 1881, The Popular Concerts. For Rea's work in the North East, see K. Barker, "The performing arts in Newcastle-upon-Tyne, 1840-1870", pp.53-70, particularly p.62 in J.K. Walton and J. Walvin (eds.), Leisure in Britain, 1780-1939, Manchester, 1983.

14. Newcastle Weekly Chronicle, June 11, 1898, Presentation Address to W.E. Adams.

15. D.G. Wright, Popular Radicalism, The Working-Class Experience 1780-1880, op.cit., p.166.

16. Newcastle Daily Chronicle, May 14, 1907. Speech by T. Burt at the ceremony to unveil the bust of W.E. Adams in Newcastle Public Library.

17. T. Burt, Pitman and Privy Councillor, An Autobiography, op.cit., p.185. See also The Northern Echo, May 14, 1907 and North Mail, May 14, 1907 for reports on speeches by T. Burt on Adams's life at the unveiling ceremony of the bust of W.E. Adams.

18. Newcastle Weekly Chronicle, Nov. 1 1879, The Children's Corner.

19. D. Vincent, "Love and death in the nineteenth century working class", op.cit., p.227. Vincent states that, working class autobiographers felt it improper or unnecessary to write about family experience.

20. Letter from Peg Adams, December 12, 1986.

21. Dictionary of American Biography, Vol.X, New York, 1964, pp.629-632.

22. Census Returns, 1871 and 1881.

23. Newcastle Weekly Chronicle, Oct. 29, 1881, The Children's Corner: "What our members of the Bath Lane schools are going to do about the disasters at sea" by Ada Eveline Adams.

24. Idem.,

25. Newcastle Weekly Chronicle, June 14, 1879, The Children's Corner.

26. Ms Eng 180, W.J. Linton to W.E. Adams, Aug. 27, 1873.

27. Letter from W.E. Adams to Alfie Edwin Adams, Bella Vista, Madeira, January 3, 1902. Kindly loaned by Peg Adams.

28. Newcastle Weekly Chronicle, March 16, 1878.

29. Ibid., Nov.1, 1879, Letter from Ada Eveline Adams, Oct.20, 1879, complaining to Uncle Toby about her brothers.

30. Ibid., Dec. 29, 1888.

31. Ibid., Dec. 30, 1893.

32. Ibid., Nov. 5, 1887, Letter from Florence Annie Smith, 14, Lily Crescent, Newcastle, Oct. 23, 1887 to Uncle Toby, The Children's Corner.

33. Ibid., Aug. 25, 1877.

34. Ibid., Sept. 1, 1877.

35. Ibid., Oct. 20, 1888. According to F.B. Smith, The People's Health, London, 1979, p.136 "The main destructive diseases (in childhood and youth) were scarlet fever, measles, diptheria and small-pox".

36. Ibid., Sept. 20, 1890.

37. Ibid., Oct. 31, 1891.

38. W.E. Adams, Memoirs, op.cit., p.552.

39. Ibid., p.562 and p.635 where he states: "Blood-poisoning, the result of scamping work in a new house, was not only nearly fatal, but the parent of a whole crop of diseases."

40. Ms Eng 180, W.J. Linton to W.E. Adams, P.O. Box 1139, New Haven, Jan.27, 1893.

41. Letter from Peg Adams, Jan. 26, 1987.

42. Newcastle Weekly Chronicle, Dec. 21, 1940, Valediction on Ernest Welles Adams's retirement.

43. Ibid., Sept. 12, 1891.

44. Ibid., Dec. 21, 1940.

45. Cowen Collection, F116. Letter from E.W. Adams to Miss Jane Cowen, Jan. 14, 1916 regarding the approval of certain proofs.

46. Newcastle Evening Chronicle, May 30, 1946, Obituary of E.W. Adams.

47. Newcastle Weekly Chronicle, Oct. 5, 1889, The Ladies' Corner: "Geraldine's Letter".

48. Ibid., March 2, 1889. See also W.E. Adams, Memoirs, op.cit., pp.628-631, for similar views. The wearing of bird carcasses as millinery decorations he considered "reprehensible".

49. Ibid, March 2, 1889.

50. Ibid., March 1, 1890; Oct. 10, 1891; July 29, 1893.

51. Ibid., Aug. 22, 1896.

52. The Methodist Who's Who, London, 1933 p.56 for the entry on the Rev. Leonard B. Dalby. I am particularly grateful to my colleague, the Rev. Dr. P. Dickinson, for his help in tracing Dalby's career.

53. Newcastle Weekly Chronicle, Jan. 2 1897, The Ladies' Corner : "Geraldine's Letter". This was one of her last. In typical fashion she was exposing the hardships and worries facing two groups of workers: domestic servants and shopgirls. The latter were, she wrote, "worse off than servants having not one master, but many masters; and at the same time have to satisfy the exacting demands of perhaps, imperious and irritable manageresses". She predicted that 'better times were coming for both".

54. Newcastle Weekly Chronicle, Jan. 1, 1898; Dec. 22, 1900; and Memorial Newspaper cuttings, Newcastle 1907, L. 920 A219, Letter from R. Welford to B. Anderton, May 2, 1907, giving Horace's address as Tynedale, Duncombe Hill, Honor Oak Park, London.

55. I am grateful to the National Union of Journalists, Acorn House, Gray's Inn Rd., London, for providing me with a copy of his application for membership.

56. I am grateful to C.A. Bassett of Beckenham Library for providing me with information on Horace's family from their holdings of electoral registers. Horace and his wife, Amy Anita, continued to live at 10, Kingshall Road, Beckenham until at least 1950.

57. Newcastle Weekly Chronicle, Nov. 5, 1887; and information kindly supplied by one of her grand-daughter's, Mrs. Sheila Dahlin of Galashiels.

58. Ibid., Jan 1, 1898.

59. Details taken from W.E. Adams's title deeds and kindly loaned by Helen Audrey Dalby, 32, Holly Avenue, Jesmond, Newcastle, June 3, 1987.

60. Ada was involved in charity work. Another grandson of W.E. Adams, Frederick William Smith, Gertrude's eldest child, was a member of the Northumberland Philarmonic Orchestra in the early years of the twentieth century.

61. Information supplied by Mrs. Sheila Dahlin of Galashiels, Feb. 14, 1990. Gerda Dahlin is a career journalist, formerly working in Denmark, Calgary and

Newfoundland. Before her present position, she was a journalist with a pressure group, the Radiation Safety Unit for Canadians in Toronto.

62. Information supplied by Mr. David Dalby, Chartered Accountant of Whitstable, Kent and a grandson of Ada Eveline, June 9, 1987.

7 An Old-Fashioned Radical

The visit to North America in 1882 represents something of a watershed in Adams's political career. On his return the long-standing "Ironside" column, suspended for the duration of the tour, was not reintroduced. Increasingly, as we observed in the last chapter, Adams retreated from politics into antiquarian pursuits and homely reforms of a more local character. The motives behind this shift of emphasis remain unclear. Health problems may have been one significant factor.[1] Secondly, he found "contemporary trends politically unhealthy, and personally distasteful".[2] Although only fifty years of age, Adams was already exhibiting features common to other notable Radicals such as George Howell and Thomas Cooper: a failure both to appreciate the complexity of late nineteenth century social problems, the wider horizons and ameliorative possibilities offered to the individual by the ongoing activities of the state; and an inability to adjust to the related and dynamic political developments suggested by the emergence of Socialism, New Unionism and the movement for independent Labour representation.[3] Equally plausible in this changing socio-political context was Adams's growing sense of disillusionment over whether working men would ever achieve their own regeneration by acting on their own behalf as a prelude to founding a Republic; and it was a doubt he expressed in correspondence to Linton in 1892[4] and expanded upon at some length in the closing chapters of the *Memoirs* under the titles of "Degeneracy" and "The Decline of Man".[5]

In general, the last two decades of the nineteenth century were a period of renewed social, economic and political upheaval. British society appeared to be less secure and settled than at any time since the hungry 1840s and the days of Chartism. Industrial competition, particularly from America and Germany, had steadily undermined the fabric of business confidence and precipitated abrasive style survival strategies by firms through wage reductions, the introduction of new technology at the expense of skill, and a speed-up and intensification of the pace of work.[6] During the mid-1880s trade recession, many groups of organised workers also experienced the highest and most prolonged unemployment for forty years. The sheer extent of urban poverty began to suggest to some politicians the limitations of Gladstonian self-help in strategies for its elimination. Finally, the expanding influence of Socialism as a solution to economic problems, the appeal of collectivist ideas amongst the unemployed, the growing strength of unskilled labour whose leaders were receptive to State intervention ideology, and the gradual evolution of the Labour Party threatened a new phase of union militancy and class conflict.

Apart from a more sympathetic view of British Imperial policies in the 1890s, Adams's political position remained unchanged throughout these more unsettled times. Indeed, the emergence of collectivist ideas more in tune with the shifting mood of the labour movement and Adams's antipathy towards them and their exponents served to undermine both the limited nature of the mid-century self-help radicalism in which he was reared and confirm him as an old-fashioned, traditional yet picturesque Radical survivor from an earlier political age. For example, in the *Memoirs* he barely mentions the Socialist developments of the 1880s. Special invective is also reserved for a small number of its leaders: John Williams of the Social Democratic Federation is dismissed as an anarchist;[7] Shaw Maxwell of the Scottish Labour Party condemned for his truculence;[8] and Keir Hardie censured, following his first appearance in Parliament complete with cloth cap, for "vanity or conceit, or the desire to appear singular".[9]

In the *Weekly Chronicle*, however, Adams was on occasions more forthcoming and his arguments opposing collectivist ideas and the role of state intervention in the affairs of society clearly articulated and reasoned. Yet in any assessment we should not at the outset be misled, according to M. Milne, into attributing these opinions to a shift in position "towards the political 'right' — to a hardening of the ideological arteries".[10] One of the difficulties the independent artisan like Adams faced with Socialist philosophy was that coming as he did from a political tradition which had emphasized independence, self-education and self-help, Socialism appeared to deny, or at least downgrade, the importance of individual liberty and the freedom of working men and women to rise by their own initiative. It is important to bear in mind therefore that what changed was not so much Adams's political standpoint as the context in which it figured. To quote Milne:

> "Hence, his political outlook was overtaken by events and he became the critic instead of the champion of 'advanced' ideas."[11]

One other significant observation should be noted here. For all his hostility to collectivist solutions to the country's problems, Adams was motivated by a commendable sense of fair play, honesty and liberal conviction about free speech sufficient to allow what other editors frequently denied: a full, fearless and frank hearing of Socialist panaceas and policies.[12]

At the beginning of 1885 the *Weekly* published under its advanced opinion column, the "Open Council", a series of articles on the rights and wrongs of State intervention in society. Auberon Herbert, one of the most libertarian of late Victorian political thinkers, opened the debate on January 3 in opposition to collectivist ideas with a seven part article on the theme "The Party of Individual Liberty"; on February 14 H.M. Hyndman of the Social Democratic Federation was given the opportunity to reply over a similar length of time under the title "The Party of Collective and Individual Liberty". Later in the year, on September 12, Adams made his first entry in the debate with the following scarcely generous definition of emerging collectivist ideas under an article entitled "State Socialism":

> "Socialism is the name given to various theories which have for their aim the abolition of that individual action on which society depends for vivacity and vitality."[13]

Adams did acknowledge in the same article the need for minimum government intervention in a complex industrial society, but felt that the limits of this process had already been reached. If a halt was not made then, he believed legislative interference of the Socialist kind would everywhere paralyse individual effort in the future. Thus the article concluded with the assertion that:

> "Faith in individual energy and mistrust of State agency should be the watchwords of modern democracy. If these watchwords are forgotten, the genuine aspirations of the people will be crushed by a network of philanthropic officialism."

By 1890, however, Adams found himself lamenting the fact that Parliament was passing a plethora of laws — "Grandmotherly Legislation" Lord Wemyss had called it — which in his view promoted the centralization of authority, curbed individual initiative and left as little as possible to individual energies.[14] As such authoritarian measures were "the very antithesis of Radical teaching", Adams felt convinced that their genesis lay firmly in the Socialist tendencies of the time:

> "It (i.e. Radicalism) and Socialism are as poles asunder. But it is Socialism which in our time is playing the winning game."[15]

Four years later in what was one of his last editorial comments on the subject, he speculated gloomily on the ethical results of a society becoming over-reliant on the idea that the State could do everything for the individual and do it better than the latter could do for himself:

> "But the constant demands now made for State interposition in nearly every sphere must sap the springs of individual action and enervate conscience. There are responsibilities with which man in virtue of his manhood is invested that he cannot shuffle off at the bidding of the State without serious damage to the body politic."[16]

Reviving industrial militancy in the North East from the mid-1880s, in which plans for independent labour representation and Socialist ideas steadily found favour, also left Adams on the defensive and increasingly out of touch. Attention has hitherto focused on the importance of one of the opening conflicts, the long and bitter coal strike of 1887. The nature of that dispute, particularly the intrusion for the first time of Socialist elements, presented the greatest challenge to Thomas Burt's control of the Northumberland Miners and, in the view of one historian, "altered the political and labour climate of the North East".[17] However, the little known but equally intense, if localised, dispute over the eviction of pit-men from their homes by the company owning the South Medomsley Colliery[18] near Consett in County Durham in the bleak mid-winter of 1885/1886, and about which voices of concern were raised at Westminster, offered a foretaste to the new phase of unbridled militancy; it also served to undermine a lingering fiction in the North East that the mutual dependency of labour and capital still led invariably to compromises in industrial matters.

The conflict at South Medomsley Colliery grew out of a wages dispute: the pit-men had already by 1885, in response to the trade depression, been working at a reduction of 6% below the country wage average; by the beginning of January 1886 the company was demanding a further abatement of 10% to which request the men, backed by their Durham Miners' Association, refused to comply; they were promptly dismissed on January 6th and "black-legs" recruited in their place.[19] Whereas elsewhere in County Durham a reasonably amicable modus vivendi had, as we have seen in Chapter Four, been reached over many years between the owners and the men, this company, established only in 1885, decided to turn the clock back to pre-1844 times. The major reason for a return to the old confrontational mentality lay with a toughening of managerial style and discipline. The general manager at South Medomsley, William Tyzack, was not untypical of a new breed of professional managers appearing on the North East's industrial scene: anxious to increase profits through new workshop practices and techniques, or at the expense of wages, they were unconcerned about the personal bonds and understandings which had emerged between workers and their employers.

New style management, for example, had already precipitated a brief but acrimonious dispute at the giant Elswick works in September 1885;[20] but the nature of that strike was nothing by comparison to the conflict between the over-zealous and abrasive Tyzack and the equally determined resistance of the men at South Medomsley. In a conflict which dragged on for nearly a year,[21] Tyzack eventually destroyed the local union branch, evicted 300 pit-men and their families from their cottages in what appeared to be the worst winter of the century[22] and imported Irish strike-breakers under heavy police escort to work in the Colliery. Violence, including shootings of non-union labour and attacks on the police in revenge for their rough handling of the wives and children of the pit-men during the evictions by the candymen, were common-place; there was also an unsuccessful attempt to blow up the Tyzack household.

Adams for the *Weekly* and Richard Ruddock, editor of the *Daily* (1878-1908), gave equal space to the views and arguments of both sides; but the tyrannical conduct of the colliery manager made it difficult for either editor to report impartially; and Tyzack's victory was eventually made absolute when he successfully sued the *Daily Chronicle* for libel at Leeds Assizes on May 17 1886; he received the colossal sum of £1,200 damages.[23]

The main result of this ugly affair was a direct accession of strength to those pit-men and artisans who were coming to favour independent labour or working class representation in Parliament to protect their interests — a concept and practice which Adams had long opposed.[24] In Newcastle the situation was rapidly becoming conducive to the reception of new political ideas. Amidst mounting unemployment,[25] social distress[26] and a general strike on both the Tyne and Wear involving over 7,000 shipwrights and boilermakers opposed to wage reductions,[27] a group of artisans, led by three talented local activists, Elijah Copland,[28] John Kier and John Hall of the Newcastle Democratic Club, were actively proselytizing the cause of independent labour representation as the most effective means of resolving their grievances.[29] In 1885, for example, during the build up to the General Election in November they had passed resolutions at well-attended meetings of a type declaring "Messrs. Burt and Broadhurst tame and complacent, marked by too little independence".[30] Significantly, apart from Joseph Cowen jr., the only other labour leaders to avoid the men's strictures at this time were Lloyd Jones, the Radical candidate for Chester-le-Street, and John Wilson, the Durham Miners' choice at Houghton-le-Spring; they were approved of because they had "declared their adhesion to the principle of land nationalization".[31]

Increasingly disaffected, these labour activists now seized on the outrages at South Medomsley to advance their cause. At a series of mass meetings of the unemployed who had assembled at The Haymarket and on The Sandhill, a popular open air site for mass meetings in Newcastle,[32] they made great play of the fact that it was "a member of the capitalist class" (A.E. Pease, the Liberal Member for York), rather than any local radically-inclined M.P., who had first raised questions in the House regarding the conduct of the police during the eviction of pit-men's families; it could scarcely have escaped their notice, too, that the influence of the *Chronicle* on the men's behalf had been singularly emasculated by a partisan judiciary. The upshot of all this political ferment finally manifested itself in early July 1886, when Joseph Cowen jr., in reply to a letter from John Hall, announced that he would not be contesting the seat following Gladstone's defeat over the Irish Home Rule Bill.[33] An abortive attempt had already been made in August 1885 to select Elijah Copland as a rival independent labour candidate; but loyalty to Joseph Cowen jr. had ultimately prevailed; and the Democratic Club had thrown its weight behind Cowen's successful stand in November 1885 as an independent Liberal.[34] News of the changed situation in 1886 removed all difficulties with regard to personal loyalty towards Cowen's Radical creed. Henceforward, the growing army of supporters of independent labour representation, spurred on by visits from Metropolitan Socialists at strategic moments in industrial disputes, were free to pursue their own preferred cause; and by 1893, sufficient groundwork had been completed for the Newcastle and Gateshead Trades Council to feel confident enough in adopting Frederick Hammill, a New Unionist and Socialist politician, as their independent Labour candidate at the next Parliamentary election.[35]

The South Medomsley evictions and the growing distress on Tyneside also coincided with an event which received national attention: the Socialist inspired riots in London's wealthy West End following a mass meeting of the unemployed in Trafalgar Square on February 8, 1886. Once again, in responding editorially to the grievances behind the discontent Adams's limited political horizons were everywhere apparent. He deplored the riots and destruction of property, but attributed the unrest to a rising simply of London's "residuum" fuelled by the violent speeches of irresponsible Socialists[36] (a reference to the activities of H.M. Hyndman, J. Burns, H.H. Champion and J. Williams who had addressed the mass meeting). As to the plight of the genuine unemployed, Adams felt that the best way forward was through a mixture of exhortations to private self-help and locally-inspired, public work schemes.[37] In contrast to men like Copland and Hall, who were beginning to put their faith in collectivist solutions to unemployment, Adams had no confidence in the capacity of the State to intervene beneficially in the operation of the economy:

> "It cannot be too distinctly understood by every man and woman in England that the State can give nothing which it requires money to get without first extracting that money from the pockets of the people. The vicissitudes of industrial and commercial enterprise are independent of Governments and cannot effectively be either controlled or modified by their interposition."[38]

The seemingly inexorable advance of Socialism in the North East was dramatically confirmed by the intrusion of its Metropolitan apostles in the bitter four month Northumberland Miners' strike between February and May 1887.[39] Aware of the Union's weak bargaining position in the depressed state of the coal trade, Adams in the *Weekly* backed Thomas Burt's conciliatory strike policy of attempting to settle the dispute through a policy of damage limitation. He offered a solution on the basis of a 12½% wages reduction which the men overwhelmingly refused to accept, although the strike was ultimately to be settled on these terms. The dispute was bitter, most particularly within the union itself: to offer any reduction had rankled with the rank and file; union officials were harassed; and Burt and his committee members only withdrew their resignation after a vote of confidence by the lodges.

The reasons for the challenge to Burt are complex, but the timely appearance of Socialist organizers did much to delay a settlement; they also exploited an already widening gulf between hard-pressed pit-men and their union leaders' middle class life-style and endless penchant for industrial compromise and cooperation.[40] Adams carried full reports of Socialist addresses held under the presidency of John Hall and the Democratic Club. Before meetings in excess of 4,000 people in Newcastle (not all of whom were striking miners) the language of class war, workers' control and the ineffectiveness of Liberal-Labour M.P.s like Burt was forcibly argued by J.L. Mahon and William Morris of the Socialist League, and John Williams, J. Hunter Watts and Tom Mann of the Social Democratic Federation.[41] Arrangements were then made to form a branch of the S.D.F. in the city.[42] In an editorial on the Socialist lectures, however, Adams was quick to reaffirm the time-tested philosophy behind Burt's industrial strategy:

> "Capital, it is true, has not always been judiciously used, but it may well be regarded as the spring of industrial effort, and exactly in proportion as it is plentiful does the position of the workman improve."[43]

For the most part the miners in Northumberland and Durham appear to have remained firmly in favour of the leadership's Liberal-Labour mentality in their political sympathies;[44] but, as R. Gregory has pointed out, those close to Tyneside were far more militant and Socialist than those in the hinterland.[45]

Reviving militancy amongst miners also overlapped at this time with a similar upsurge of feeling amongst hitherto poorly or non-unionised labour: the Tyneside engineers' labourers and shipyard helpers. In the wake of the 1886 boilermakers' strike, as business activity began to improve again,[46] Edward Pease, a Fabian Socialist from

London, sensing that Tyneside was a good area for unionism, started to organise non-craft labour into a new general union, the National Federation of Labour.[47] By 1889, it was catering for dockers, gas and chemical workers, and builders' labourers. Here was a foretaste of what was to become known by the time of the great London dock strike in the summer of 1889 as the advent of New Unionism. As such its appearance gave an entirely new twist to the meaning of collective bargaining, for it represented a challenge not only to employers but also to the more traditionally minded union leaders, like R. Knight, T. Burt, W. Crawford and J. Wilson. The latter objected both to the socialist views of Ben Tillet and Tom Mann, the charismatic leaders, and their supporters, and to the New Unionists' aggressive organizing tactics, not least their enforcement of the closed shop and rallying call for a legal, nationwide eight-hour working day.[48]

Adams had always firmly supported the right of workers to organize themselves in trade unions and to use industrial action to improve their circumstances.[49] He gave unequivocal support in editorials in the *Weekly* both to the struggles of the London dockers in August[50] and the North East's railway servants' agitation in November 1889,[51] two groups of down-trodden and unskilled workers who had much to gain from the upsurge of New Unionist activity. Whilst approving of such advances, he nevertheless regarded the demand for a closed shop on the docks and elsewhere as "symptomatic of the growth of arrogance and despotism in the workshop";[52] and when the statutory eight-hour day question became the dominant issue at the Trade Union Congress Annual Meeting at Newcastle in September 1891, he opposed the campaign on the grounds that it was both impractical and might subvert individual liberty.[53] Not surprisingly, such antipathy placed Adams alongside the "old" rather than the "new" trade unionists, a position he himself had made explicit in an editorial a year earlier:

> "The old Unionists did not meddle so much with politics and State-tinkering as the apostles of the new creed, but their progress was steady and sure, and they commanded confidence. Now matters are changed. The new Unionists, eager and ardent theorists, seek to accomplish impossibilities, and cooler-headed men have no sympathy with such Quixotic tendencies. Tyranny and arrogance cannot be tolerated in the men any more than in the masters."[54]

Adams felt so strongly about New Unionist tyrannies that he gave a cautious welcome to the appearance of William Collison's National Free Labour Association in 1893, which attempted to protect the rights of these who did not join trade unions.[55] Individual freedom he tried to explain in his *Memoirs* was now imperilled:

> "I remember how we old Radicals fought tooth and nail against employers who denied to their workers the right of combination. It is the right to abstain from combining that is now denied ... The dominant idea of working men, or rather of working men's societies, is that nobody should be allowed to do anything outside his own trade ... The life of the wretched exiles in Siberian mines is scarcely more weary, monotonous and despairing than that to which some of our modern trades unionists would condemn all mankind."[56]

By the time of the Association's third annual congress held at Newcastle in October 1895, when socialists had become sufficiently alarmed to feel the need to send Ben Tillett and other like-minded trade unionists northwards to denounce Collison,[57] Adams suggested the following possible scenario:

> "The Free Labour Convention which has this week been held in Newcastle may be regarded as evidence of revolt — of revolt, not against trades unionism, but against the indefensible practices of modern trades unionists. Evils sometimes bring their own remedies. It was natural that the folly and the tyranny, the excesses and the outrages of the new unionists should raise up a spirit of opposition ... When people in the assertion of their own rights have learnt to respect the rights of others, there will be no need for a Free Labour Association."[58]

Well before that date,however, Adams appears to have become a politically disillusioned man. Correspondence in November 1892 with Linton suggests his faith in human progress had been dented and hopes for mankind considerably chastened by contemporary developments in society. Linton tried in vain to be reassuring:

> "I do not like to hear you "losing heart". Why, Man! did you ever in your greenest days suppose the millenium would come in your own days? Think how much has been done, not how little. If not up yet to the mark we sit, surely we may say that we could expect the one generation to change the next; noting too how history is made, a time if reaction always following that of action, a torpid time the active."[59]

Education was to be an important corner-stone in the realization of an *English Republic*;[60] but the Liberal's Education Act of 1870, which provided mass, compulsory elementary education, had fallen short of a "creative moral advance for the people".[61] What Adams now lamented was the fact that generations of school children were being educated at great public expense — "coddling"[62] he called it — but were bereft of a clear sense of public citizenship and of duty to themselves, their neighbours, kindred and to the world.[63] Commenting adversely in his *Memoirs* on the extravagance of the London School Board, he observed nostalgically that his own inexpensive education at least provided him with the tools of knowledge:

> "My own education never cost much more than sixpence a week. It was not much of an education; but it sufficed. It supplied me at any rate with the tools of knowledge. And the tools of knowledge are above all that the State right to be expected to provide gratis."[64]

It was the failure of the educational system to produce socially-conscious and responsible citizens that Adams found most disturbing. "There are evidences of intellectual improvement beyond a doubt" he noted towards the end of his *Memoirs*; but then posed the question: "where are the evidences of moral improvement?"[65] About what should be taught in schools, Adams made clear in the *Weekly* in August 1898:

> "What is wanted is not that children should be instructed in Euclid or in botany, but that they should be educated in such a manner as will develop their moral faculties — taught the difference between right and wrong, encouraged to show tenderness and consideration for others, and given a fair chance to become in after years better men and women than many of them become now."[66]

He therefore condemned the multitudes' pursuit of self-gratification and love of pleasure consequent on the insufficiency of modern education in "cultivating the intellect, while neglecting the conscience".[67] In addition, as he survived into the Edwardian age Adams attacked those cultural or literacy agencies which pandered to the lowest tastes of the educated urban masses: he castigated in turn the Press for its "vulgar sensationalism";[68] periodicals for their "vilest indecency in print and illustration";[69] and plays and novels for their "gross immorality"[70] and "disgusting rubbish".[71] He also deplored the hedonistic nature of that late nineteenth century Tyneside working class world surrounding professional football and supporters' rowdyism when "their favourite team gets beaten",[72] attendant gambling and heavy drinking;[73] it had become a self-enclosed culture in which amusement and indulgence were big business,[74] and intellectual or self-improving pastimes "but little patronised".[75]

Another unpleasant reflection in the *Memoirs* related to the conduct of new workshop practices.[76] The strike-prone North East had become in the early 1890s "the real storm centre"[77] of intensified conflict between skilled workers and hostile employers. A new wave of mechanisation coincided with attempts by the former to regain ground lost to the latter on a broad front of issues ranging from wages to the regulation of apprenticeships, machine manning, piecework and the eight-hour day.[78] Long imbued with a sense of the nobility of work and honest endeavour,[79] Adams now despaired at the growing dissatisfaction and disinterest exhibited by craftsmen and apprentices in the yards. However, coming from an occupation which had remained relatively untouched by mechanization during his workshop days,[80] Adams, the journalist, was in no position to appreciate the real nature of the problems confronting alienated skilled craftsmen as they struggled to control specialised engineering work processes which, because of increasing levels of automation and efficiency drives by management, only required semi or even unskilled labour.[81]

Adams's naivety is seen, for example, in the three month Engineers' demarcation dispute and lock-out by the management at the beginning of 1892.[82] The highly skilled Amalgamated men refused to accept the employers' decision of handing over as much engineering work as possible to the plumbers, who worked longer hours for less pay. As the dispute dragged on he criticised the engineers for their irresponsible behaviour:

> "The difficulty arises from petty jealousy and utter lack of an accommodating spirit among the workmen themselves. Will it ever be possible for them to understand there is something more worthy of consideration than a selfishness which can only issue in a beggar-thy-neighbour policy?"[83]

Even though industrial unrest became chronic, Adams still hoped that:

> "a sense of duty will hold in check sinister considerations. the progress of machinery is inevitable."[84]

The final indignity for Adams came in the General Election of July 1892 when C.F. Hamond, a popular local Conservative, topped the poll in Newcastle with John Morley in second place and James Craig, the other Liberal candidate, third.[85] Deepening class divisions were making it difficult to sustain the view that Liberalism was really the party of the 'people' and its M.P.s the representatives of a community of economic and social interests. Despite attempts by the local Liberal executive, led by the far-sighted radical-Liberal, R. Spence Watson, to secure the adoption of Arthur Henderson, a popular trade unionist, local Liberal councillor and a future Labour Party leader, as Morley's running mate in 1895, a majority of the Newcastle Liberal "One Thousand" unwisely selected once again the wealthy merchant and right winger, James Craig.[86] A nucleus of independent labour supporters amongst the swelling ranks of Newcastle's Socialists also made the historic decision in August 1893, backed by the Trades

Council, to adopt Frederick Hammill as their next Independent Labour Party candidate.[87] For their part, the local Conservative Association, encouraged by Hamond's success, resolved to run two candidates in 1895, the second being W.D. Cruddas, chairman of the local Association and a director of Armstrong's Elswick engineering works. Such confidence was founded upon a dramatic strengthening of local organization and support for popular Conservatism, particularly through the activities of the Party's Primrose League (founded 1883).[88] By the time of Hamond's victory in 1892, the city had seven branches or habitations and over 3,000 League members. A year later some 6,000 members had been enrolled. According to Martin Pugh, the habitations covered all parts: from the poverty of Saint Andrews to the villadom of Jesmond; although a heavy concentration was to be found amongst skilled engineers and mechanics in the giant Elswick works[89] — a consideration possibly in Cruddas's decision to stand. In the General Election of 1895, which saw a national swing to the Conservatives, both Morley and Craig were roundly defeated and the two Conservatives returned.[90]

It is not surprising, therefore, in view of all these developments, that a disheartened Adams retreated from politics into good works at a local level.[91] Apart from becoming actively involved in a number of nationwide testimonial schemes designed to raise funds to help surviving radicals like G.J. Harney (1896), Edward Rymer and Edward Truelove (1898),[92] all in old age and failing health, Adams's only entry into public affairs came in connection with an impassioned defence of British imperial policy in South Africa. As we observed in Chapter Four, Adams had been a reluctant imperialist: he doubted the wisdom of extending British possessions and responsibilities over various parts of the globe; but, following British defeat of the despotic and tyrannical Burmese ruler, King Theebaw, and the annexation of Burma in 1885, he appeared to be coming round to the view that

> "All the same there seems to be a sort of 'manifest destiny' in the expansion of the British Empire."[93]

In the light of these comments it is not difficult to understand why the scramble for Africa through the 1890s was a phenomenon which largely met with his approval. Although aware of the great commercial potential which the opening up of that vast Continent now offered, Adams supported British expansion, as he had in the 1870s, on the grounds that it would be used to end slavery and advance the cause of civilization. For example, when in May 1890 the African explorer Henry Stanley was made a freeman of Newcastle, Adams carried an editorial on the forthcoming attractions of Africa:

> "There is another side to the picture, however, than that of commerce, and it is terrible to think that, through the supineness of our people, civilization in Africa has been retarded so many years, millions of lives being meanwhile sacrificed in all the horrors of tribal warfare and Arab marauding."[94]

He therefore welcomed wholeheartedly moves initiated in 1895 to put an end to slavery in the British East African protectorates of Zanzibar and Pemba as doing justice to its "dusky tribes".[95] Such a policy was also made all the more urgent in Adams's view because of the pillage and murder of the indigenous population long associated with the ivory trade:

> "Every tusk, piece and scrap in the possession of an Arab trader has been steeped and dyed in blood. Every pound weight has cost the life of a man, woman, or child."[96]

However, when this civilizing mission was increasingly challenged by the Boers in Southern Africa from 1896, it drew all the old radical invective for which Adams had earned his reputation in past struggles against privilege and oppression. It was quite incomprehensible for Adams how anybody could side with the Boers. "These men" he wrote:

> "are born slave-holders who have inflicted brutal injury on the black races of the lands over which they trekked."[97]

He also condemned the manner in which an "iniquitous" Boer oligarchy had ostracised and dominated the Uitlanders (foreign residents), who were now denied the vote and taxed six or seven times the amount the Boers imposed upon themselves.[98] Uitlander opposition in December 1896 took the form of an unsuccessful raid into the Transvaal by Dr. Jameson at the head of a troop of under five hundred men. In welcoming the raid Adams offered these prophetic comments:

> "The type of civilization of which the Boers are enamoured is not a pleasant one, and though the transformation may be delayed, it is inevitable."[99]

Adams's views were not however shared by all the prominent Radical-Liberals in the North East. For the first time he found himself opposing the views of R. Spence Watson, Thomas Burt and Charles Fenwick, who argued at a series of peace meetings that the war was unjust or simply dictated by British designs to secure gold from the rich mines of the Boer dominated Transvaal.[100]

W.E. Adams died peacefully at the Bella Vista Hotel in Funchal on the mid Atlantic island of Madeira on May 13, 1906 in the presence of his eldest daughter, Gertrude

Amy Smith.[101] That he should die and be buried here, rather than in England, was perhaps a fitting end to a life that had so many trans-Atlantic alignments. Equally appropriate was the inscription upon his gravestone which, in words borrowed from the poet Leigh Hunt, embodied his own being: "Write me as one who loves his fellow-men." To one admirer Thomas Cairns, the Newcastle Liberal M.P. elected in 1906, who drew inspiration from a visit to the grave in 1907, the inscription was not only simple and true but even indicative of saintliness: "I like that present tense"; he wrote, "it suggests immortality".[102]

Back home in Newcastle, as a mark of respect, a W.E. Adams Memorial Committee was formed, under the presidency of Alderman Dr. Henry Newton, the object of which was to launch a fund so as to enable a commemorative marble bust of Adams to be placed in the Newcastle Free Library. To this end the sum of over 100 guineas was rapidly raised and a promising young Newcastle sculptor, Christian Neuper, commissioned to prepare the bust from the details of old photographs. On the first anniversary of Adams's death, a large company assembled at the Library to witness the unveiling of the marble bust, with pedestal, by his life-long friend the Northumberland Miners' leader and Morpeth M.P., Thomas Burt.[103] The pedestal bears the inscription: "W.E. Adams 1832-1906. Journalist and Author, Member of the Public Libraries Committee for 32 years." It was also very fitting that this memorial should find a shrine in Newcastle Library, because Adams was one of its earliest friends. It still remains there today.

Far from being the marginal man in nineteenth century radical politics, W.E. Adams came to play a key role in many of its activities. Along with a small band of fellow artisans as ardent as himself, he entered Chartism determined to remove privilege and oppression. His literary talents and access to print-based materials as a working compositor soon marked him off as a local leader who, before he was out of his teens, was presiding over branch meetings, corresponding with M.P.s regarding the treatment of Chartist prisoners, offering material help to the struggling peoples of Europe and liaising with Chartist leaders on how best to ensure the continued survival of Chartism in the 1850s. By the end of that decade, inspired by his Brantwood Republican experience, Adams became a convinced internationalist of the Mazzinian kind; and the latter's views on duty and citizenship now propelled him to consider the needs of the entire nation and not just the working classes.

In working as a journalist first for Charles Bradlaugh and then Joseph Cowen jr., Adams found himself in a unique and powerful position to influence the nature and tone of provincial Radicalism, as well as to contribute to the success and popularity which these two public figures enjoyed. At the *Weekly Chronicle* he dedicated his life to the cause of universal suffrage, freedom of speech and conscience, breaking the shackles that generally bound men to the old order in Church and State, and advancing the cause of international human rights. One important result was to confirm "Radical Tyneside" as an important force in the emergent character of Mid-Victorian Liberalism.[104]

Rarely the platform orator, Adams could wield a pen with great effectiveness and determination. Such talents enabled him in a personal way to make two modest contributions to the course of nineteenth century political history. Firstly, as the author of the 1858 pamphlet on "Tyrannicide", he helped bring down a Whig government led by the aristocratic Lord Palmerston and troubled the authorities over what precisely constituted freedom of speech in the supposedly more relaxed political climate of the 1860s. Secondly, his editorials and personal involvement played a crucial role in the process of consciousness-raising during the campaign for that extension of the miners' franchise which led directly to the election in 1874 of Thomas Burt, the miners' M.P. for Morpeth, as the first working man to enter Parliament. Not surprisingly, Adams's *Weekly* remained the "pit-men's bible" for as long as men like Burt were the miners' representatives.

Adams always remained wedded to a radical individualist tradition which derived from the teachings of Tom Paine. He therefore deplored measures which would restrict the freedom of the individual. Drawing on "the pregnant lines of Byron", his own philosophy echoed that of the great Poet:

> "I wish men to be free,
> As much from mobs as kings, from you as me."[105]

Consequently, the arrival of Socialism found him hostile because he believed its collectivist ethos would simply work to paralyse the individual's own ability and effort to shape his or her own destiny.

Adams was, very properly, greatly respected in social and political circles in the North East for his personal integrity, independent mind and wide-ranging association with movements of progress, culture and humanity. As well as a leading campaigner for a free Library, he was something of a proto-conservationist with a deep love of the countryside and concerned that parks for the people or arboreal areas should be created in the city; he was also in the avant-garde of those who encouraged youth movements and the need for special facilities for the young. The Dicky Bird Society, uniquely his own creation in the *Weekly*, did much to spread a little kindness from its epicentre in Newcastle to many other urban areas of England, as well as in rural parts, by encouraging children to be kind to all living things. Through him, the *Weekly* became an important and constituent element in that Radical-Liberal matrix which made for community politics in Newcastle until the early 1890s.

At the unveiling ceremony in 1907, Burt paid tribute to Adams's personal strengths. "He had about him" be believed:

> "no deception, no duplicity; he was transparently straightforward and honest."[106]

For Burt, nothing more appropriate could have been selected for Adams's epitaph than the words inscribed on his Madeira tombstone. Touchingly though, the member for Morpeth added one final comment: "In the words of the same poem" he declared, "may his tribe increase".[107]

Notes

1. W.E. Adams, Memoirs, op.cit., p.552 where he notes that his "health was permanently injured".

2. J. Saville and J. Bellamy (eds.), Dictionary of Labour Biography, Vol.VII, op.cit., p.3.

3. T. Cooper, The Life of Thomas Cooper, (Reprinted with Introduction by J. Saville), Leicester, 1971, pp.393-4; F.M. Leventhal, Respectable Radical, George Howell and Victorian Working Class Politics, op.cit., p.190.

4. Ms Eng. 180, W.J. Linton to W.E. Adams, P.O. Box 1139, New Haven, Nov. 21, 1892. Linton tried to reassure Adams, who was losing heart at the lack of political progress towards the Republic.

5. W.E. Adams, Memoirs, op.cit., Chapter LVII, "Degeneracy" pp.581-590 and Chapter LVIII, "The Decline of Man", pp.591-602.

6. For the destruction of craft control and the imposition of new work practises in North East engineering and ship-building, see, for example, J. Zeitlin, "Engineers and Compositors : A Comparison" in R. Harrison and J. Zeitlin (eds.), Divisions of Labour, Skilled Workers and Technological Change in Nineteenth Century England, Brighton, 1985, pp.184-249; and W. Knox, "Apprenticeship and De-Skilling in Britain, 1850-1914", International Review of Social History, Vol.XXXI, 1986, Part 2, pp.166-184.

7. W.E. Adams, Memoirs, op.cit., pp.567-8.

8. Ibid., p.568.

9. Ibid., p.60.

10. J.O. Baylen and N.J. Gossman (eds.), Biographical Dictionary of Modern British Radicals, Vol.III, op.cit., M. Milne, p.16.

11. Idem.,

12. Adams also defended the Socialists' right to hold open-air public meetings like that on Sunday mornings in Dod Street in the East End of London. See, for example, Newcastle Weekly Chronicle, Sept. 26, 1885. "The London Police and the Socialists". In a short editorial piece on the Dod Street demonstration, conspicuous for the high-handed and discriminatory police action in attempting to prosecute Socialists for public obstruction, Adams made this comment: "In any case, the Socialists have as much right to propagate their doctrines, whatever we may think of them, as any other class of the community."

13. Newcastle Weekly Chronicle, Sept. 12, 1885, State Socialism.

14. Ibid., May 24, 1890, Grandmotherly Legislation.

15. Idem.,

16. Ibid., Sept. 1, 1894, Great Principles.

17. L.J. Satre, "Thomas Burt and the Crisis of Late-Victorian Liberalism in the North East", Northern History, op.cit., p.180.

18. I am particularly grateful to Dr. Raymond Challinor of Whitley Bay, Tyne and Wear, for drawing my attention to the importance of this conflict.

19. Newcastle Weekly Chronicle, Jan. 9 and Jan. 16 1886.

20. Ibid., Sept. 5, 1885, The Strike at Elswick. The dispute arose over the appointment of a new manager, Mr. McDonnell, who was said to have "indiscriminately dismissed some men, grossly insulted others and made life for the men unbearable by new payment rates and practices on piece work". A sign of the changing times can be glimpsed in the language of the men. John Ramsay, chairman of the strike committee, total a mass meeting on the Town Moor that "they had now entered into what he should call a gigantic struggle between capital and labour".

21. The Newcastle Weekly Chronicle carried reports almost every week on the situation at South Medomsley during 1886.

22. The severity of the winter was the subject of a special five column feature in the Newcastle Weekly Chronicle, March 6, 1886.

23. Ibid., May 22, 1886, South Medomsley Evictions: Local Libel Case at Leeds Assizes.

24. Ibid., May 22, 1869, "Ironside" on George Odger, the candidate for Stafford. Adams welcomed his appearance as a candidate but warned that workingmen should come forward first as "Englishmen, they should be citizens ... men fitted by character and capacity to discharge the duties of legislators". See also Newcastle Weekly Chronicle, Jan 31, 1885 again condemning the idea of class representation to Parliament.

25. Ibid., Jan. 30 1886, The Local Distress, Newcastle. According to the report 1500 men were unemployed, but "if they took the number out on strike, there would not be less than 15,000 men unemployed in Newcastle".

26. Idem., According to the Mayor, Benjamin Browne, "over 1,100 families of respectable working people were in absolute poverty". Soup kitchens, Sunday

free meals, the distribution of coal and public works' schemes (excavating and paving streets) were Newcastle Distress Fund Committee's attempt at relieving the distress.

27. Ibid., Jan. 9, 1886, Strike of Shipbuilding on the Tyne and Wear. It lasted until the end of Feb. 1886 when a compromise settlement negotiated by R. Knight, involving a range of wage reductions betwen 2 1/2 % — 7 1/2%, was finally accepted by the boilermakers and shipwrights.

28. Elijah Copland was a widely respected Newcastle artisan. In the winter of 1884-1885, for example, at a time of much hardship and suffering, he had been appointed honourary Secretary of the Newcastle Relief Fund by the Council. Alderman W.H. Stephenson, the Mayor in 1884/85, said of him that "he was a man with a good head on his shoulders". See Newcastle Weekly Chronicle, April 11, 1885, The Newcastle Relief Fund.

29. Newcastle Weekly Chronicle, April 25, 1885, Labour Representation for Newcastle; May 2, 1885; June 27, 1885; Aug. 22, 1885; and Aug. 29, 1885. Copland argued that both Liberals and Conservatives were equally hostile to labour representation.

30. Ibid., April 25, 1885, Labour Representation for Newcastle.

31. Ibid., May 2, 1885, Newcastle Democratic Club.

32. Ibid., Jan. 30, 1886, March 20, 1886.

33. Ibid., July 3, 1886, Mr. Joseph Cowen and the Representation of Newcastle.

34. Ibid., Aug. 29, 1885, Local Election News; and Nov. 28, 1885. Copland was a proposer of Cowen jr.

35. Ibid., Aug. 26, 1893. Adoption of Mr. Hammill by the Trades Council. This attempt at independent Labour representation took place against a background of organised working class involvement in local government and election to school boards. See I.G. Hunter, "Municipal Socialism and independent labour on Tyneside, 1883-1914", Bulletin of the Society for the Study of Labour History, Vol.51 No.3, 1986, pp.9-10.

36. Newcastle Weekly Chronicle, Feb, 1886, The Riots in London.

37. Ibid., Feb. 20, 1886, The Distress.

38. Ibid., Feb. 13, 1886, The Riots in London.

39. L.J. Satre, "Thomas Burt and the Crisis of Late-Victorian Liberalism in the North East", Northern History, op.cit., particularly pp.174-183

40. Ibid., pp.178-181.

41. Newcastle Weekly Chronicle, March 5, 1887, Socialists in Newcastle; and March 12, 1887. For Morris's visit in early April, see E.P. Thompson, William Morris: Romantic to Revolutionary, London, 1977, pp.441-445.

42. Ibid., Nov. 12, 1887, Socialist Demonstrations in Newcastle.

43. Ibid., March 12, 1887, Editorial comment on the Socialists.

44. A.W. Purdue, "The Liberal and Labour Parties in North-East Politics, 1900-14: The Struggle for Supremacy", International Review of Social History, op.cit., pp.4-5.

45. R. Gregory, Miners and Politics, 1906-14, London, 1968, pp.71-72.

46. According to J. Hinton, Labour and Socialism: A History of the British Labour Movement, 1867-1974, Brighton, 1983, p.45. "Unemployment fell from its peak in 1886, reaching very low levels in 1889 and 1890."

47. H. Pelling, A History of British Trade Unionism, Second Edition, Middlesex, 1973, pp.96-97.

48. J. Hinton, Labour and Socialism: A History of the British Labour Movement, 1867-1974, op.cit., pp.45-51. See also L.J. Satre, "Thomas Burt and the Crisis of Late-Victorian Liberalism in the North East", Northern History, op.cit., pp.192-193.

49. J.O. Baylen and N.J. Gossman (eds.), Biographical Dictionary of Modern British Radicals, Vol.III, op.cit.., M. Milne p.17.

50. Newcastle Weekly Chronicle, Aug. 31, 1889, The London Strikes. Adams regretted, however, the fact that "noted metropolitan Socialists have interfered in this struggle".

51. Ibid., Nov. 30, 1889, The Railway Servants' Agitation.

52. W.E. Adams, Memoirs, op.cit., p.555.

53. Newcastle Weekly Chronicle, Sept. 12. 1891, The Eight Hour Day.

54. Ibid., Sept. 13, 1890, The New Trades Unionists.

55. G. Alderman, "The National Free Labour Association : Working Class Opposition to New Unionism in Britain" in W. Mommsen and H.G. Husung (eds.), The Development of Trade Unionism in Great Britain and Germany, 1880-1914, London, 1985, pp.302-311.

56. W.E. Adams, Memoirs, op.cit., pp.555-557.

57. G. Alderman, "The National Free Labour Association: Working Class Opposition to New Unionism in Britain" W. Mommsen and H.G. Husung (eds.), The Development of Trade Unionism in Great Britain and Germany, op.cit., p.305.

58. Newcastle Weekly Chronicle, Oct. 12, 1895, The Gossip's Bowl.

59. Ms Eng 180, W.J. Linton to W.E. Adams, P.O. Box 1139, New Haven, Nov.21, 1892.

60. F.B. Smith, Radical Artisan, W.J. Linton, 1812-97, op.cit., pp.103-104.

61. Ibid., p.209.

62. W.E. Adams, Memoirs, op.cit., pp.109-110.

63. Newcastle Weekly Chronicle, Oct. 6, 1900, The Gossip's Bowl.

64. W.E. Adams, Memoirs, op.cit., p.110.

65. Ibid., p.582.

66. Newcastle Weekly Chronicle, Aug. 20, 1898, The Gossip's Bowl.

67. W.E. Adams, Memoirs, op.cit., p.584.

68. Idem.,

69. Ibid., p.585.

70. Ibid., p.589.

71. Ibid., p.590.

72. Ibid., p.600.

73. Ibid., p.600 and p.597. Adams wrote that "to Durham, Northumberland and Lancashire belong the distinction of being the three most dissipated counties in the kingdom".

74. Ibid., p.599.

75. Idem., See also G. Stedman Jones, Languages of Class, Studies in English Working Class History 1832-1982, Cambridge, 1983, particularly Chapter IV, "Working-class culture and working-class politics in London, 1870-1900: Notes on the remaking of a working class", which suggests some important similarities between working class culture in late nineteenth century London and Newcastle.

76. W.E. Adams, Memoirs, op.cit., pp.548-559, Chapter LIV, "The Laws of the Workshop".

77. J. Zeitlin, "Engineers and Compositors : A Comparison" in R. Harrison and J. Zeitlin (eds.), Divisions of Labour, Skilled Workers and Technological Change in Nineteenth Century England, op.cit., p.223.

78. Idem.,

79. W.E. Adams, Memoirs, op.cit., pp.549-550.

80. W. Knox, "Apprenticeship and De-Skilling in Britain, 1850-1914", International Review of Social History, op.cit., p.171.

81. Ibid., pp.173-183.

82. Newcastle Weekly Chronicle, Jan. 30, 1892, Strike of Skilled Workmen; and April 30, 1892, The Strike: Its History and Cost. A sub-headline noted: "Half a Million of Money Wasted".

83. Ibid., Jan. 30, 1892, Strike of Skilled Workmen.

84. Ibid., April 6, 1895, Industrial Unrest.

85. A.W. Purdue, "Parliamentary Elections in North East England 1900-1906: The Advent of Labour", M.Litt. thesis, University of Newcastle, 1974, p.80.

86. Ibid., p.82. According to Purdue p.85 among the factors contributing to Henderson's failure to be adopted were the financial question (Craig, through his own money and his ability in fund raising, was a "golden source", Henderson was not), the Liberal Newcastle Daily Leader's campaign against him, and a conviction that Craig was more the sort of person suited to being a Liberal candidate than was Henderson.

87. Newcastle Weekly Chronicle, March 18, 1893, The Independent Labour Party and its Work; and Aug 26, 1893, Adaption of Mr. Hammill by the Trades Council.

88. M. Pugh, The Tories and the People, 1880-1985, Oxford, 1985, particularly p.38 and pp.125-128 for the Primrose League activities in Newcastle.

89. Ibid., pp.127-128. At Elswick, the 700 League members of 1891 had grown to 1,500 by 1894.

90. See Newcastle Weekly Chronicle, July 20, 1895 Election Result: C.F. Hamond — 12,833; W.D. Cruddas —12,170; J. Morley — 11,862; J. Craig — 11,154; F. Hammill — 2,302. According to A.W. Purdue, "Parliamentary Elections in North East England 1900-1906: The Advent of Labour", M. Litt. thesis, op.cit., p.86. "Liberal opinion was inclined to blame defeat upon the Socialist intervention". However, Purdue's analysis of the voting suggests otherwise: "more votes were split between Hammill and Hamond than between Hammill and any other candidate". The Conservatives again won both seats in the 1900 General Election.

91. The meeting in Newcastle, in April 1895, of the annual conference of the I.L.P. provoked an exceptional editorial blast in the Weekly against the idea of nationalization. See Newcastle Weekly Chronicle, April 20, 1895, A Socialist Conference. Adams asserted that such a scheme "is one of the grossest manifestations of selfishness the world has yet witnessed".

92. See, for example, Newcastle Weekly Chronicle, Nov. 21, 1896. Testimonial for G.J. Harney. Adams was a member of the committee which raised £200 to mark the completion of his eightieth year in February 1897.

93. Ibid., Jan. 9, 1886, The Annexation of Burma.

94. Ibid., May 17, 1890, Does England Care?

95. Ibid., Dec. 28, 1895, Review of the Year's Events.

96. Ibid., May 31, 1890, Stanley's Remedy for Slavery.

97. Ibid., Oct. 14, 1899, War!

98. Idem.,

99. Ibid., Jan. 4, 1896, The Jameson Raid.

100. Ibid., Jan. 27, 1900, Gold! See also Dec. 23, 1899 for Peace Meetings addressed by Burt and Fenwick in Newcastle. Joseph Cowen jr. was, like Adams, anti-Boer.

101. Ibid., May 19, 1906, Death of Mr. W.E. Adams. His wife died in January 1907.

102. Newcastle Evening Chronicle, March 30, 1907.

103. Newcastle Daily Chronicle, May 14, 1907.

104. J. Vincent, The Formation of the Liberal Party, 1857-1868, Middlesex, 1972, pp.262-263.

105. W.E. Adams, Memoirs, op.cit., p.227.

106. The Northern Echo, May 14, 1907, Eulogy of late Mr. W.E. Adams by Mr. T. Burt.

107. Idem.,

BIBLIOGRAPHY

MANUSCRIPT SOURCES

Bishopsgate Institute, London:

Bradlaugh Papers (National Secular Society Collection) : Two letters from W.E. Adams to Hypatia Bradlaugh Bonner.

George Howell Collection : Letters (17) from W.E. Adams to George Howell.

Caractacus (W.E. Adams), "The Province of Authority in Matters of Opinion", London, 1875.

Cambridge University Library:

The Madden Ballads Collection. Vol.23 containing pieces printed by Thomas Willey of Cheltenham, Nos. 403-553.

Houghton Library, Harvard University, U.S.A.:

Ms. Eng. 180, Letters (118) to W.E. Adams from W.J. Linton, 1855-1897.

Public Record Office, London:

Correspondence and Papers relating to Gloucestershire in HO 45/OS2410D (1848) Part III.

Board of Trade Papers B.T.41 (Land Company Members), Box Nos. 136, 474, 475 and 476 (1847 and 1848).

Newcastle-upon-Tyne, Central Reference Library:

W.E. Adams, "The Struggle for a Free Library in Newcastle-upon-Tyne, 1870-1880", Notes and Newspaper cuttings (120 leaves).
Reports of proceedings and copy of presentation address to William Edwin Adams, with List of Subscribers, June 6, 1898.
Memorial to W.E. Adams Correspondence (including obituary notices), concerning the memorial bust of W.E. Adams in the Public Reference Library, 1907.
W.E. Adams, "Tyrannicide: Is It Justifiable?" London, 1858.
"An Argument for Complete Suffrage", London, Manchester, Newcastle, 1860.
"The Slaveholders War: An Argument for the North and the Negro", Manchester, 1863.
"Bonaparte's Challenge to Tyrannicides. By the Author of Tyrannicide: Is It Justifiable?" A Suppressed Pamphlet, 1867.
"History of the Dicky Bird Society" by Uncle Toby, Newcastle-upon-Tyne, 1887.
The Cowen Collection: Letters (12) from Joseph Cowen to W.E. Adams.

Staffordshire Polytechnic Library:

The Holyoake papers, Microfilm copy with Introduction by E. Royle, Cambridge, 1969. Letters (14) from or about W.E. Adams to G.J. Holyoake.

CONTEMPORARY PRINTED SOURCES

i. Books:

W.E. Adams — Memoirs of a Social Atom, London, 1903, 2 Vols. Reptd. in one with an Introduction by J. Saville, New York, 1969.

W.E. Adams — Our American Cousins: being personal impressions of the people and institutions of the United States, London and Newcastle, 1883.

W. Archer — William Charles Macready, London, 1890.

H.C. Black — Notable Women Authors of the Day, Glasgow, 1893.

H. Bradlaugh Bonner — Charles Bradlaugh, A Record of his Life and Work, London, 1908.

T. Burt — Pitman and Privy Councillor, An Autobiography, London, 1924.

W. Cobbett — Rural Rides, London, 1830, Reptd. with an Introduction by G. Woodcock, Middlesex, 1967.

T. Cooper — The Life of Thomas Cooper, London, 1972, Reptd. with an Introduction by J. Saville, Leicester, 1971.

J. Dellow — Memoirs of An Old Stager, Newcastle, 1928.

W. Duncan — The Life of Joseph Cowen, London and Newcastle, 1904.

R. Fynes — The Miners of Northumberland and Durham, Blyth 1873, Rept. Sunderland, 1923.

R.G. Gammage — The History of the Chartist Movement from its Commencement Down to the Present Time, London, 1854, First Edition — See also facsimile of the Second Edition, 1894, with an Introduction by J. Saville, London and New York, 1969.

G. Hodgson — From Smithy to Senate: The Life Story of James Annand, Journalist and Politician, London, 1908.

C. Ignotus — The Golden Decade of a Favoured Town, London, 1884.

E.R. Jones — The Life and Speeches of Joseph Cowen, M.P. London, 1885.

J.B. Leno — The Aftermath, London, 1892, Reptd. in D. Thompson (ed.), Chartist Biographies and Autobiographies, London, 1986.

W.J. Linton — Memories, London, 1895, Reptd., New York, 1970.

J. McCabe — Life and Letters of G.J. Holyoake, London, 1908.

J. Stuart Mill — On Liberty, London, 1859, Reptd. with an Introduction by G. Himmelfarb, Middlesex, 1974.

G. Rowe — The Illustrated Cheltenham Guide, Cheltenham, 1845, Reptd. with an Introduction by S. Blake, Gloucester, 1981.

G.A. Sala — America Revisited, London, 1885.

H.A. Solly — These Eighty Years, London, 1893.

T.W.P. Taylder — History of the Rise and Progress of Teetotalism in Newcastle-upon-Tyne, Newcastle, 1886.

A. Watson — A Newspaper Man's Memories, London, 1925.

W.R. Williams — The Parliamentary History of the County of Gloucester (1213-1898), Hereford, 1898.

(ii) Chartist Periodicals and Contemporary Newspapers:

Animal World, London, 1875-1901.
Beehive, London, 1862-1867.
The Cabinet Newspaper, London, 1858-1860.
The Cheltenham Chronicle, 1845-1860.
The Cheltenham Examiner, 1845-1860.
The Cheltenham Free Press, 1845-1860.
The Cheltenham Journal, 1845-1860.

Cooper's Journal: or, Unfettered Thinker and Plain Speaker for Truth, Freedom and Progress, London, 1850, Reptd. New York, 1970.

The Democratic Review of British and Foreign Politics, History and Literature, London, 1849-1850, Reptd. London, 1968.

The English Republic, London, Leeds, Brantwood, 1851 and 1854-1855, Reptd. London, 1891 (ed. Kineton Parkes)
The Investigator, London, 1857-1859.
National Reformer, London 1860-1865.
Newcastle Weekly Chronicle, Newcastle, 1862-1908.
The Northern Star, London, 1845-1852.
Notes to the People, London, 1851-1852, Reptd. New York, 1968.
The People's Paper, London, 1852-1858.
The Reasoner and Herald of Progress, London, 1846-1861.

The Red Republican, London, 1850, continued as The Friend of the People, London, 1851. Reptd. with an Introduction by J. Saville, London, 1966.

iii. Articles in other Nineteenth Century Periodicals:

W.E. Adams — "Morris Dancers at Cheltenham", Notes and Queries, London, Sixth Series, July-December, 1881, Vol.IV.

Winter's Magazine, London, 1893.

iv. Re-printed Documents:

J. Burnett (ed.) — Destiny Obscure: autobiographies of childhood, education and family from the 1820s to the 1920s, London, 1982.

L. James (ed.) — Print and The People, 1819-1851, Middlesex, 1987.

W.H. Maehl (ed.) — R. Gammage: Reminiscences of a Chartist. Society for the Study of Labour History, Aids to Research, No.4 Manchester, 1983.

E. Royle (ed.) — The Infidel Tradition, London, 1976.

A.V. Seaton (ed.) — Journal Of An Expedition to the Feroe and Westman Islands and Iceland, 1833 by G.C. Atkinson, Newcastle, 1989.

D. Vincent, (ed.) — Testaments of Radicalism: Memoirs of Working Class Politicians, 1790-1885, London, 1977.

UNPUBLISHED SECONDARY MATERIAL

Theses:

O.R. Ashton — "Radicalism and Chartism in Gloucestershire, 1832-1847", Ph.D University of Birmingham, 1980.

A. Courtenay — "Parliamentary Representation and General Elections in Cheltenham Spa, 1832-1848: A Study of a Pocket Borough", M.Phil. The Open University, 1991.

A.W. Purdue — "Parliamentary Elections in North East England, 1900-1906: The Advent of Labour", M.Litt. University of Newcastle, 1974.

E.I. Waitt — "John Morley, Joseph Cowen and Robert Spence Watson: Liberal Divisions in Newcastle Politics, 1873-95." Ph.D University of Manchester, 1972.

PUBLISHED SECONDARY MATERIAL

(i) Books:

P. Adelman — Victorian Radicalism, The Middle Class Experience, 1830-1914, London, 1984.

E. Allen, J.F. Clarke, N. McCord and D.J. Rowe — The North East Engineers' Strike of 1871, Newcastle, 1971.

R.D. Altick — The English Common Reader, 1800-1900, Chicago, 1957.

P. Bailey — Leisure and Class in Victorian England, London, 1978.

T. Bennett, G. Martin, C. Mercer, J. Woollacott (eds.) Culture, Ideology and Social Process, Milton Keynes, 1981.

Benwell Community Project, Final Report Series, No.6, The Making of a Ruling Class, Newcastle, 1978.

J.M. Bourne Patronage and Society in Nineteenth Century England, London, 1986.

A. Briggs (ed.) Chartist Studies, London, 1959.

A. Briggs Victorian Cities, Middlesex, 1968.
A Social History of England, Middlesex, 1983.

L. Brown Victorian News and Newspapers, Oxford, 1985.

R.B. Bushaway By Rite, Custom, Ceremony and Community in England, 1700-1800, London, 1982.

R. Colls & P. Dodd (ed.) Englishness: Politics and Culture, 1880-1920, London, 1986.

J. Cooper Animals in War, London, 1983.

G. Crossick (ed.) The Lower Middle Class in Britain, London, 1977.

G. Crossick An Artisan Elite in Victorian Society, London, 1978.

S. Easton (ed.) Disorder and Discipline: Popular Culture from 1550 to the Present, London, 1988.

M. Ellison Support for Secession, Chicago, 1972.

J. Epstein The Lion of Freedom: Feargus O'Connor and the Chartist Movement 1832-1842, London, 1982.

E.J. Feuchtwanger Democracy and Empire, Britain 1865-1914, London, 1985.

P.S. Foner British Labour and the American Civil War, New York, 1981.

F.E. Gillespie Labor and Politics in England, Durham, N. Carolina, 1927.

C. Godfrey Chartist Lives — The Anatomy of a Working Class Movement, New York, 1987.

R. Gregory Miners and Politics, 1906-14, London, 1968.

D. Hardy Alternative Communities in Nineteenth Century England, London, 1979.

D. Harker Fakesong: The Manufacture of British 'Folk song', 1700 to the Present Day, Milton Keynes, 1985.

B. Harrison Drink and the Victorians, London, 1971.

Peaceable Kingdom, Stability and Change in Modern Britain, Oxford, 1982.

R. Harrison & J. Zeitlin (eds.) — Divisions of Labour, Skilled Workers and Technological Change in Nineteenth Century England, Brighton, 1985.

S. Harrison — Poor Men's Guardians, London, 1974.

G. Hart — A History of Cheltenham, Leicester, 1965.

J. Hinton — Labour and Socialism: A History of the British Labour Movement, 1867-1974, Brighton, 1983.

S. Humphries, — Hooligans or Rebels? An Oral History of Working Class Childhood and Youth, 1889-1939, Oxford, 1981.

L. James — Fiction for the Working Man, London, 1973.

D. Jones — Chartism and the Chartists, London, 1975.

G. Stedman Jones — Languages of Class: Studies in English Working Class History, 1832-1982, Cambridge, 1983.

N. Kirk — The Growth of Working Class Reformism in Mid-Victorian England, London, 1985.

J. Knott — The First Hundred Years, Newcastle-upon-Tyne City Libraries, Newcastle, 1980.

S. Koss — The Rise and Fall of the Political Press in Britain, Vol.I, London, 1981.

T.W. Laqueur — Religion and Respectability, Sunday Schools and Working Class Culture, London, 1976.

A.J. Lee — The Origins of the Popular Press in England, 1855-1914, London, 1976.

F.M. Leventhal — Respectable Radical, George Howell and Victorian Working Class Politics, London, 1971.

T. Matsumura — The Labour Aristocracy Revisited: the Victorian Flint Glass Makers, 1850-1880, Manchester, 1983.

N. McCord (ed.) — Essays in Tyneside Labour History, Newcastle, 1977.

N. McCord — North East England, London, 1979.

G.S. Messinger — Manchester in the Victorian Age, Manchester, 1985.

J. Millard — Ralph Hedley, Tyneside Painter, Newcastle, 1990.

M. Milne — Newspapers of Northumberland and Durham, Newcastle, 1971.

W. Mommsen & H.G. Husung (eds.) — The Development of Trade Unionism in Great Britain and Germany 1880-1914, London, 1985.

A.W. Moss	Valiant Crusade, The History of the RSPCA, London, 1961.
A.E. Musson	The Typographical Association, London, 1954.
T.J. Nossiter	Influence, Opinion and Political Idioms in Reformed England, 1823-1874, Brighton, 1975.
H. Pelling	A History of British Trade Unionism, Middlesex, 1973.
A. Plummer	Bronterre: A Political Biography of Bronterre O'Brien, 1804-1864, London, 1971.
B. Porter	Plots and Paranoia, A History of Political Espionage in Britain 1790-1988, London, 1989.
I. Prothero	Artisans and Politics in Early Nineteenth Century London: John Gast and his Times, London, 1981.
M. Pugh	The Tories and the People, 1880-1985, Oxford, 1985.
K. Robbins	Nineteenth Century Britain. England, Scotland and Wales. The Making of a Nation, Oxford, 1989.
J.W. Rounsfell	On the Road: Journeys of a Tramping Printer, with an Introduction by A. Whitehead, Horsham, 1982.
E. Royle	Victorian Infidels, Manchester, 1974.
D. Rubinstein	Before the Suffragettes, Women's Emancipation in the 1890s, Brighton, 1986.
D. Rubinstein (ed.)	People for the People, London, 1973.
J. Saville	1848: the British State and the Chartist Movement, Cambridge, 1987.
R. Samuel (ed.)	People's History and Socialist Theory, London, 1981.
A.R. Schoyen	The Chartist Challenge: a Portrait of George Julian Harney, London, 1958.
F.B. Smith	Radical Artisan, W.J. Linton 1812-97, Manchester, 1973. The People's Health, London, 1979.
T.R. Tholfsen	Working Class Radicalism in Mid-Victorian England, London, 1976.
D. Thompson	The Chartists, London, 1984.
E.P. Thompson	William Morris: Romantic to Revolutionary, London, 1977.
J. Trenherz	Hard Times, Social Realism in Victorian Art, London, 1987.

E.S. Turner — All Heaven in a Rage, London, 1964.

M. Vicinus — The Industrial Muse, London, 1974.

D. Vincent — Bread, Knowledge and Freedom: A Study of Nineteenth Century Working Class Autobiography, London, 1981.
Literacy and Popular Culture, England 1750-1914, Cambridge, 1989.

J. Vincent — The Formation of the Liberal Party, 1857-1868, Middlesex, 1972.

J.K. Walton & J. Walvin (eds.) — Leisure in Britain 1780-1939, Manchester, 1983.

J.T. Ward — Chartism, London, 1973.

H. Weisser — British Working Class Movements and Europe, 1815-1848, Manchester, 1975.

J.H. Wiener (ed.) — Innovators and Preachers, The Role of the Editor in Victorian England, Westport, 1985.

D.G. Wright — Popular Radicalism: The Working Class Experience, 1780-1880, London, 1988.

(ii) Articles

F.A. D'Arcy — "Charles Bradlaugh and The English Republican Movement, 1868-1878", Historical Journal, 25 (2), June 1982.

O.R. Ashton — "Clerical Control and Radical Responses in Cheltenham Spa, 1838-1848", Midland History, Vol.VIII, 1983.

"The Mechanics' Institute and Radical Politics in Cheltenham Spa, 1834-1840", Cheltenham Local History Society Journal, No.2, 1984.

"Chartism in Gloucestershire: the contribution of the Chartist Land Plan, 1843-1850", Transactions of the Bristol and Gloucestershire Archaeological Society, Vol.104, 1986.

"Chartism and Popular Culture: an Introduction to the Radical Culture in Cheltenham Spa, 1830-1847", Journal of Popular Culture, Vol.20, No.4, 1987.

T. Bennett — "Popular Culture: Divided Territory", Social History Society Newsletter, Autumn, 1981.

P. Brock — "Polish Democrats and English Radicals, 1832-1862: A Chapter in the History of Anglo-Polish Relations", Journal of Modern History, Vol.25, Part 2, 1953.

"Joseph Cowen and the Polish Exiles", Slavonic and East European Review, Vol.XXXII, 1953.

R.B. Bushaway — "The Ideology of Custom in Eighteenth Century England" in "Custom, Crime and Prerequisites", Bulletin of the Society for the Study of Labour History, Vol. 52, No.1, 1987.

G. Claeys — "Republicanism versus commercial society: Paine, Burke and the French Revolution debate", Conference Report, Bulletin of the Society for the Study of Labour History, Vol.54, No.3, 1989.
"Mazzini, Kossuth, and British Radicalism, 1848-1854", Journal of British Studies, Vol.28 (3), July, 1989.

P.A. Dunae — "Penny Dreadfuls: Late Nineteenth Century Boys' Literature and Crime", Victorian Studies, Vol.22, No.2, Winter, 1979.

R. Gagnier — "Social Atoms: Working Class Autobiography, Subjectivity and Gender", Victorian Studies, Vol.30, No.3, Spring, 1987.

K. Harris — "Joseph Cowen — The Northern Tribune", Bulletin of the North East Group for the Study of Labour History, No.5. 1971.

B. Harrison — "A World of Which We Had No Conception: Liberalism and the English Temperance Press; 1830-1872", Victorian Studies, Vol.XIII, Dec. 1969.

M. Heaney — "Morris Dancers at Cheltenham", The Morris Dancer, No.17, Nov. 1983.

A. Humphreys — "G.W.M. Reynolds: Popular Literature and Popular Politics", Victorian Periodicals Review, Vol.16, Part 3/4, Fall, 1983.

I.G. Hunter — "Municipal Socialism and independent labour on Tyneside, 1883-1914." Bulletin of the Society for the Study of Labour History, Vol.51, No.3, 1986.

W. Knox — "Apprenticeship and De-Skilling in Britain, 1850-1914, International Review of Social History, Vol.XXXI, Part 2, 1986.

J.F. Kutolowski — "English Radicals and the Polish Insurrection of 1863-64", Polish Review, XI, 1966.

"Mid-Victorian Public Opinion, Polish Propaganda and the Uprising of 1863", Journal of British Studies, VIII, May, 1969.

W.H. Maehl — "The North-Eastern Miners' Struggle for the Franchise, 1872-74", International Review of Social History, vol.XX, 1975.

K. McClelland — "A Politics of the Labour Aristocracy? Skilled Workers and Radical Politics on Tyneside, c.1850-74",

Conference Report. Bulletin of the Society for the Study of Labour History, No.40, Spring, 1980.

N. McCord — "Some Aspects of North-East England in the Nineteenth Century", Northern History, Vol.VIII, 1972.

A. Metcalfe — "Organised Sport in the Mining Communities of South Northumberland, 1880-1889", Victorian Studies, Vol.25, No.4, Summer, 1982.

M. Milne — "Strikes and Strike-Breaking in North-East England, 1815-1844: The Attitude of the Local Press", International Review of Social History, 22(2), 1977.

A.L. Morton — "W.E. Adams, Memoirs of a Social Atom, Introduction by J. Saville, (Augustus M. Kelley, 1968)", Review Article. Bulletin of the Society for the Study of Labour History, No.17, 1970.

G. Pollard — "Novels in newspapers: some unpublished letters of Captain Mayne Reid", Review of English Studies, Vol.XVI, Part II, 1942.

A.W. Purdue — "The Liberal and Labour Parties in North-East Politics, 1900-14: The Struggle for Supremacy", International Review of Social History, Vol.XXVI, Part 1, 1981.

"Jarrow Politics, 1885-1914: The Challenge to Liberal Hegemony", Northern History, Vol.XVIII, 1982.

I. Prothero — "Chartism in London", Past and Present, Vol.44, 1969.

"London Chartism and the Trades", Economic History Review, 2nd series, XXIX, No.2, Mary, 1971.

C. Reid — "Essays in Review: Class and Culture", Bulletin of the Society for the Study of Labour History, No.34, Spring 1977.

E. Rymer — "The Martyrdom of the Mine", with an Introduction by R. Neville, History Workshop Journal, No.1, Spring, 1976.

R. Samuel — "The Bishopsgate Institute", History Workshop Journal, No.5, Spring, 1978.

L.J. Satre — "Thomas Burt and the Crisis of Late-Victorian Liberalism in the North-East", Northern History, Vol.XXIII, 1987.

K. Tiller — "Charterville and the Chartist Land Company", Oxoniensa, Vol.L.1985.

N. Todd — "Black-on-Tyne: The Black Presence on Tyneside in the 1860's", Bulletin of the North East Group for the Study of Labour History, No.21, 1987.

D. Vincent — "Love and death and the nineteenth century working class", Social History, Vol.5, No.2, May, 1980.

H. Weisser — "Chartist Internationalism, 1845-1848", The Historical Journal, XLX, No.1, 1971.

iii. Biographical Dictionaries

J.O. Baylen & N.J. Gossman (eds.) — Biographical Dictionary of Modern British Radicals, Vol.III, 1870-1914, Brighton, 1988.

J. Burnett, D. Vincent, D. Mayall (eds.) — The Autobiography of the Working Class: An Annotated, Critical Bibliography, Vol.1, 1790-1900, Brighton, 1984.

J.F.C. Harrison & D. Thompson — Bibliography of the Chartist Movement, 1837-1976, Brighton, 1978.

J. Saville & J. Bellamy (eds.) — Dictionary of Labour Biography, London, Vol.1, 1972 and Vol. VII, 1984.

C. Wood (ed.) — The Dictionary of Victorian Painters, Woodbridge, 1978, Rept. 1981.

Dictionary of National Biography, Vol.I, 1901-11, London, 1920.

Dictionary of American Biography, Vol.X, New York, 1964.

The Methodist Who's Who, London, 1933.

Index